Structuralism and Hermeneutics

Structuralism and Hermeneutics

T . K . SEUNG

COLUMBIA UNIVERSITY PRESS

New York

Clothbound editions of Columbia University Press books are Smyth-sewn and printed on permanent and durable acid-free paper.

Library of Congress Cataloging in Publication Data

Seung, T. K., 1930–
    Structuralism and hermeneutics.

    Includes bibliographical references and
index.
    1. Structuralism.   2. Structuralism
(Literary analysis)   3. Hermeneutics.   I. Title.
B841.4.S45   149′.96   81-10274
ISBN 0-231-05278-2   AACR2
ISBN 0-231-05279-0   (paper)

Columbia University Press
New York   Guildford, Surrey

For Kwihwan

My Relentless Critic
and
Resourceful Counselor

Contents

Preface

THE ART OF interpretation may be as old as mankind itself. In ancient Greece and Rome, it was used for deciphering oracles and omens. During the Middle Ages and the Renaissance, it was used for the exegesis of the Bible and hermetic pagan texts. In our own world, it is no longer geared only for the special task of unraveling oracular messages or obscure texts. It is now used for the interpretation of a whole age or culture. This enormous expansion of the hermeneutic art has been dictated by her new role as the handmaiden for the newly emerging human sciences or *Geisteswissenschaften*.

The emergence of these new sciences around the turn of the last century had been inspired by the grand ambition of elevating human studies to the august level of scientific inquiry. There were two alternatives for realizing this ambition: (1) to transfer the established methods of natural science to human studies, or (2) to transform the native method of these disciplines into a scientific procedure. The first alternative has been taken by behavioral sciences, which have thrived on empirical observations and generalizations. The second alternative has been adopted by what may be called the interpretive sciences, that is, those disciplines whose cognition ultimately involves the process of interpretation.

To many disciplines of human studies, such as literary criticism, art history, and cultural anthropology, the technique of interpretation has been as native as anything can be. It is not only that the ultimate phase of their investigations must involve questions of interpretation, but also that even the factual questions of exploration and discovery in these disciplines cannot be settled without using the technique of interpretation. From the inception to the conclusion of their inquiries, these disciplines cannot take a single step without relying on the art of interpretation. Hence it was assumed by the pioneers of human sciences that the elevation of these disciplines to the truly scientific level could be achieved by transforming their art of interpretation into scientific method.

The scientific transformation of the hermeneutic art has been the common goal for the various formalist-structuralist programs of interpretation that have dominated human studies in our century—such as New Criticism in literary analysis, the formalist programs in art history and musicology, the gestalt and Freudian psychology, structuralism in linguistics and anthropology, etc. In this volume, these formalist-structuralist programs shall be called structural programs, and the word "structuralism" shall be used to refer not only to the French structuralist movement, but to all the structural programs of interpretation in Europe and America.

In structural programs, the art of interpretation has been transformed into the art of structural analysis; to interpret a cultural object has become equivalent to analyzing its structure. This methodological equivalence has appeared to give the hermeneutic art its scientific stature and establish a respectable parity of human sciences to natural sciences. For natural sciences have drawn their ultimate power from their analyses of the structure of nature, and the standard scientific procedures of observation and experiment have provided only ancillary forces to this ultimate power.

In natural science, the immense power of structural investigations is derived from the universality of natural struc-

tures. For example, the structure of a carbon atom is never
constrained or compromised by space and time; it is the same
in any part of the spatiotemporal continuum. Because of this
structural universality, to know the structure of one carbon
atom is to know the structure of all carbon atoms. Since the
universality of natural structures has been the fundamental
premise for natural sciences, structural programs have been
constructed on a corresponding premise, namely, the universality of cultural structures. For example, the New Critics have
assumed that the poetic structure of ambiguity and ambivalence
they have found in modern European poetry is the structure
of all poetry. But this assumption of structural universality has
lately been eroded, and its erosion has produced a series of
violent reactions against the original scientific spirit of structural programs.

The eruption of these antiscientific reactions has constituted the emergence of post-structuralism (or post-formalism).
To explore and explicate the nature of this transition from structuralism to post-structuralism is the objective of this book. It
begins with the task of clarifying the historical connection of
structural programs to the German hermeneutic tradition, and
then explicates the nature of structural analysis. This explication is followed by an extensive discussion of historical relativity, which has become perhaps the most controversial issue
since the advent of post-structuralism. The outcome of this
discussion seems to show that it is impossible even to talk
about subjectivism and relativism without presupposing an
objective framework. One way or another, the very espousal of
relativity seems unavoidably to entail transcendence.

This objectivist conclusion has had to be pitted against
Jacques Derrida's theory of signs and his deconstructivism,
which have been hailed by many as solid justification of subjectivism and relativism. Thus I have concluded this volume
with an exhaustive critique of Derrida's position. My critique
of Derrida and relativism is also a critique of the rampant ir-

rationalism and antiscientism that have been provoked by the decline of structuralism. In all fairness, I should admit, the eruption of post-structuralist irrationalism can be accepted as a necessary reaction and even be used as a healthy antidote to the naive scientific optimism and dogmatism that have nurtured the various structural programs. But to exalt this irrationalism as the guiding spirit of a new era is to invite and establish an intellectual anarchy.

As long as this anarchy is confined within a few professional journals, it may not exact any tolls heavier than deranging a few feeble-minded pedants. But when it invades classrooms and ravages the tender minds of young students, it can produce disastrous consequences. This invasion, I fear, has already begun on many campuses across the nation, where shallow tricks in obscurantism and shady gimmicks for specious arguments have been paraded as the trendy fashion of Nietzschean plays. If this book can be of any use to anybody in his or her fight against this invasion, I shall count it as its greatest fortune.

In the course of composing this volume, I have received generous and precious assistance from many friends and various sources. Especially I would like to express my gratitude to the following persons and institutions. I am grateful to Aloysius Martinich for his ceaseless help in clarifying my endless questions in linguistics. Even when he went to California for a summer vacation, he allowed me to interrupt his vacation with my further queries and manuscript, which he read with care, setting aside his own work. On complex questions in the philosophy of logic, I had the comfort of relying on Herbert Hochberg. On technical issues in philosophy of science, I had the privilege of being instructed and assisted by Robert Causey. For many questions on Greek mythology, I had the benefit of David Francis' expert counsel. For the intractable problem of deciphering Derrida's writings, I had the fortune of threshing out my questions with Louis Mackey, James Holquist, and Gayatri Spivak, and of firming up my answers with the kind help of Dina Sherzer and Mary-Farr Baker. My frequent discussions with Charles Guignon have left clear imprints on my treatment of Heidegger and Saussure. I am also grateful to John Silber for his repeated encouragement from the inception of my project to its completion.

The first draft of this volume was written with a generous grant from National Endowment for the Humanities and The University of Texas Research Institute. I am grateful to these two institutions and their directors, David Coder and Chet Lieb. Apart from this official capacity, Chet Lieb has been firmly in support of this project. Finally I would like to thank William Livingston, Dean of Graduate Studies at the University of Texas, and Byung-Hak Kim of IBM, for their kind assistance in the production of the typescript and photocopies of my manuscript.

T. K. Seung
Austin, Texas

Structuralism and Hermeneutics

CHAPTER ONE

Programs for
the Human Sciences

THE FORMALIST PROGRAMS of interpretation that have dominated the various branches of the humanities in our century were originally conceived as scientific or quasi-scientific projects in the burgeoning human sciences. These new sciences were the attempts to elevate the studies of human affairs to the august level of natural science. During their formative years around the turn of the last century, these new sciences were given various labels: *Geisteswissenschaften* (Wilhelm Dilthey), *Kulturwissenschaften* (Heinrich Rickert), and *Geschichtswissenschaft* (Wilhelm Windelband).

The pioneers of these new sciences had a long, serious debate on the difference between their sciences and natural science. Wilhelm Dilthey maintained that nature is the domain of brute force, which can never be truly understood. To understand (*verstehen*) means to know something from the perspective of its inside; but nature has no inside, according to Dilthey. Those things which have no inside can only be explained. To explain (*erklären*) something is to subsume it under general laws. In Dilthey's view, thus, *Geisteswissenschaft* is the science of *Verstehen*, whereas *Naturwissenschaft* is only a science of *Erklärung*.[1]

Dissatisfied with Dilthey's differentiation of human sciences from natural science, Wilhelm Windelband proposed his own differentiation.[2] While the knowledge of general laws is the goal of natural science, he claimed, the knowledge of particular historical facts is the goal of history. In his words, natural science is nomothetic; history is idiographic. The nomothetic function is to explain (erklären) particular natural phenomena by subsuming them under general laws; the idiographic function is to understand (verstehen) particular historical phenomena in their particularity. The difference between Verstehen and Erklärung is not simply that of knowing from the inside and knowing from the outside. These two types of knowledge involve two different kinds of things to be known: natural objects or events that can be fully explained by their subsumption under general laws, and cultural objects or historical events that cannot be adequately explained by the same method.

If the human sciences are idiographic, as Windelband claims, they cannot produce universal truths. They have to be content with proposing and verifying particular assertions, one by one. The question of whether a science can produce universal or particular truths is the question of its epistemic power. A universal truth is far more powerful than a particular one; the force of the former is equivalent to that of an unlimited number of the latter. For example, the universal assertion, "All men are mortal," has the same force as an infinite number of particular assertions which can be generated from this universal assertion, e.g., "Socrates is mortal," "Plato is mortal," "Aristotle is mortal," etc. Because a universal assertion can proclaim, in one stroke, what can be said only in an infinite number of particular assertions, the glory and power of the natural sciences have been the universal character of their theorems and theories.

If Windelband's thesis is right, the human sciences can never expect to achieve the same kind of glory and power as the natural sciences have achieved. Hence his thesis is a fatal blow to the pious aspirations of those pioneers who have struggled to elevate the new sciences of human affairs to the level of the natural sciences. Despite all their aspirations and pretensions, the practice of these new sciences cannot be any different from the practice of history, one of the oldest intellectual disciplines, which is forced to track down one particular truth after another in the most prosaic manner. It does not seem to be even justifiable to regard the human sciences as sciences, because the nomothetic character of natural science has been so widely and so firmly accepted as an essential feature of all sciences. As a matter of fact, Windelband refers to the human sciences simply as history in the title of his rectorial address *Geschichte und Naturwissenschaft* (History and Natural Science), in which he tries to counter Dilthey's differentiation of natural and human studies with his own.

The simplest way to tackle Windelband's stricture on the possibility of elevating human studies to the scientific level is to prove it wrong by producing a body of universal truths about human affairs. This direct approach has been championed by behavioral scientists, who have tried to discover inductively general laws of social behavior. However, this inductive approach has not produced the sort of exciting results that have been produced by natural science. In the first place, the laws that can be inductively established in the behavioral sciences are severely limited in their scope; in the second place, they are usually no more than statistical reformulation of rather well-known trends and tendencies. These laws neither seem to have the awesome epistemic power of natural laws, nor does their recognition seem to generate much excitement of discovery.

Beside this inductive approach, however, there is another way of overcoming Windelband's disheartening stricture on the prosaic character of the human studies and instill some truly scientific excitement into them. This is to locate the scientific character of science not in its method of inductive generalization, but in its method of systematic analysis, of analyzing a complex whole into its components. For example, the great variety of geometrical shapes can be analyzed into a few elements, such as points, lines, planes, and volumes. The vast welter of material substances can be analyzed into molecules, atoms, and subatomic particles. This method of analysis is used in almost every branch of natural science; it is used in determining the anatomical structure of animal bodies as well as the astronomical structure of the solar system.

The aim of scientific analysis is not simply to determine the constitutive elements of an object, but to discover its constitutive form or structure. For example, chemical analysis of a molecule is meant to determine its structure as well as its components. Furthermore, the behavior of molecular components is to be understood mainly within the framework of their molecular structure. Hence scientific analysis is essentially formal or structural; its ultimate aim is to determine the formal, structural properties and relations of natural objects.

The method of structural analysis can be called Cartesian, because it was essential to René Descartes' conception of scientific method. On the other hand, the method of inductive generalization should be called Baconian, since it was advocated by Francis Bacon. These two methods have been inseparable in the development of modern science.

In ancient Greece, however, structural analysis was regarded as far more indispensable for scientific inquiry than inductive generalization. Euclid's science of geometry, for example, is based on the structural analysis of geometrical objects; but it is not dependent on inductive generalization. In the *Republic* Plato performs his structural analysis of city states, but his analysis is not supported by the inductive method. His theory of Forms is a structural theory of reality and cognition; the ultimate nature of reality is structural, and formal-structural analysis is the key to its understanding.

Aristotle is said to have had much more respect for the

inductive method than Plato did, but the most fundamental method for Aristotle's scientific investigations was also the method of structural analysis. He defines scientific cognition as the intellectual intuition of *essence* in its Aristotelian sense, that is, the recognition of the formal cause or structure of scientific objects. His *Poetics* has given us his structural analysis of poetry in general and tragedy in particular; his *Politics* has given us his structural analysis of city states in general and monarchy in particular; his logical treatises have given us his structural analysis of judgment and inference; his *Metaphysics* has given us his structural analysis of the Aristotelian substance or being qua being. His theory of substance and its essence is no less emphatically structural than Plato's theory of Forms.

The method of inductive generalization gained its present eminence during the formative period of modern science, especially through the preaching of Francis Bacon, the self-appointed advocate of modern scientific method. Even in the development of modern science, however, structural analysis has been the cutting edge in such epoch-making discoveries as Copernicus' theory of the heliocentric system or Harvey's theory of the circulation of the blood. Furthermore, it has provided the matrix of explanation for natural phenomena by constructing theoretical models in which those phenomena can be rendered intelligible. Inductive generalization has mainly served a subordinate role to structural analysis.

If the method of structural analysis is the most essential feature of natural science, the whole question of how to elevate the studies of human affairs to the level of scientific cognition turns out to be the question of how to incorporate that method into the organization of those studies. It is this idea that has inspired the various formal-structural programs such as New Criticism, the formalist programs in art and music history, structural linguistics, structural anthropology, structural poetics, psychoanalysis, phenomenological analysis, etc.

The common premise for these formalist programs has been

the structural view of reality and its cognition. This premise is even older than Plato and Aristotle; it goes back to the Pythagoreans. In our own day, Ferdinand de Saussure has reaffirmed the premise by using the distinction between *langue* (language) and *parole* (speech). *Langue* is language as a systematic whole; *parole* is an individual utterance in that language. Saussure maintains that a language cannot be properly understood as long as it is regarded as a collection of *paroles*; it must be approached as a *langue*.[3] This structural approach to the study of language has been the methodological foundation for structural linguistics. Roman Jakobson has faithfully accepted it in producing structural phonology, in which the phonetic values of phonemes are determined in a systematic contrast with one another.[4]

Martin Heidegger has also reaffirmed this structural approach for the understanding of human existence; it can be understood by articulating the nature of our mood and feelings, our thoughts and aspirations, our failings and fallings in the structural context of our entire life. He describes the character of this structural approach by deliberately using the Greek word *logos*, probably the most ancient word for structure—that which binds together many different elements into a coherent whole.[5] The New Critics have preached a similar idea: every poem should be analyzed as a systematic whole, and all its parts, such as imagery or diction, should be understood in the structural context of this whole.

Formalists have also assumed the universal validity of their formal structures. For example, the New Critical criteria of paradox, irony, and ambiguity have been assumed to constitute the formal structure not of any particular poem, but of all poems. The same assumption of universal validity has been made about Freud's formal structure of the human psyche, Heidegger's formal structure of human existence, etc. Because of their presumed universality, I shall refer to the formal structures which have been discovered and employed in various programs as formal, structural, or formal-structural universals. Formal-structural universals are meant to perform a cognitive function quite different from that of inductive universals. Since the inductive universals are obtained by abstracting general features and leaving particular features out of account, they are useful only for understanding generality and useless for understanding particularity. Formal-structural universals are not used for understanding any generality; the formal-structural analysis of a poem or a sonata is for the sake of understanding that poem or that sonata in its concrete particularity. Formal-structural universals are concrete, whereas inductive universals are abstract. Since formal-structural analysis operates with concrete universals, it can perhaps perform what Windelband has called the idiographic function of *Verstehen*.

A formalist program consists of two phases: the theoretical and the practical. The practical phase is to make use of established formal-structural universals in analyzing some particular entities such as a poem or a sonata. This phase is concerned neither with the discovery of formal-structural universals nor with the demonstration of their validity, both of which belong to the theoretical phase. This phase involves what I would like to call the logic of formal-structural analysis, and I shall try to illustrate the complexity of this logic by a careful scrutiny of Claude Lévi-Strauss' structuralism. I am singling it out for scrutiny because it clearly stands out as the most ambitious formalist program of our century. After all, it has been conceived as *les sciences humaines* for analyzing the overall formal structure of human culture rather than any segment of it.

Lévi-Strauss has given two different rationales for his structuralist program. One of them runs as follows: All human institutions and conventions are governed by the structural universal of binary opposition, because they are extensions of language and because the fundamental structure of language is binary opposition. The other rationale runs as follows: Binary opposition is the universal structure of all languages and all other human institutions and conventions, because it is the fundamental structure of the human mind.

Although these two rationales have not been clearly discriminated from each other by Lévi-Strauss and his followers, it is important to articulate their difference because they produce two different types of structural universals. One type is linguistic; the other is psychological. These two types of structural universals in turn generate two different types of structuralism: linguistic and psychological, having their respective fundamentums in the structure of language and the structure of mind. In linguistic structuralism, the structure of language determines even the structure of mind. In psychological structuralism, the converse of this relation holds; the structure of mind determines that of language.

LINGUISTIC STRUCTURALISM

In *Structural Anthropology*, Lévi-Strauss is eager to provide a secure scientific foundation for the study of social and cultural phenomena by using the scientific method of structural linguistics, which has revolutionalized the study of language.[6] For this purpose, he adopts two premises and tries to reformulate the scientific study of human affairs in terms of them. As his first premise, he assumes that structural linguistics has established a set of structural universals for all languages, especially binary opposition. As his second premise, he assumes that the entire human culture is an extension of language. From these two premises, it follows that anthropology, or rather the entire set of the human sciences (*les sciences humaines*), should be reconceived as an extension of structural linguistics. His own work is called *Structural Anthropology* because it is meant to be the application of linguistic structure to anthropology.

Lévi-Strauss was evidently impressed with the extensive use of binary opposition especially in structural phonology.[7] Roman Jakobson and his followers have maintained that the phonological values of phonemes are learned and recognized not as isolated individual items but as members of an organized system of polarities and oppositions. In this system, the most basic stratum is the distinction between consonants and vowels.[8] Vowels then are claimed to be differentiated by two pairs of oppositions: compact vs. diffuse, and acute vs. grave. These two pairs of oppositions are then claimed also to be operative in a systematic differentiation of consonants. For the uninitiated, it is much easier to see the operation of binary opposition in the domain of consonants than in that of vowels. For example, many consonants are paired in terms of the binary opposition of voiced and voiceless, e.g., /d/ vs. /t/, /b/ vs. /p/, /v/ vs. /f/, /g/ vs. /k/, etc. The contrast between the voiced and the voiceless is only one of the various binary oppositions used in the systematic organization of consonants.

The operation of binary opposition in syntax is also impressive, although it may not be so pervasive as in phonology. Sentence forms can be divided into various binary oppositions, such as affirmative vs. negative, active vs. passive voice, conjunction vs. disjunction, etc. Most sentences can be analyzed into the two components of subject and predicate, and the parts of speech can be divided into substantives (e.g., nouns, pronouns, verbs, adjectives, and adverbs) and connectives (e.g., prepositions and conjunctives). Noam Chomsky's distinction between the surface and the deep structure of a sentence can be regarded as another application of binary opposition to syntax.

Although structural linguistics has been mostly limited to phonology and syntax, it is not hard to detect the operation of binary opposition in semantics and pragmatics. A. J. Greimas has tried to demonstrate the universality of binary opposition in semantics by arguing that the basic semes, or semantic units, are defined and recognized in binary oppositions, e.g., "light" vs. "dark," "male" vs. "female," "human" vs. "animal," "horizontal" vs. "vertical," etc.[9] I do not know of anybody who has consciously tried to demonstrate the operation of binary opposition as the universal structural principle in pragmatics. But the principle of binary opposition may be lurking in Roman Jakobson's distinction between the addresser (speaker) and the addressee (hearer), between message and context, and between code and contact.[10]

Should we then rest assured that binary opposition is the universal structural principle in linguistics? By no means. Although the operation of this structural principle is quite extensive and prominent on all levels of language, there are too many linguistic relations that cannot be subsumed under binary opposition. For example, the phonemes /m/, /n/, or /l/ cannot each be paired up with another phoneme in binary opposition as in the case of /d/ vs. /t/.[11] To be sure, the phonological values of even these phonemes can be described by using a system of two-value discrimination. For example, the sound of /m/ can be described in terms of the presence or absence of each of the following qualities: vocalic ($-$), consonantal ($+$), sonorant ($+$), continuant ($-$), coronal ($-$), anterior ($+$), voiced ($+$), nasal ($+$), etc. However, this system of phonological discrimination is employing not the principle of binary opposition but that of binary distinction.

Although these two principles look alike, they are quite different. Binary distinction is the simplest logical device for discrimination, namely, between having a quality or attribute and not having it, or between belonging to a class and not belonging to it. It underlies every assertion or denial. There can be no more pervasive logical principle than this one. But the principle of binary opposition does not have the same universal scope as the principle of binary distinction. The former is a slightly more complex logical device than the latter, as we shall soon see.

When Lévi-Strauss and his followers claimed that binary opposition is the universal structural principle of all languages, they evidently assumed that the principle of binary opposition is the same as the principle of binary distinction. But their confusion is understandable, because the two can be easily mistaken for each other. As a matter of fact, the confusion of the two principles and its clarification have constituted some epochal moments in the development of Western philosophy.

Aristotle was the first to see the gravity of this confusion and explain the difference between these two principles. Whereas binary distinction asserts a two-term relation, he points out, binary opposition expresses a three-term relation. For example, the binary opposition of odd and even requires the domain of natural numbers as a substratum, which serves as a third term. In contrast to this, the binary distinction between odd and non-odd does not require the domain of natural numbers as a third term, because non-odd means not only the even numbers, but also size, shape, length, weight, rocks, trees, donkeys, and whatever else does not belong to the class of odd numbers.

Binary distinction can be expressed by using two symbols: a positive term and the negation sign, e.g., A and −A. Binary opposition, however, requires three symbols: two positive terms and their relation. For example, let A stand for odd, and B for even; these two symbols alone cannot express their opposition any better than can any other pair of positive terms, such as "goat" and "goal." To be sure, we do feel a direct opposition between odd and even, whereas we do not feel it between goats and goals. This directly felt opposition is derived from our sense of natural numbers, which serves as the relational term in the opposition of odd and even. Since there is no relational term that can establish the opposition between goats and goals, these two terms cannot constitute a binary opposition. Binary distinction requires no relational term, because the relation between a positive term and its negation is established by the negation itself. Even when one of the two terms in a bipolar opposition stands for the privation of what is represented by the other term (e.g., light vs. darkness), both terms function as positive terms (i.e., darkness is not defined as non-light), insofar as this opposition is accepted as binary.

Aristotle himself does not use the expressions "binary opposition" and "binary distinction"; his own terms are "contrariety" and "contradiction." It appears that he introduced and elaborated on this terminological distinction because many pre-Socratic thinkers had made the same sort of mistake as Lévi-Strauss and his followers are now making. As we shall soon see, most pre-Socratic schools had had a penchant for seeing all things in the universal schema of binary opposition. This obsession with binary opposition tended to produce logical chaos in pre-Socratic Greece, just as it has done in post-Sartrian France. Aristotle's distinction between contrariety and contradiction was one of his valuable logical instruments (*organon*) in establishing rigorous order in Greek thought.[12]

Kant revived Aristotle's distinction in his criticism of Leibnizians for their metaphysical claim that there is no evil in reality.[13] The Leibnizians of his day defined evil as the conflict and opposition of incompatible forces in reality, and argued for the impossibility of evil for the following reason. They assumed that every conflict in the world could be defined as the combination or coexistence of a positive and a negative attribute, which are logically opposed; for example, the positive attribute of being wise and the negative attribute of not being wise. The combination of such a logically opposed pair of attributes in one subject is logically impossible; it violates the principle of non-contradiction. Whatever violates a logical principle is logically impossible; it cannot exist in any possible or conceivable world. Hence the Leibnizians concluded that the existence of evil is impossible absolutely.

This optimistic view of the world, Kant claims, reflects a logical confusion. He explains the nature of this confusion by using the distinction between a logical and a real opposition. He says that the Leibnizians' definition of conflict is valid of logical oppositions but not of real oppositions. For the constitution of a real opposition requires much more than the logical relation of one positive attribute to its negation. A real opposition is the conflict between two positive attributes, neither of which is simply the logical opposite (negation) of the other. For example, the conflict between two persons or parties is not a mere logical opposition, but a real one. The existence of a real opposition is clearly possible—as clearly as the existence of a logical opposition is impossible. By overlooking the distinction between these two types of opposition, Kant has shown, the Leibnizians had thought that the impossibility of evil could be deduced from the logical principle of non-contradiction.

Kant's valuable lesson was soon forgotten, and Hegel made a mistake which was exactly the opposite of the Leibnizians' error. He assumed that all logical oppositions were real oppositions. This assumption is the logical foundation for his so-called dialectical logic. The dialectic of thesis and antithesis can take place only in the domain of real opposition, e.g., the conflict of master and slave and their reconciliation in the sphere of interpersonal relationship. On the other hand, the logical opposition of a positive attribute and its negative within a given subject, e.g., the presence of redness in your eye and its absence, is just impossible; it can neither take place in reality nor be resolved in a synthesis.

In a logical opposition, there is no room for the operation of a third term as the synthesis of the two opposite terms: there is no tertium quid in a contradiction. But the operation of a third term as the agent of mediation and reconciliation is possible in a real opposition because it is a three-term relation. Thus Hegel's dialectical logic cannot operate in the domain of logical opposition. But he claimed his dialectical logic as the universal principle of all oppositions and negations, thereby exalting it as the ultimate logic of all reality. This mistaken claim was based on the erroneous assumption that all logical oppositions are real.[14]

The same mistake underlies the first premise of Lévi-Strauss' linguistic structuralism, that is, his assumption that binary opposition is the most extensive structural universal of all languages. In Aristotle's terms, this is the confusion between contradiction and contrariety; in Kant's terms, it is the confusion between logical and real oppositions. Through this confusion, Lévi-Strauss has assumed that binary opposition can serve as the most basic structural universal of his linguistic structuralism.[15]

The second premise in Lévi-Strauss' linguistic structuralism is the assumption that all human institutions and conventions are extensions of language. For example, kinship is a kind of language. In support of this assumption, he gives two different arguments. In the first one, he claims that the kinship system is a language because it is a semantic system or a system of signification.[16] In this claim, he appears to confuse the two meanings of the expression "a system of signification." This expression can mean either a system of the signifiers or a system of the signified. Language is a system of signifiers, but it is not a system of the signified. Kinship is a system of the signified, but it is not a system of signifiers. Of course, the language of kinship is a system of signifiers, but kinship itself cannot perform the same function of signification as that of the language of kinship.

The label "a semantic system" can be properly attached to a system of signifiers, but not to that of the signified. If every system of the signified were to be regarded as a language, everything that is named in the universe, e.g., rocks and pebbles, plants and animals, stars and angels, etc., would be regarded as extensions of language. This would be extending the notion of language to an intolerable extent.

Perhaps realizing this intolerable consequence of his first argument, Lévi-Strauss soon drops it and presents another one. His second argument is to claim that kinship is a kind of language because it is a system of communication, namely, the communication or exchange of women.[17] Of course, the kinship system he has in mind is not the complicated systems in our so-called civilized societies, but the simple ones in the primitive world, where a moiety is divided into two opposing sections, each of which is further divided into bipolar counterparts. In those primitive societies, the structural principle of binary opposition may very well be to facilitate and regulate the exchange of women or, in some cases, of men. However, can other institutions and conventions of the same primitive societies also be regarded as systems of exchange, e.g., the conventions of dividing the world into different spatial regions, of organizing monthly and annual calendars, of regulating rituals and festivals, etc.? What is exchanged through these conventions?

There are many conventions and institutions in any society which are not primarily concerned with the exchange function. Their primary function is to organize the natural and social orders: exchange relations are but one type of ordering system. Even the function of kinship in primitive societies cannot be limited to the exchange of women; its obvious function is to establish and articulate the various relationships among the kin, which are emotional as well as economic, ethical as well as political. In any society, the overall function of kinship is far more complex than the exchange function. That function may often be one of those served by human institutions, but there are no grounds to support the claim that it is universal, or even central.

Even if the exchange function were the central function of kinship or any other human institution, this would still not warrant our regarding these institutions as semantic systems. The exchange function is indeed one of the many ways language has been used, but it is not its *essential* function that can be taken as its defining characteristic. The only function that can be regarded as its defining characteristic is the semantic function, or the function of signification. Surely, as we have just seen, this function can be performed not by the institution of kinship but by the language of kinship. Hence Lévi-Strauss' second argument in support of the second premise of his linguistic structuralism is as unsound as his first argument.

Beside these two arguments, it is quite possible that Lévi-Strauss had another in the back of his mind, namely, the thesis that our world is constituted by our language. This thesis has been fashionable among some linguists and philosophers such as Edward Sapir, Benjamin Whorf, Martin Heidegger, and Ludwig Wittgenstein. This thesis appears to be especially true of the cultural world; every cultural object or convention appears to be instituted through the power of language. Hence it seems plausible to conclude that the structure of the world is the same as that of language, or that the structure of language is reflected in that of the world.

In a certain sense, the structural isomorphism between language and the world is a truism. But the meaning of this truism cannot be correctly captured until the meaning of the expression "the structure of language" is clarified. This expression can mean different things, such as the phonological structure, the sentence structure, or the semantic structure. If a language has words for recognizing twenty-four different grades of kinship, this semantic structure will be obviously reflected in the structure of kinship which is expressed through that language. However, it is difficult to see how the phonological or sentence structure of that language can also be reflected in the structure of kinship. If two languages have the same semantic structure but different sentence structures, are they supposed to produce the same or different structures of kinship?

Lévi-Strauss has avoided this complex problem of determining what is really meant by the magic phrase "linguistic structure" by making two big assumptions: (1) binary opposition is the fundamental structure of every language on all levels (hence there is no need to distinguish one kind of linguistic structure from another, for example, semantic from syntactic structure), and (2) all languages have the same fundamental structure (hence there is no need to differentiate the structure of one language from that of another). This is a gross oversimplification of the nature of linguistic structure—too gross to justify "the structure of language" as a universal framework for the structural analysis of the cultural world.

PSYCHOLOGICAL STRUCTURALISM

In *The Savage Mind*, Lévi-Strauss drops the second premise of his linguistic structuralism, and retains only its first premise.[18] There he claims that binary opposition is the structural universal of all primitive institutions and conventions, because it belongs to the structure of the primitive mind. In his *Structural Anthropology*, Lévi-Strauss had already considered this psychological approach as an intriguing possibility:

> Both [anthropological and linguistic researches] could thus ascertain whether or not different types of communication systems in the same societies—that is, kinship and language—are or are not caused by identical unconscious structures.[19]

Lévi-Strauss is not content with finding a mere *similarity* between the structure of language and that of other institutions. He is eager to establish their *identity* by tracing them back to their common source, namely, the unconscious structure of human mind. This unconscious mental structure will be regarded as the ultimate ground of all structures in his psychological structuralism, the same pivotal role played by the structure of language in his linguistic structuralism.

In psychological structuralism, language no longer occupies a privileged position. It is one of the institutions and con-

ventions whose structures are to be explained in terms of the
structure of the human mind. In linguistic structuralism, language is regarded as the universal *explanans* (that which explains everything); in psychological structuralism, it becomes
only an *explanandum* (that which is to be explained) along
with all other features of human culture.[20]

In psychological structuralism, the principle of binary opposition is not the sole structural principle; it is always in need
of its complement, the principle of homology, which is sometimes called the principle of analogy or equivalence. This second principle was not available for linguistic structuralism,
since it had never been used in structural linguistics. Hence
the principle of homology can be regarded as one of the *structural* differences between the two versions of Lévi-Strauss'
structuralism.[21] Here is an example of homologies: pure (sacred) and impure (profane), male and female, superior and inferior, fertilizing (rains) and fertilized (land), bad season and
good season. Every one of these bipolar oppositions is supposed
to be homologous with or equivalent to every other. This is the
system of homologies the Murngin tribe used in organizing
their world.[22]

The principle of homology is indispensable to the primitive
mind, because the principle of binary opposition is insufficient
for its structural organization of the world. As Saussure said,
the purpose of the structural approach is to see all things not
as isolated items but as members of an integrated system. To
see and order all things in polarities is only one-half of the
primitive mind's structural attempt to organize its world; the
other half is to establish the structural relations between those
polarities. This second half is accomplished by the principle
of homologies and equivalences.[23]

There is still one more difference between Lévi-Strauss'
linguistic and psychological structuralism. In *Structural An-
throplogy*, he never draws the boundary of his structural universal; the principle of binary opposition is meant to be ap-

plicable to all cultures, whether they are primitive or advanced. Because of his confidence in the transcultural validity of his structural universal, he uses it in analyzing not only primitive but also advanced cultures, for example, in his analysis of the Oedipus myth as well as of Zuni myth.[24] He betrays the same confidence in his structural analysis of Baudelaire's sonnet "Les Chats."[25] In linguistic structuralism, the scope of his structural universal is assumed to be as global as language itself.

In *The Primitive Mind*, binary opposition is clearly confined to the structure of primitive mentality. Lévi-Strauss says that the totemic classification which employs extensively binary opposition prevails only in the "cold" societies and not in the "hot" societies.[26] The distinction between the "cold" and the "hot" societies is presumably meant to be equivalent to the standard distinction between primitive and advanced cultures. In hot societies, he observes, the totemic classification and the rigid use of binary opposition become impossible because there historical development is given supremacy over atemporal classificatory systems.

Lévi-Strauss' admission that the primitive and the advanced cultures are constituted by different mental structures amounts to his rejection of innate psychological structuralism. Innate psychological structuralism is the thesis that all human minds have the same innate structure whether they are nurtured in primitive or advanced cultures. Descartes became the father of this innatism by advocating his doctrine of innate ideas. Kant's theory of a priori concepts and intuitions was the first architectonic formulation of innate psychological structuralism. Noam Chomsky's theory of deep structure is a revival of Cartesian innate psychological structuralism; he calls his generative grammar Cartesian linguistics.[27]

Lévi-Strauss' psychological structuralism follows a line of thought that underlies Hegel's philosophy of history. Hegel rejects Kant's doctrine that the structure of the human mind is fixed; he maintains that it changes and evolves in the course of human history. Moreover, he tries to demonstrate that the changing structure of the human mind has been manifested in the changing structure of human culture. I am not sure whether Lévi-Strauss accepts any theory of evolution concerning the human mind or culture. On two counts, however, he is a Hegelian: (1) in rejecting the universal innatism of human thought and (2) in presupposing the isomorphism or even identity between the structure of the human mind and that of human culture.

For these reasons, Lévi-Strauss' psychological structuralism presents a view of the human mind, language, and culture which is fundamentally different from the one reflected in the innatism of Descartes, Kant, and Chomsky. In terms of theoretical consequences and implications, his linguistic structuralism is much closer to this innatism than his psychological structuralism. In his linguistic structuralism, he assumes the unlimited structural uniformity of all languages and cultures, and leaves no room for the historical transformation of their structures. This is the same sort of structural permanence that is entailed by every form of innatism. However, we should not overlook the difference in the ultimate source of structural permanence. For psychological innatism, it is the structure of human mind; for linguistic structuralism, it is the structure of language. We shall now see what ramifications these two concepts of structure have had for the development of structuralism.

CHAPTER TWO

Types of Psychological Structure

AS WE HAVE seen, the psychological structure that is delineated in Lévi-Strauss' *Savage Mind* is a conceptual structure constituted by the two classification principles of binary opposition and homology.[1] It is, in his own words, a system of classification, namely, the totemic classification.[2] A system of classification is a conceptual structure, although not every conceptual structure is a system of classification. How does the conceptual structure of primitive mentality differ from that of civilized mentality? Concerning this difference, Lévi-Strauss says that the totemic classification becomes impossible in "hot" or advanced societies,[3] but he does not say what kind of conceptual structure becomes possible in those societies. Until the conceptual structure of advanced cultures is spelled out, Lévi-Strauss' psychological structuralism shall remain incomplete.

We can perhaps fill in this missing feature of Lévi-Strauss' psychological structuralism by using G. E. R. Lloyd's impressive survey of pre-Socratic thought.[4] In *Polarity and Analogy*, Lloyd has demonstrated how the conceptual structure of ancient Greece was governed by the two structural principles of polarity and analogy (homology), the two structural universals in Lévi-Strauss' psychological structuralism. If we can reconstruct the conceptual structure of post-Socratic Greek thought and specify its difference from the conceptual structure of pre-Socratic thought, we may be able to formulate the structural difference that may generally obtain between primitive and civilized mentalities.

PRE-SOCRATIC CONCEPTUAL STRUCTURE

We can begin this structural account by reviewing Lloyd's survey. He has shown that the two structural principles of polarity and analogy (homology) are the basic modes of thinking and feeling not only in primitive societies, as Lévi-Strauss and other ethnologists have claimed, but also in the early stages of such illustrious cultures as those of ancient Greece and China. Yin and yang was the central polarity in pre-Confucian China. In ancient Greece, almost every pre-Socratic school of thought had its own favorite polarity: odd and even of the Pythagoreans, day and night of Heraclitus, hot and cold of Anaxagoras, love and strife of Empedocles. To be sure, as Lloyd observes, these polarities employ more abstract concepts than those used in primitive societies, e.g., land-side and water-side.[5] Nonetheless, their formal structure is the same as Lévi-Strauss binary opposition.

Since it is difficult to order the entire natural and social world on the axis of a single polarity, there is the natural tendency to multiply polarities in an endless chain of isomorphism and correspondence. For example, the ancient Chinese polarity of yin and yang, which had originally meant the shady side and the sunny side, was multiplied and expanded into a long series of similar polarities: light and darkness, warm and cool, day and night, sun and moon, south and north, east and west, front and behind, heaven and earth, right and left, male and female, life and death, joy and sorrow, etc.[6] According to Aristotle's account, the Pythagoreans had used nine other polarities beside odd and even: limited and unlimited, one and many, right and left, male and female, resting and moving, straight and crooked, light and darkness, good and bad, square and oblong (*Metaphysics* 986a22).

The proliferation of polarities in general produces some serious conceptual problems. As we have seen, the principle of homology is used to establish an interrelation among the various polarities. But the use of this ordering principle can be unduly overstrained. For example, the principle of homology can work quite well in the binary organization of a moiety, if it is divided into only a limited number of clans and tribes, say, two, four, eight, or ten. Now suppose that a moiety is divided into 84 tribes and that it consists of 42 binary oppositions. You can easily see how difficult it would be to establish the interrelation of these 42 binary oppositions with the single principle of homology. Furthermore, this problem of unwieldy complexity is conceptual as well as practical; it is a problem in establishing a conceptual order as well as in establishing a social order.

The principle of homology operates with the logic of similarity and association: to say that one polarity is homologous or equivalent to another means that the former is similar to or associated with the latter. But the categories of similarity and association are not precise but vague, not rigid but flexible, which is at once their virtue and their vice. Because they are vague, they can be used to establish the similarity and association of any two entities. Hence they are exceedingly flexible. However, their flexibility may also spell confusion and contradiction, when these categories are used transitively. For example, a lion is similar to (associated with) an eagle (both are brave and lordly); an eagle is similar to (associated with) a sparrow (both are beaked and winged); therefore a lion is similar to (associated with) a sparrow.

This sort of transitive error in the logic of homology can be avoided by explicitly specifying the points of similarity and association, that is, by pinpointing the aspects in which two entities are said to be similar to or associated with each other. But explicit specification cannot be introduced into a system of homologies without destroying its very essence, which is the implicit (unspecified) and intuitive use of the categories of similarity and association. In this implicit and intuitive use, these two categories operate as one, whereas they are clearly distinguishable in an explicit conceptual system. For this reason, I intend to use the expression "similarity-association" to refer to the joint operation of similarity and association in a system of homologies. A system of homologies will be transformed into a system of universal concepts, as soon as its implicit use of similarity-association is explicitly spelled out in conceptual terms.

To multiply polarities in an extended chain of homologies and equivalences is to extend the logical chain of similarity-association, which is usually meant to be transitive. This extended chain can produce conceptual confusions or even contradictions. Let us consider the Murngin table of homologies:[7]

Pure, sacred:	male	superior	fertilizing (rains)	bad season
Impure, profane:	female	inferior	fertilized (land)	good season

In this table, the bad (rainy) season is associated with male and superior, while the good (dry) season is associated with female and inferior. This association implies that the bad (rainy) season, which is the season of famine, isolation, and danger, is superior to the good (dry) season, which is the season of abundance and festivity. Lévi-Strauss explains how this apparent confusion has been produced by conflating two systems of association, the natural and the social:

> On the natural plane, however, the good season is subordinate
> to the bad, while on the social plane the relation between the

corresponding terms is reversed. If the good season is said to be
male on the grounds that it is superior to the bad season and
that men and the initiated are superior to women and the uninitiated (a category to which women also belong) then not only
power and efficacy but sterility as well would have to be attributed to the profane and female element. This would be doubly
absurd since social power belongs to men and natural fertility
to women. The other alternative is equally contradictory but its
inconsistency can at least be disguised by the double division
of the whole society . . .[8]

This is the sort of dilemma that cannot be avoided in any extended use of homologies.

G. E. R. Lloyd points out another pervasive problem in the
logic of binary oppositions: that is the tendency to ignore the
distinctions between different modes of opposition, or at least
not to draw them explicitly.[9] For example, some polarities
allow no intermediates, e.g., odd and even, while others do
allow them, e.g., black and white. The logical law of the excluded middle holds for the former but not for the latter; every
number is either odd or even, but not every color is either black
or white. The opposite terms which allow intermediates are
usually established by a bipartite division on one continuum,
e.g., the division of people into young and old, rich and poor,
or strong and weak. Such a basis of continuum does not underlie the polarities without intermediates.

Since the bipartite division of a continuum can be made
at any point on the continuum, any continuum-based binary
opposition can take on different values in different contexts.
For example, a person who is young, rich, or strong in relation
to another person, can be old, poor, or weak in relation to a
third person. Unless their relational contexts are discriminated,
these polarities of continuum may appear to violate the logical
law of contradiction. The notorious feature of Heraclitus' discourses was his alleged violation of this logical law. In most
cases, Lloyd says, the alleged contradictions are only rhetorical.
They dissolve as soon as they are seen in the right relational

contexts: "Although Heraclitus asserts, for example, that 'sea is the purest and foulest water' (Fr. 61), he adds by way of explanation that 'for fish it is drinkable and healthy, but for men it is undrinkable and deadly.'"[10]

If the different modes of binary opposition are not discriminated from one another, one cannot tell when and where the logical laws of contradiction and the excluded middle can or cannot be used. That can create serious confusions and contradictions in any system of polarities. These problems in the logic of polarities reflect the same kind of conceptual weakness that we have seen in the logic of homologies, namely, the lack of precision inherent in the use of the coverall category of similarity-association. That weakness can be overcome by introducing a system of explicit specifications, which will transform a simple system of homologies into a complex system of distinction and discrimination.

Let me try to explain the nature of this conceptual transformation with an example. In ancient China, as we have seen, the original polarity of yin and yang multiplied into many different pairs, producing some serious confusion. For a long time, those multiplying polarities were assumed to belong to the same conceptual level. The inherent conceptual confusion in this primitive system was soon overcome by organizing those numerous polarities into a systematic order. This organization was established by admitting only one original polarity on the first level and then dividing and subdividing it on successive levels. That is, the polarity of the first level divides itself into two on the second level; each of these two again divides itself into two polarities, producing four polarities on the third level; each of these four again divides itself on the fourth level; and so forth. The *I Ching* (Book of Changes), whose exact composition date is still unknown, embodies the result of having divided the original polarities of yin and yang on five successive levels. It is a codification of sixty-four symbols, which can be systematized on six layers of increasing complexity.[11]

The Chinese polarities in the *I Ching* constitute a system of subordination; before the *I Ching*, they constituted a system of coordination. A system of subordination has many levels or strata; a system of coordination has only one level or stratum. The transformation of the latter into the former seems to underlie the transition from the primitive to the advanced culture. Let me illustrate this point with the conceptual transformation of Greek thought from the pre-Socratic to the post-Socratic Greece.

POST SOCRATIC CONCEPTUAL STRUCTURE

Since the pre-Socratics employed the logic of polarities and homologies, they tended to create the same sort of conceptual confusion as do the primitive thinkers of today. We will now consider Plato's and Aristotle's achievements as their attempts to clarify and eliminate those confusions. In the *Sophist* and *Statesman*, Plato converts the pre-Socratic device of polarity into his own device of division (*diairesis*) by showing that any class of objects can be divided and subdivided any number of times. For example, the general class of art can be divided into (1) productive art and (2) acquisitive art; the latter can be further divided into (1) the art of acquisition by exchange and (2) the art of acquisition by capture; the latter can be further divided into (1) the art of capture by contention and (2) the art of capture by hunting; and so on (*Sophist* 218D–221C).

Plato's technique uses a series of binary oppositions; each division or subdivision is a bisection of a class or subclass. But the various binary oppositions used in Plato's technique are not linked with one another in a horizontal plane of equivalences, as in the case of pre-Socratic thought. Instead, they are ordered in one hierarchy. This hierarchical ordering of binary oppositions transforms ancient Greek thought from a system of coordination into a system of subordination.

Plato finally constructs his most comprehensive system of subordination by designating the notion of *being* as the highest category, and the bipolar categories of identity (sameness) and difference (otherness) and rest (permanence) and motion (change) as the ultimate polarities (*Sophist* 254B–259B). These two pairs of bipolar categories are the two most comprehensive ways of articulating the nature of being. Hence they are subordinate to the highest ontological category of being, while all other polarities are subordinate to them. Thus Plato's hierarchy of polarities is governed by a single idea.

Aristotle reformulates Plato's technique of division and subdivision into his theory of genus and species, which produces the Aristotelian hierarchy of natural kinds. In this Aristotelian hierarchy, the schema of binary opposition is no longer important because the division of a genus into species is not always a matter of bisection. Hence Aristotle's hierarchy of genus and species is not a hierarchy of binary oppositions; nonetheless it is a system of subordination. In this system, Plato's notion of division and subidivison (*diairesis*) is transformed into Aristotle's notion of essential definition (*horismos*), that is, the definition of a specific essence by determining its genus and differentia.[12]

Aristotle's system of categories is also a system of subordination. There is a conceptual hierarchy among the Aristotelian categories of substance, quantity, quality, relation, place, time, position, state, action, and affection (*Categories* 1b25–2a3). The concept of *substance* is the apex of this categorial system; all the other Aristotelian categories are ways of articulating the nature of substance. Hence the notion of substance in Aristotle's categorial system plays a role analogous to the one played by the notion of being in Plato's categorial system. However, the categories of bipolar opposition play no more significant role in Aristotle's categorial system than they do in his hierarchy of genera and species.

Aristotle treats the problem of polarities as a separate issue by classifying them into four groups: (1) correlatives, (2) con traries, (3) positives and negatives, and (4) affirmatives and negatives (*Categories* 11b15–13b35). Among these four groups, he is especially fascinated with contraries, probably because this group covers most of the pre-Socratic polarities. He uses his categorial hierarchy in sorting out various types of contraries: some of them belong to the category of substance, some to that of quantity, some to that of quality, some to that of relation, and so on. By this conceptual operation, he establishes a hierarchical order among the different types of polarities. This is the Aristotelian way of transforming the pre-Socratic polarities from a system of coordination into a system of subordination.

Of all his categories, Aristotle observes, only the category of substance is ontologically ultimate; that is, substances alone can have independent existence, while the other categories designate those entities whose existence is dependent on the existence of substances. But a substance itself is not made of contraries; contrary attributes such as disease and health, black and white, can be predicated of or present in substances (*Categories* 14a15–18). In Aristotle's view, the pre-Socratics made the mistake of assuming that contraries such as odd and even, light and dark, were the ontological ultimates (*archai*), from which all things were made (*Metaphysics* 1075a27–34). The aura of ontological ultimacy that had been associated with the pre-Socratic polarities is thus thoroughly exorcised in Aristotle's ontological hierarchy—much more thoroughly than even in Plato's ontological system.

Both Plato's and Aristotle's systems can be called architectonic; in fact, they were the first architectonic systems in the West. The replacement of the logic of coordination with that of subordination made it possible for them to build architectonic systems. This was the fundamental transformation of conceptual system in ancient Greece. With this transformation, even the relation of two terms in a binary opposition was converted from a horizontal to a vertical relation. In Plato's system, for example, the binary opposition of the soul and the body, the eternal and the temporal, or the intelligible and the sensible designates not a simple relation of two equal terms but the order of their inequality.

There was one more conceptual instrument which was indispensable for the transformation of conceptual structure in ancient Greece. That was the notion of definition developed by Socrates.[13] In Plato's dialogues, Socrates is always in search of definitions, e.g., the definition of friendship, love, courage, justice, or virtue. Definitions become possible only with a clear distinction between universals and particulars. In the course of defining the nature of virtue, Socrates asks Meno to "tell me what virtue is as a whole (*kata olou*) and stop making one [essence of virtue] into many [instances of virtue]" (*Meno* 77A–B). In making this request, Socrates is presupposing that there is an essence of virtue which is distinct from its particular instances, and that this abstract entity has its own unity as much as the concrete entities. This is an epoch-making revolution in human thought, which is generally known as the distinction between universals (abstract entities) and particulars (concrete entities).[14]

The distinction between universals and particulars is not known in the logic of primitive thought; for that reason, Lévi-Strauss calls the totemic system of classification the science of the concrete.[15] For the same reason, the science of the concrete is incapable of specifying explicitly the exact nature of similarity and equivalence in its system of homologies and polarities. The Socratic method of definition produces the science of the abstract by establishing a system of abstract concepts. Abstract concepts establish definitional identity, while concrete ideas only ensure homologous resemblance. By virtue of those concepts, it becomes possible to spell out explicitly in what regards two things are alike or different. What was a matter of unspecified and vague equivalence in the science of the

concrete is transformed into that of defined and specified identity in the science of the abstract.

The binary opposition is the dominant principle in the
science of the concrete; so is binary distinction in the science
of the abstract. For example, whereas the binary opposition
between virtue and vice is the primary concern for the former,
the binary distinction between what is virtue (or its definitional
essence) and what is not virtue is the primary objective of the
latter. To be sure, the binary opposition between virtue and
vice is not forgotten in the Socratic art of definition, but it is
treated only as a special case of the binary distinction between
what is virtue and what is not.

The Socratic art of definition employs binary distinction
as its method; e.g., the definition of justice is achieved by distinguishing what is just from what is not. The method of binary
distinction demands a different kind of attention from that of
binary opposition. In a binary opposition, one's attention is
equally divided between the two terms. In a binary distinction,
however, it is mainly focused on the positive term. In the Socratic art of definition, the device of binary distinction is used
mainly to focus attention progressively on the object of definition. This definitional procedure articulates the scope of a
concept or universal.

This notion of categorial scope is essential material for the
construction of an architectonic system, because its stratifica-
tion must depend on the different scopes of universals. For
example, the category of being is the highest universal in Plato's
categorial system, since its scope is broad enough to encompass
all other categories. The notion of conceptual scope is also
indispensable for the Aristotelian hierarchy of genera and species, because the inclusion of different species in one genus,
or their exclusion from other genera, can be determined by the
scope of those species and genera.

This is not to say that the notions of various classes or

natural kinds are not operative in primitive or pre-Socratic thought. On the contrary, their operations there are extensive. But those notions are ordered differently; their main function is to establish bipolar contrasts. In Lévi-Strauss' words, there is the "logical subordination of resemblance to contrast."[16] For example, the binary opposition of male vs. female, or eagle vs. turtle, is to indicate a bipolar contrast as an ultimate fact. Although one polarity may be considered equivalent to another, no bipolar opposition allows a third term that can establish the similarity of the two opposed terms in any binary opposition. But the Socratic art of definition exalts the category of *resemblance* as the ultimate one, by relentlessly seeking the common essence that underlies the apparent difference. Hence the Socratic art reverses the order of pre-Socratic thought by subordinating contrast (or difference) to resemblance (or unity). It is this conceptual reversal that prepared for the emergence of such post-Socratic architechtonic systems as Plato's and Aristotle's.

Lévi-Strauss has called the science of the concrete *bricolage*. In its crude simplicity, primitive thought indeed looks like a *bricoleur*, if the articulate systematic thought of advanced cultures is compared to an engineer. I have tried to spell out the implications of this metaphorical description by comparing pre-Socratic with post-Socratic thought. The central difference between these two types of thought is structural; they operate with different principles of conceptual organization. One is the principle of coordination; the other is the principle of subordination. The function of the former is to highlight contrast and opposition; the function of the latter is to accentuate unity and resemblance. Hence the principle of subordination produces a unitary conceptual system, while the principle of coordination accumulates only a cluster of binary contrasts.

The metamorphosis of the logic of coordination into the logic of subordination underlay the full flowering of ancient Greek thought. Socrates often compared his art of dialogical inquiry to the art of midwifery; his art of definition was midwife to the conceptual metamorphosis of ancient Greek thought. Of course, the Socratic art of definition did not come out of nowhere. It appears to have evolved from the Sophistic tradition. As practitioners and teachers of the new art of rhetoric, the Sophists were keenly conscious of the power of language and developed a penchant for precise distinction, thereby preparing the intellectual milieu for the Socratic art of definition.

Some of the Sophists were already raising the fundamental semantic question of the relation between words and objects, and formulating some intriguing theories of verbal meanings, as attested by Plato's dialogue *Cratylus*. Even Plato's theory of Forms was addressed to this semantic question: the Forms were claimed to be the ultimate source of verbal meanings. Aristotle's theory of categories was also addressed to the same question: it was meant to be a systematic classification of verbal expressions in accordance with the objects to which they are related, that is, a systematic account of how words are related to objects (*Categories* 1b25).

The Sophists also developed the forms of proofs and arguments as instruments of persuasion. These forms had not been necessary for the discourses of pre-Socratic thinkers in general, who only had to pronounce their words of truth and wisdom instead of having to prove them. This is reflected in the transformation of Greek prose style. The pre-Socratic prose style had been predominantly the *lexis eiromene*, "in which the component parts are 'strung together' in coordination"; by the time of the Sophists, it was becoming more and more the *lexis katestrammene*, "in which long and highly organized sentences are built up by subordination of clauses."[17]

The subordination prose structure became indispensable to the Sophists; their proofs and arguments are made by subordinating one clause to another, or one sentence to another. The coordination prose structure would have been sufficient, had they only needed to pronounce their words like the pre-

Socratic sages.[18] As to these sages, many of them wrote not in prose but in verse, which is far less suitable for proofs and arguments than prose. The transformation of Greek prose style is most noticeable in Greek historical writings, e.g., the contrast between Herodotus and Thucydides. The former employs the coordination prose structure extensively; the latter heavily employs the subordination structure.[19] Furthermore, it is well established that Thucydides' prose style had been developed under the influence of the Sophists.

From these considerations, we may conclude that the transformation of a system of coordination into a system of subordination constituted the structural transformation of ancient Greek culture form its pre-Socratic to its post-Socratic era. Insofar as the structure of pre-Socratic Greek culture was governed by a system of coordination, it resembled the structure of primitive cultures.[20] Beyond this, is there any structural difference between them? We cannot settle this question without considering the problem of temporality and historicity.

TEMPORALITY AND HISTORICITY

As a preliminary, let us consider the question of logical and temporal orders in syllogistic arguments and prose styles. In a syllogistic argument, there is a logical order in the sequence of premises and conclusion; this logical order determines the temporal sequence in which the premises and the conclusion are presented. Consider the following syllogism: "All men are mortal. Therefore Socrates is mortal. Socrates is a man." As a syllogism, this one sounds quite odd, because its temporal sequence does not coicide with its logical order. Let us now consider the following statement: "Socrates was mortal. He was wise. He was brave." The temporal order of these three sentences can be altered without affecting the semantic content of the statement. The temporal order in this case is arbitrary and immaterial. In the case of a syllogistic argument, however, the temporal order of its sentences is neither arbitrary nor immaterial. The former may be called the order of chance or the aleatorial order; the latter may be called the order of reason or the rational order.

The distinction between these two types of temporal order can be further illustrated with Lévi-Strauss' own favorite example of thematic variations in a musical composition.[21] Let us consider a musical piece composed of six variations on a given theme. These six variations can be organized in two different ways: the aleatorial and the rational modes. In an aleatorial mode, the sequence of those variations is a matter of chance; it can be determined by casting dice (alea means a game with dice). In a rational mode, the sequence of those variations is determined by some ordering principle; for example, they can be ordered in terms of rhythm, tempo, intensity, or complexity. A rational mode can give the sense of progression or development, whereas an aleatorial mode cannot. The former can have a cumulative effect, but the latter cannot. Hence the former can also be called a progressional, developmental, or cumulative mode, while the latter can be labeled a nonprogressional, nondevelopmental, or noncumulative mode. No doubt, there can be more than one aleatorial or rational mode for organizing these different variations on a given theme.

Lévi-Strauss applies these two modes to historical events in his distinction between "hot" and "cold" societies, which roughly corresponds to the standard distinction between primitive and advanced cultures.[22] In hot societies, the sequence of historical events has a sense of progression or development; in cold societies, their sequence is devoid of such a sense. For this reason, primitive cultures appear to be static, whereas advanced cultures appear to be moving toward a certain goal.[23]

Now it is interesting to note that a system of coordination can be realized in either of these two historical modes. Suppose that the history of a primitive tribe has manifested a series of polarities and that the historical sequence of those polarities has had no cumulative effect. Furthermore, those polarities are equivalent to one another, or rather they are different ways of expressing the same ultimate polarity, for example, good vs. evil. The history of this primitive tribe can be regarded as a nonprogressional system of coordination. In this system, synchrony can be said to prevail over diachrony, to use Lévi-Strauss' technical terms.

Let us now imagine another primitive tribe whose history is different from that of the other tribe in one regard. Its history is also a series of polarities, which are equivalent to one another. But the sequence of those polarities has had cumulative effect. Let me illustrate the nature of their cumulative effect with Aeschylus' trilogy. The three tragic events of this trilogy can be regarded as equal manifestations of the same polarity, love vs. hate. In spite of this equality, the order of their sequence cannot be changed without altering their narrative effect; the first event provides the background for the occurrence of the second event, which in turns performs the same role for the occurrence of the third and final event. The trilogy constitutes a meaningful development of events, which build up cumulative effect. If the history of this primitive tribe develops in this manner, it can be regarded as a progressional system of coordination. In this system, diachrony can be said to prevail over synchrony.

In his theory of cold societies, Lévi-Strauss generally assumes that a system of coordination is always nonprogressional. This assumption is also operative in his transformational account of myths, in which the sequence of occurrence has no importance. For example, it is immaterial whether the tragedy of Oedipus Tyrannus occurs before or after that of Antigone in the cycle of Theban myths, as long as they manifest the same polarity.[24] Against this general assumption of his non-

progressional view of primitive societies, Lévi-Strauss sometimes seems to entertain the possibility of a progressional view.
In his transformational account of the myth of Asdival, for
example, he talks of "regression" and "progression." These
words seem to belong to a progressional view.[25]

A system of subordination can also be realized in either
a progressional or a nonprogressional historical mode. For illustration, let us compare Aristotle's system of genera and species with Darwin's. Although both are systems of subordination, they take different historical modes. Darwin's system is
realized in a progressional mode; Aristotle's in a nonprogressional mode. The former develops in history; the latter does
not. The former is evolutionary; the latter is stationary.

Plato's view of history is as nonprogressional as Aristotle's.
In his *Republic*, Plato constructs the ideal pattern of all possible
city states. This ideal state, which consists of three different
classes, is clearly a system of subordination. In books 8 and 9,
Plato tries to explain all the different forms of government,
which have appeared in history, as different manifestations or
distortions of this ideal pattern. For example, he regards plu-
tocracy and democracy as degenerate forms of the ideal state
that emerge on the usurpation of philosopher-kings' governing
role by some other classes, such as a few rich people and the
poor multitude. His theory of degeneration is a theory of transformation; every transformation of the ideal state is its degeneration. Hence he advocates a rigid adherence to established
ideal standards and conventions, as rigid as Egyptians are alleged to have been (*Laws* 656D–E). His view of Egyptian history
is very much like Lévi-Strauss' view of primitive history.

It has been said by many that the progressional view of
history is a Judeo-Christian legacy.[26] Ancient Jews did indeed
develop an eschatological view of history, the idea that their
history was a continuous, cumulative movement for the ful-
fillment of the covenant between Abraham and his God, or the

coming of the Messiah and his kingdom. The early Christians transformed this one-stage Judaic view into their two-stage eschatology by dividing world history into the Age of the Father and the Age of the Son. In the twelfth and thirteenth centuries, this two-stage view was elaborated into a three-stage eschatology by the addition of the Age of the Spirit.[27]

Ancient Romans had also developed an eschatological view of history. Virgil's *Aeneid* and Livy's *History of Rome* are impressive monuments to Roman eschatology. The eschatological character of the *Aeneid* becomes obvious when it is compared with Callimachus' *Aetia*, which served as a model for the composition of Virgil's epic. In the *Aetia*, Callimachus recounts the legendary beginnings and causes of Greek cities, but these initial causes are presented without any bearings on the direction of their development. In the *Aeneid*, Virgil tries to show how the entire destiny of Rome had been planned in her very beginning and how this destiny had been fulfilled and vindicated in Roman history. Callimachus' *Aetia* is etiological; Virgil's *Aeneid* is teleological or eschatological.

Livy's eschatology covers not only the rise of Rome but also her decline. In his view, neither rise nor decline had been accidental or episodic; they had been cumulative and progressional. This progressional view of history is hard to find among ancient Greek historians. For example, Thucydides tries to diagnose the causes of the Peloponnesian War, but these causes are not conceived in the context of the historical destiny of Athens or Sparta. Herodotus' aim is to chronicle for posterity the great deeds of both friends and foes during the Greco-Persian Wars, but those deeds are not seen in the context of development of Greece or Persia. The work of a Greek historian is generally limited to the investigation of one event or one series of events without an eschatological overtone.

This difference between Greek and Roman historical perspectives seems to reflect the difference in their political experiences. Whereas the history of ancient Greece was the story

of contending city states and their fluctuating fortunes, that of
Rome was the story of her steady rise and fall over a long period
of time. Even the Greek historian Polybius, who had initially
formulated the eschatological view of Roman history and influenced the historical views of Livy and other Roman historians, composed his *Universal History* in order to capture the
historical essence of the cumulative Roman development.[28] In
his *Universal History*, even Chance (*Tyche*) plays the role of
Providence; it has its own cumulative effect in fulfilling the
Roman destiny.[29]

The view that the idea of progress was not known in ancient Greece has been challenged by Ludwig Edelstein.[30] He
has argued that the idea of progress had been entertained by
many Greek thinkers from Xenophanes through Plato and Aristotle down to the Hellenistic thinkers. Edelstein's thesis has
been partially accepted and disputed by E. R. Dodds.[31] A clear
understanding of these claims and disputes requires some
futher distinctions and clarifications in the progressional view
of history.

First, a progressional view of history is not necessarily tied
down to the idea of progress. For the progression of historical
events can be toward evil as well as good, decline as well as
progress. The word "progression" is value-neutral; all it means
is that historical progression is cumulative or moves toward a
certain point.[32] For example, Dodds disputes Edelstein's view
of Lucretius as an apostle of progress on the ground that Lucretius was conscious of not only progress and improvement
but also corruption and degeneration.[33] This point, though true,
presents no problem in ascribing a progressional view of history
to Lucretius, because his notion of decline is as cumulative as
is his notion of progress.

Second, historical progression can be partial or total. For
example, Edelstein says that Xenophanes believed in the progress of human knowledge and science.[34] In spite of this belief,
Xenophanes may not have entertained the idea of progress

about the other aspects of human history. In that event, his notion of historical progression was partial. Plato and Aristotle also seem to have believed in the progress of human knowledge, although they did not subscribe to the idea of total historical progression. When Plato talks of the battle of gods and giants, that is, the continuous pre-Socratic dispute between idealists and materialists, he clearly gives the impression that his own theory is a historical synthesis of this battle (*Sophists* 246A–250C). When Aristotle examines all the pre-Aristotelian theories of reality in book 1 of his *Metaphysics*, he also gives the impression that his theory of four causes brings all those previous theories into their final perfection. In both Plato and Aristotle, the notion of progression appears to be limited to the development of human knowledge; theirs was the notion of partial historical progression.

Ancient Greeks appear to have accepted only the notion of partial historical progression until Polybius' *Universal History*. After Polybius, especially among Roman poets and historians, the notion of total historical progression became popular and influential. This notion was joined to the notion of Judeo-Christian eschatology when Christianity was introduced into the Roman Empire. The conjunction was formalized in Saint Augustine's *City of God*. For the exposition of his Christian eschatology, Augustine employs the Roman notion of two cities, the heavenly and the earthly cities. This notion was especially popular among Roman Stoics such as Cicero and Seneca. Whereas Romans believed in the joint destiny of their two cities and their harmony (the earthly city was believed to be the replica of the heavenly city), Augustine depicts a perpetual strife between his two cities. In his Christian eschatology, the earthly city is branded as the City of the Devil, which is destined to be vanquished by the City of God at the Last Judgment.

Let us now try to recapitulate our classification of conceptual systems. First, they can be divided into systems of coordination and systems of subordination. Second, these types of conceptual systems can be associated with two different types of historical sequence: the aleatorial or nonprogressional, and the rational or progressional. A system of coordination can be realized in either a progressional or a nonprogressional historical mode. Since a system of coordination realized in a nonprogressional historical mode is supposed to be a system of homologous binary oppositions, it can be called a system of nonprogressional binary oppositions. For the same reason, a system of coordination realized in a progressional historical mode can be called a system of progressional binary oppositions. A system of subordination can also be realized in either of the two historical modes; it can become either a system of progressional subordination or nonprogressional subordination.[35]

These are the four different types of psychological structure which are implicitly or explicitly operative in Lévi-Strauss' characterization of hot and cold societies. Of course, he has used only one of them in delineating the structure of primitive mentality in The Savage Mind, but the other three are needed in fully rounding out the contour of his psychological structuralism.

CHAPTER THREE

Structure of a Greek Myth

ONE OF THE haunting questions about Lévi-Strauss' structuralism has concerned its applicability to European culture. The difficulty of resolving this question arises from the ambiguity of what is meant by "Lévi-Strauss' structuralism" and "European culture." European culture has had a long history. Some of its phases may belong to what Lévi-Strauss calls cold societies; some other phases may belong to what he calls hot societies; still others may belong to the transitional stage between the two. Moreover, the expression "Lévi-Strauss' structuralism" can mean either his linguistic or his psychological structuralism. Since this distinction between the two versions of his structuralism has not been recognized, the problematic expression may simply refer to the structural analysis that employs the schema of binary oppositions and their equivalences. This version of his structuralism may be called its simplified form.

In this simplified form, structuralism means a system of nonprogressional binary oppositions. This primitive form is likely to apply to European culture in its earliest stage, because the organizational principle for ancient European culture is not likely to be much different from the one governing the structure of today's primitive societies. But the same primitive form is unlikely to apply to modern European culture, since it is a product of hot societies. As such, its principle of organization is most likely to be the principle of subordination rather than coordination. We can test these conjectures and projections by examining Lévi-Strauss' analyses of the Oedipus myth and Baudelaire's sonnet "Les Chats," two well-known attempts to apply his structuralism to European culture. For the convenience of our test, the Oedipus myth is a legacy of ancient European culture, while Baudelaire's sonnet is a product of modern European culture. If our hypothesis about the structure of European culture and its transformation is correct, the structural analysis of these cultural objects should produce quite different results.

THE THEBAN MYTHS

What Lévi-Strauss calls the Oedipus myth is not the story of Oedipus alone, but the whole cycle of Theban myths, which begins with the founding of Thebes by Cadmus and ends with Antigone's defiance of Creon over the burial rite of her brother Polynices. The expression "the Oedipus myth" can be easily taken to refer to the myth of Oedipus Tyrannus rather than this whole cycle of Theban myths. In order to avoid this sort of misunderstanding, let us call these myths the Theban myths rather than the Oedipus myth.

Lévi-Strauss sets out his structural analysis of the Theban myths in the accompanying chart.[1] According to Lévi-Strauss, the four columns represent the two bipolar oppositions which run through the entire cycle of Theban myths, namely, the opposition between the overrating of blood relations vs. the underrating of blood relations, and the opposition between the denial of man's autochthonous origin vs. the persistence of his autochthonous origin. The first of these binary oppositions is described in the two columns on the left side; the second, in the two columns on the right side. In the Theban myths, trag-

Structural Analysis of the Theban Myths

I	II	III	IV
Cadmus seeks his sister Europa, ravished by Zeus			
		Cadmus kills the dragon	
	The Spartoi kill one another		
	Oedipus kills his father, Laius		Labdacus (Laius' father) = *lame* (?)
			Laius (Oedipus' father) = *left-sided* (?)
		Oedipus kills the sphinx	
			Oedipus = *swollen-foot* (?)
Oedipus marries his mother, Jocasta			
	Eteocles kills his brother, Polynices		
Antigone buries her brother, Polynices, despite prohibition			

edies and misfortunes seem to take place whenever one of
these bipolar terms overpowers the other. This line of thought
is in accord with Lévi-Strauss' thesis that the function of bipolar
structure is to maintain the symmetry of social and mental
orders, and that the disturbance of this symmetry is to be
avoided and remedied under any circumstances.[2]

   We shall test the validity of this structural analysis by using
Terence Turner's exhaustive critique of it.[3] Turner's critique
is divided into two segments, the substantive and the methodological. His substantive criticism is that Lévi-Strauss' two
polarities do not correctly capture the substance of the
"mythemes":

> Cadmus' search for his sister and Antigone's burial of her brother
> are simply acts conforming to the normal obligations of kin. The
> former was undertaken at the behest of a father . . . while the
> latter owed its dramatic quality as a strong assertion of blood
> ties (as distinct from "over-assertion") to its violation of Creon's
> prohibition, which was itself rather an "underrating" of blood
> relationships. Oedipus' incestuous relationship with his mother
> is surely to be regarded as a destructive combination of incom-
> patible relationships (one of blood and one of marriage) rather
> than as the "overrating" of a blood relationship.[4]

Turner makes a similar substantive argument against the validity of the polarity between the denial of the autochthonous
origin of man and the persistence of the autochthonous origin
of man.

   It is not entirely correct to hold that Cadmus and Antigone
did not overrate their blood relationships because they were
performing acts conforming to the normal obligations of kin.
Although the obligations were normal, they had to be performed under extraordinary circumstances. It is not the nature
of obligations but that of circumstances that makes the behavior
of Cadmus and Antigone extraordinary. They had to risk their
own lives. To overrate blood relationship may simply mean to

place an unusually high value on that relationship. By this standard, Cadmus and Antigone may be said to have overrated their blood relationships.

Oedipus' blood relationship with his parents was indeed undervalued by his parents when he was cast away as an unwanted infant; it was overvalued when he married his own mother. Even after his return to plague-ridden Thebes, the central question about his relation with the Thebans was whether he was an insider or an outsider, one of their own or a stranger to them. In those days, this was essentially a question of kinship; in primitive societies, to be an insider is the same as to be a blood relation. Hence the blood relationship can be regarded as a central axis whose polarity structures the tragic fate of Oedipus as much as those of Cadmus and Antigone.

It should be admitted that Lévi-Strauss' characterization of this polarity is not quite appropriate; perhaps it can be better described as the polarity of natives vs. strangers, insiders vs. outsiders, or kin vs. aliens. When Cadmus leaves his home in search of his sister, he does not undertake this ordeal on his own. It is in obedience to his father King Agenor's command that he and his two brothers set out on their hazardous journey. Agenor is the first one to experience conflict, by forcing his three sons into exile for the recovery of his daughter, and by risking the safety of the former for the sake of the latter. This forces Cadmus into a conflict with his father and makes him an exile in search of his sister. Out of these tangled relationships of father and son, brother and sister, home and exile, Cadmus founds the city of Thebes. The myth of the Spartoi, who spring from the dragon's teeth and fight among themselves, is the story of an intrafamilial feud that can be regarded as a continuation of the conflict between Cadmus and his father.

The polarity of kinfolk and strangers should not be considered a unique feature of Theban myths. It was a matter of overriding concern in most neolithic cultures, because the integrity and security of those cultures came to be endangered by the rapidly increasing traffic between the communities which had long developed under the insulation of paleolithic immobility. This concern can also be detected in the Homeric epics. Paris' elopement with Helen was, first of all, a serious violation of his relation with his host Menelaus, serious enough to bring about the Trojan expedition of the Achaean forces. In those days, the host-guest relation was evidently one of the precarious institutions devised and sanctioned to cope with the newly developing mobility between the natives and strangers. The bipolar conflict between natives and strangers, hosts and guests, native city and alien city, runs through both the Homeric epics, from Helen's elopement to Troy to Odysseus' return to Ithaca.

Lévi-Strauss' first polarity turns out to be a familiar my-theme as soon as it is restated in an appropriate language. His second polarity is also a familiar one, because it concerns the bipolar opposition between mortals and immortals. The au-tochthonous origin of man means his mortality, because he is born from the earth or comes from dust; the denial of his au-tochthonous origin is the denial of this mortality on the ground that his origin is not earthly but divine. This polarity is also a recurrent mytheme in many cultures other than the ancient Greek, and can take on many different shapes, such as the polarities of sacred vs. profane, divine vs. human, heaven vs. earth, etc.

Lévi-Strauss is quite right in observing that the second polarity is concerned with the question of origin, namely, whether the Thebans are born of the divine or of the earthly. The city of Thebes was founded by Cadmus under Apollo's guidance, and this attests to divine sanction of the Thebans. But the five Spartoi, who survived their destructive feud and became the founding fathers of the Theban nobility, were born from the dragon's teeth, and that seems to indicate the earthly origin of the Thebans. This ambiguity on the question of origin is also an overriding concern in the tragic fate of Oedipus.

Throughout his career, Oedipus is keenly conscious of his resourceful intellect, which establishes his close affinity with Apollo, the god of intellect. Even more significant than his intellect is his godlike courage to use his intellect for noble causes rather than the petty cause of his own comfort and profit. However, this Apollonian affinity is clearly infected by his ignorance and other earthly flaws, as clearly as his physical beauty is marred by his physical deformity.

Assuming that these two polarities correctly capture the thematic substance of Theban myths, let us now try to determine their relation to each other. The two polarities seem to be concerned with the same question of birth and origin. Initially, birth and origin may have been the only criteria used in differentiating kinfolk from strangers; subsequently, those criteria may have been extended from the immediate community of human beings to the cosmic community which includes immortals. In that event, the second polarity is an analogical extension of the first polarity.[5] Hence Lévi-Strauss claims a homological (or analogical) equivalence of the two polarities.[6]

SYNCHRONY VS. DIACHRONY

Notwithstanding Turner's substantive criticism, Lévi-Strauss' structural analysis of the Theban myths appears to be substantively correct. Let us now turn to Turner's methodological critique: the diachronic order of the myths is totally suppressed by their synchronic order.[7] The synchronic order of the Theban myths can be found by reading horizontally the chart that tabulates Lévi-Strauss' structural analysis of those myths; their diachronic order can be found by reading the same chart vertically. Let us now suppose that its vertical order is rearranged by changing the sequence of those myths. This change in vertical or diachronic order cannot dictate a corresponding change in Lévi-Strauss' structural analysis. In other words, his structural analysis should be valid of the rearranged sequence of Theban myths, if it is valid of the original sequence of those myths. Methodologically, Turner holds, Lévi-Strauss' structural analysis is incapable of accounting for diachronic orders because it is exclusively synchronic.

This methodological critique of Lévi-Strauss' structural analysis is absolutely correct. However, the importance of this critique depends on the importance of the diachronic order of those myths. If their diachronic order is immaterial, it can be ignored without any serious consequence. On the other hand, if it is significant, it cannot be ignored without distorting our understanding of those myths. In the last chapter, we distinguished between two different modes of diachronic order: (1) a progressional or cumulative one and (2) a nonprogressional or noncumulative one. If the cycle of Theban myths embodies a progressional order, its diachronic order must be taken into account. On the other hand, if it embodies a nonprogressional order, its diachronic order need not be taken into account. Hence our problem boils down to the question: what type of temporal order is operative in the cycle of Theban myths?

Turner maintains that the sequence of the Theban myths plays an important role in establishing their cumulative effect. For example, he says, "Labdacus' death is the operator that brings about the transformation of the earlier configuration of relations into the later. . . ."[8] In a nonprogressional diachronic order, every myth is self-contained; it can have no effect on other myths. Turner is saying that this is not the way the Theban myths are organized, and that the order of their sequence is to establish their interdependence and continuity. On this point, Turner appears to be clearly right. There is an assured sense of progression in the diachronic order of Theban myths, insofar as they are considered as episodes in the development of a single myth cycle.

If the cycle of Theban myths embodies a progressional

diachronic order, to ignore or suppress it is indeed a serious defect of Lévi-Strauss' structural analysis. This progressional order may very well be the crucial differentia between ancient Greek culture and primitive cultures. As Lévi-Strauss assumes, both types of culture may be organized on the same structural universal of binary opposition. However, the same system of bipolar coordination may be realized in a progressional mode in one of them and in a nonprogressional mode in the other. In that event, Lévi-Strauss' structural analysis of ancient Greek myths or culture can be partially but never wholly adequate so long as his analysis is governed by the nonprogressional schema of binary oppositions.

In addition to this inadequacy, there are a couple of other points in whose regard Lévi-Strauss' structural analysis fails to do justice to the complexity of the Theban myths. Let us reconsider the polarity between kinfolk and strangers. This polarity takes on a far more complex form in the Theban myths than the simple dichotomy it usually assumes in most primitive societies. For example, when Cadmus is forced to leave his native city and found a new one for his home in exile, he becomes an alien to the home of his birth and a native of a strange land. He has to leave his own kin and establish a new kinship with the Spartoi, who have sprung from the dragon's teeth. Old ties are severed and new ties established. The bipolar opposition of kinfolk vs. strangers now becomes a complex double dichotomy. Whereas the simple or single dichotomy of kinfolk and strangers gives a person a single identity, the complex or double dichotomy gives him a double identity.

The complexity of this bipolar opposition becomes even more obvious in the life of Oedipus. He was born in Thebes but raised in Corinth; he is a native of Thebes by birth but of Corinth by nurture. When he kills his father Laius, he thinks that he is killing a stranger. When he runs away from a stranger Polybus, king of Corinth, he thinks that he is running away from his father. Of course, both Laius and Polybus are at once fathers and strangers to Oedipus in different respects. Oedipus is a man of exile in perpetuity. Even when he returns to Thebes, he is still regarded as an outsider by himself and others. He is an alien in his own home.

The same complexity of bipolar opposition also underlies the tragic fate of Antigone; she is caught between her ethical obligation to her brother and her political obligation to her uncle. Her uncle Creon is an outsider to Antigone, because he is an uncle through her mother. Most patriarchal tribes are exogamous; a bride is obtained from outside. Hence all her relatives remain outsiders to the tribe of her bridegroom. But Creon was not an outsider pure and simple; he had been living with Antigone in the same house and been enthroned as king of her native city. Neither was her brother Polynices any longer a legitimate native of Thebes by the time of his death. On the death of Oedipus, both of his two sons wanted to be king of Thebes, and finally agreed to rule in alternate years. They had also agreed that one would go into exile during the year of the other's reign. The first year fell to Eteocles, and Polynices went to Argos. Once on the throne, however, Eteocles decided not to yield the kingship to Polynices, in violation of their agreement. In retaliation for this violation, Polynices tried to invade and conquer Thebes with the army of Argos. Since he was killed in this battle, he had made himself practically an outsider and an aggressor to his own native city of Thebes by the time of Antigone's tragedy. In spite of this political development, Antigone still feels her obligation to Polynices as her blood relation. Because of these complexities in familial and political ties, her tragic fate also involves questions of double rather than single identity.

In the Homeric epics, the bipolar conflict between kinfolk and strangers is a simple dichotomy, totally free of the complexities found in the Theban myths. Homeric heroes may travel to alien lands, but never attempt to make their homes in those lands. Hence their nativeness is exclusively determined by *nativity*. But the fate and circumstances of Cadmus, Oedipus, and Creon are never so simple; their nativeness is determined by their mobility as much as their nativity. This difference between the Theban and the Homeric myths reflects the difference in their cultural contexts. The Theban myths were probably the products of the period of migration, during which the ancient Greek cities were settled and founded by immigrants from Asia. The Homeric myths were the sagas of ancient Greece after this settlement, when they had established their roots in their respective native cities.

This thematic difference between the Homeric and the Theban myths cannot be captured by Lévi-Strauss' structural analysis without introducing the distinction between the simple form of bipolarity and its complex form. This difference between the two forms of the same polarity cannot be explained away as two different ways of manifesting the same polarity. The simple and the complex forms can never be structurally equivalent; in Lévi-Strauss' structuralism, two forms can manifest the same structure only if they are structurally equivalent.

It may also be advisable to take note of the distinction between the internal and the external world in understanding the operation of Lévi-Strauss' two polarities in the Theban myths. For example, the polarity between kinfolk and strangers in the story of Oedipus appears not only in his relation with Thebans but also in his relation to himself. He is a native and a stranger not only to Thebans but to himself, insofar as he does and does not know his own identity. Hence the polarity generates his inner struggle as well as his conflict with Thebans.

The same thing can be said about the polarity between mortals and immortals, or the heavenly and the earthly. It appears not only in Oedipus' and his fellow mortals' relation to immortals, but within his own self. The battle between his divine and earthly selves carries even greater tragic pathos than the struggle between him and his external world. That this battle is carried through to the bitter end really means that the divine self in Oedipus finally triumphs over his earthly self. What is crushed by the tragic ending is not the divine self (child of Apollo), but the earthly self (child of the dragon). For this reason, at the end of *Oedipus at Colonus*, the old, blind hero has every right to be transformed into a divinity in the depth of the sacred grove.

The compounding of inner and outer conflict also takes place in *Antigone*; the heroine feels the conflict between the divine and the human law within her heart as well as between herself and the external authority of the king. But this complexity of inner and outer cannot be found either in the myths of Cadmus and Spartoi or in the Homeric myths. I am fairly certain that it was introduced by Sophocles. The consciousness of the inner world, which is the necessary condition for producing inner conflicts, was most likely not yet known to the original makers of the Theban and Homeric myths. Only by the time of Sophocles and Socrates did the ancient Greeks perhaps achieve an awareness of their inner world, thereby adding a new dimension to their cultural context.

This polarity between the inner and the outer world cannot be reduced to either of Lévi-Strauss' two polarities, because it is not equivalent to either of them. Furthermore, it can be used in differentiating the two versions of Theban myths, Sophocles' and the pre-Sophocles version. This procedure is contrary to Lévi-Strauss' method, which refuses to recognize the difference between the earlier and the later versions of a myth, because "we define the myth as consisting of all its versions."[9] Since his structural analysis takes seriously only the common structure of all the different versions of a given myth and simply ignores their structural difference, it has no way of providing a structural account of their difference. Structural analysis is always blind to the problem of difference and diversity because it is solely concerned with the question of resemblance. The inability to account for diversity is not limited to Lévi-Strauss' structuralism; this weakness is shared by all formalist programs.

By leaving out of account all features of diversity and particularity, it is indeed possible to establish certain elements of uniformity and universality in all the myths of mankind. The structure of binary opposition is surely one of the most plausible candidates, because almost every myth involves some sort of conflict. Although this structure may assume many different forms, such as good vs. evil, heaven vs. earth, light vs. dark, kinfolk vs. strangers, etc., Lévi-Strauss' structural analysis seeks out the common structure by excluding the differentiae. That is, the uniformity and universality of structure are established by systematic exclusion and abstraction. By analogy, we can see a uniform color in all visual objects if we look at them through a pair of tinted glasses which can systematically reject all other colors

UNIFORMITY VS. DIVERSITY

The systematic exclusion or suppression of differentiae is a far more serious defect of Lévi-Strauss' structuralism than its suppression of temporality. With the suppression of diachrony, as we have seen, it is impossible to account for the cumulative effect of myths or historical events. However, the suppression of diversity can produce far more extensive problems, because the category of difference is absolutely universal. Everything is different from everything else in some respect. In fact, the category of diachrony is only a special case of this universal category, because the concept of diachrony is none other than the concept of difference in time or different moments in time.

By suppressing this universal category, it is possible to establish the unrestricted universality of certain structural elements for the whole of mankind. For the suppression of the difference logically entails the assertion of uniformity. If one is not aware of this systematic exclusion, one can easily be misled to believe that Lévi-Strauss' structuralism has demonstrated the absolute uniformity of human culture. Instead of demonstrating the uniformity of human culture, Lévi-Strauss has simply suppressed its diversity.[10]

In our examination of Lévi-Strauss' structural analysis, we have made a few attempts to explain structural differences by appealing to their cultural contexts. For example, we have tried to render a contextual account of the structural difference between the Theban and the Homeric myths, and between Sophocles' version of the Oedipus cycle and its pre-Sophoclesian version. This sort of contextual appeal is inadmissible in Lévi-Strauss' structuralism because it rests on the presupposition that the differentiation and variation of formal structures are dictated by the contingency of contextual circumstances. This presupposition is incompatible with Lévi-Strauss' assumption of invariant formal structures.

In Lévi-Strauss' structuralism, formal structures are conceived as necessary and ultimate entities. Their existence and invariance are matters of necessity that cannot be controlled by the force of contingency. They are so ultimate that they cannot be explained by anything other than themselves. Every structure is its own reason. Instead of being an *explanandum*, every structure is meant to be an *explanans*. In this regard, Lévi-Strauss' formal structures behave much like the theoretical structures of natural science. They are ultimate entities in the scheme of explanation; they are meant to explain natural phenomena instead of being explained by something else.

Although Lévi-Strauss has never said that he is adopting the natural scientist's notion of structure, he has often described the nature of his structural analysis in such a way that the structures in his investigations occupy the same place that the theoretical structures of natural science do in the scientific investigations of nature. The structures of myths and conventions are supposedly hidden under their diverse surface manifestations. Once they are disclosed, they are supposed to articulate the intelligibility of manifold cultural phenomena. The notion that the understanding of reality is ultimately the problem of discovering the ultimate structure has, Lévi-Strauss feels, been validated by Marxism, geology, and psychoanalysis: "All three demonstrate that understanding consists in reducing one type of reality to another; that the true reality is never the most obvious. . . ."[11] The essential function of scientific research is to discover the true structure of reality that usually lies hidden under the surface of the obvious appearance; "scientific explanation is always the discovery of an 'arrangement'."[12]

The ultimacy of structure in natural science is due to the divorce between structure and teleology. Because of this divorce, there is no point in inquiring into the reasons, purposes, or functions of the structures of natural objects and phenomena. Although this divorce is justifiable in natural science, which presupposes the nonteleological character of the natural world, it appears to be unjustifiable in cultural sciences. Before anything else, the world of culture is the world of values, purposes, and functions.

Once the teleological character of cultural world is accepted, the ultimacy of formal structures becomes impossible to uphold. In the teleological scheme, formal structures exist not for their own sake but for the sake of fulfilling some functions. Their role or value is extrinsic (instrumental) rather than intrinsic. The functional and contextual accounts of social and cultural structures are meant to explicate the extrinsic role or value of those structures by articulating their teleological nexuses. Going against this teleological approach, Lévi-Strauss exalts the intrinsic role of social and cultural structures: "the 'structuring' has an intrinsic effectiveness of its own whatever the principles and methods which suggested it."[13]

To a casual observer, Marx's notion of social structure and Freud's notion of psychic structure may appear to be nonteleological views—as nonteleological as the structure of geological strata. Freud especially often talks of the various strata of the human psychic structure as if they had been formed without any teleological considerations, just like the formation of geological structures. In his reflective moments, however, Freud does spell out the teleological character of those psychic strata. Although the libido and its pleasure principle are given by nature, he holds, the ego and its reality principle are formed to cope with the helplessness of the libido and the harshness of the external reality. Likewise, the formation of the superego is for the sake of coping with the aggressive instinct. Hence the Freudian tripartite structure of the human psyche is accountable on the teleological premise that it serves to fulfill what Freud calls the program of becoming happy.[14]

The teleological character of social structures in Marx's theory is far more pronounced than that of Freud's psychic structure. Marx emphatically claims that the ultimate structure of every society is its class structure, that is, the relation of the exploiting and the exploited classes, and that every class structure is a form of production, that is, it provides the social framework for the coordination of productive forces. Because production is the ultimate function of all social structures, Marx maintains, every social structure is overthrown by a revolution as soon as it ceases to fulfill this function.[15] There could be neither revolution nor contradiction in any society but for its value-laden character. Indeed, there is neither any contradiction between two geological strata nor any revolution from one stratum to another, precisely because those strata are totally free of all teleological relations.

Like the Marxian contradictions and their resolutions, social conflict and equilibrium can exist only in the world of values.[16] In most cases of Lévi-Strauss' structural analysis, conflict and equilibrium are the objects of his central concern; his schema of binary opposition is usually either to articulate the nature of conflict or to explicate its resolution in an equilibrium. Hence his structuralism cannot dispense with the teleological character of social and cultural structures. However, this teleological character is clearly incompatible with the ultimacy of those structures that appears to be presupposed by his structuralism. This brings us to the inevitable question: How can Lévi-Strauss maintain the ultimacy of social and cultural structures and at the same time acknowledge the value-ladenness of the social and cultural world?

Perhaps this question is meant to be answered by his repeated claim that the maintenance of binary structures in primitive societies is the ultimate end in itself. Whenever the symmetry of binary organization is disrupted by such contingent events as migrations and wars, he maintains, it is restored by the instinctive self-reorganization of that society—as instinctive as the self-reorganization of a living organism.[17] The maintenance of binary structure would thus appear to be the ultimate end of primitive social life. On this point, however, Lévi-Strauss is ambiguous; he also seems to imply that the symmetry of binary structure is valued in primitive societies because it provides social equilibrium. The restoration of a disrupted binary structure is for the sake of restoring the disrupted social equilibrium. In this case, social structure is not an end in itself but a means for the maintenance of social equilibrium.

If the binary structure is regarded only as a means of maintaining social equilibrium, structural analysis cannot be fundamentally different from functional analysis. The latter also stands on the premise that social structures are not ends in themselves but are meant to serve certain functions. This premise stands on a further one that every social structure is to be understood in the teleological context of organizing human life in meaningful forms. Lévi-Strauss' structuralism can now be taken as a special case of this teleological approach to culture.

What makes Lévi-Strauss' structuralism special is the simplicity of the social structures under its analysis; the binary structure may very well be the simplest kind of social structure that can assure equilibrium. The social problems and conflicts of primitive societies are so simple that they can be resolved simply by maintaining the symmetry of binary social structure. It is quite likely that primitive societies take the critical step toward becoming advanced societies by losing this simplicity. Our examination of the Theban myths seems to show that the culture depicted in those myths had already begun to lose this social simplicity.

Before leaving Lévi-Strauss' analysis of the Theban myths, it may be instructive to compare it with Aristotle's structural analysis of tragedy, because Aristotle uses Sophocles' *Oedipus Tyrannus* as a paradigm of tragedy in his analysis. He identifies six structural elements of a tragedy: plot, characters, diction, thought, spectacle, and melody. Of these six components, he regards the plot as the most important, "the life and soul of tragedy," which is followed by characters as the second, thought as the third, diction as the fourth, and melody and spectacle as the least important (*Poetics* 1449b32–1460b20). He then considers the unity of a plot, which gives unity to the whole play by subordinating all other structural components (*Poetics* 1451a16–35). He distinguishes between simple and complex plots: a simple plot is free of peripety (the reversal of fortunes) and discovery (of tragic truth), while a complex plot has one or both of them (*Poetics* 1452a13–17). He observes that the plot of a good tragedy must be not simple but complex, and that the third part of a complex tragic plot is suffering (*Poetics* 1452b10–31).

This is a rough summary of Aristotle's analysis. What stands out even in this summary is its architectonic character. When he identifies the six components of a tragedy, he specifies the hierarchical order among those components. In the logic of totemic structuralism, they would be left on one plane of coordination. The schema of polarities is totally absent in Aristotle's structural analysis; the central category in his analysis is the category of unity, e.g., the unity of the drama which is secured by the unity of its plot. Thus a logic of architectonic unity pervades Aristotle's structural analysis of *Oedipus Tyr-*

annus, and this logic is a logic of subordination, the subordination of all components to a single unity.

It is difficult to say whether or not Aristotle would have used the same logic in analyzing the structure of the entire Theban myth cycle. However, we may safely assume that his logic of architectonic unity represents a much more complex culture than the one represented by the simple symmetry of binary opposition.

CHAPTER FOUR

Structure of a French Sonnet

PERHAPS IT IS unfair to take Lévi-Strauss' structural analysis of the Theban myths as a serious test of his structuralist program. He presented it more or less as a casual attempt. A serious, systematic attempt was reserved for the structural analysis of Baudelaire's sonnet "Les Chats," for which Lévi-Strauss even enlisted the collaboration of the eminent structural linguist Roman Jakobson.[1] Here is the full text of that sonnet:

Les amoureux fervents et les savants austères
Aiment également, dans leur mûre saison,
Les chats puissants et doux, orgueil de la maison,
Qui comme eux sont frileux et comme eux sédentaires.

Amis de la science et de la volupté,
Ils cherchent le silence et l'horreur des ténèbres;
L'Érèbe les eut pris pour ses coursiers funèbres
S'ils pouvaient au servage incliner leur fierté.

Ils prennent en songeant les nobles attitudes
Des grands sphinx allongés au fond des solitudes,
Qui semblent s'endormir dans un rêve sans fin;

Leurs reins féconds sont pleins d'étincelles magiques,
Et des parcelles d'or, ainsi qu'un sable fin,
Étoilent vaguement leurs prunelles mystiques.

Here is my literal translation of this sonnet:

> The fervent lovers and the austere scholars
> Love equally, in their mature season,
> The powerful and gentle cats, pride of the house,
> Who like them are cold-sensitive and like them sedentary.
>
> Friends of knowledge and of sensuous rapture,
> They search for the silence and horror of darkness;
> Erebus would have taken them for his funeral steeds,
> If they could to servitude incline their lordliness.
>
> They assume in musing noble attitudes
> Of great sphinxes stretched out in the depth of solitudes,
> Who seem to fall asleep in a dream without end;
>
> Their fecund loins are full of magic sparks,
> And particles of gold, just like a fine sand,
> Star-stud vaguely their mystic pupils.

The organization of this sonnet presents various possibilities of binary opposition. The octave can be opposed to the sestet. The octave can be divided into two quatrains; the sestet can be divided into two tercets. One quatrain can be opposed to the other quatrain; one tercet can be opposed to the other tercet. In more than one way, the structure of this sonnet appears to be dyadic; it can be a fertile ground for exploiting the structural principles of binary oppositions and their correspondences. But a closer look of the same sonnet can detect triadic features of its structure. The sonnet is composed of three sentences; this punctuation scheme gives it a ternary structure. Its rhyme scheme (aBBa CddC eeFgFg) is also ternary. As a triadic structure, the poem can defy the application of Lévi-Strauss' structural principles.

Through its structural complexity this little sonnet presents a far more difficult problem of structural analysis than the Theban myths. Lévi-Strauss and Jakobson make two series of attempts at its structural analysis: one in their "demonstration proper" and the other in their "recapitulation" of that demonstration. The recapitulation does not really sum up the results of the demonstration proper, but presents another series of structural accounts quite different from those given in the demonstration proper.[2] Each of these two series contains three structural accounts of "Les Chats," which we may call (1) the ternary analysis, (2) the binary analysis, and (3) the isometric analysis.

TERNARY ANALYSIS

Our authors open their structural analysis of the sonnet by recognizing the ternary structure in its rhyme and punctuation scheme. They describe its rhyme scheme as aBBa (the first quatrain) CddC (the second quatrain) eeFgFg (the sestet). The capital letters indicate the strong or "masculine" rhymes, and the lower-case letters indicate the weak or "feminine" rhymes. Our authors recognize not only the triadic but the progressional character of its punctuation scheme: the three complex sentences which make up the sonnet show an arithmetical progression in the number of their independent clauses and definite verbs. The first sentence has one independent clause and one definite verb (*aiment*); the second sentence has two of each (*cherchent, eut pris*); the third sentence has three (*prennent, sont, étoilent*).

The ternary analysis in the demonstration proper is not fully worked out; it is presented in the following single sentence: "The ternary division of the sonnet implies an antinomy between the stanzas with two rhymes and with three rhymes."[3] This sentence is ambiguous, because the expression "the ternary division" can mean the ternary division of either the rhyme scheme or the punctuation scheme. But the ternary division of the punctuation scheme cannot contribute anything to the generation of an antinomy (or opposition) in the rhyme scheme, because the two schemes operate in complete independence.[4] The ternary division of the rhyme scheme may be said to prepare for the antinomy in question. That is, the division of the sonnet into three rhyme units makes it possible to separate those units into two groups: the units with two rhymes (the two quatrains) and the unit with three rhymes (the sestet). In that case, the ternary division of the rhyme scheme may be said to underlie the binary grouping. This appears to be what is meant by the ambiguous word "imply."

In the recapitulation, our authors present a quite different ternary analysis of the sonnet. There they do not even mention its rhyme structure, and make use of only the ternary division of the punctuation scheme. Incidentally, our authors call the ternary division of the sonnet its first division, and the binary division its second division. They now claim that the ternary division establishes an opposition between the two quatrains and resolves it in the sestet.[5] The opposition between the two quatrains is characterized as the opposition between passivity and activity. The passivity of the first quatrain is represented by the lovers and the scholars, while the activity of the second quatrain is represented by Erebus. This opposition is said to be overcome by the sestet, in which the cats actively assume passivity. This triadic account of the sonnet's structure is clearly progressional. In this regard, it is in accord with the progressional character of the sonnet's punctuation scheme.

The opposition between the two quatrains is thematic rather than structural; it concerns the thematic content of the sonnet rather than its content-neutral structure. The resolution of this thematic opposition is also thematic. Hence the triadic structure that has been used in the ternary analysis of the recapitulation can be called a thematic structure. In contrast to this, the antinomy which our authors have claimed in the sonnet's rhyme scheme belongs not to its thematic structure but to its nonthematic structure, which is content-neutral. For the rhyme structure of a poem does not affect its thematic content. Thus, there are really two different types of structure, although both of them are referred to by the same word "structure."

This ambiguity in the meaning of the word "structure" can also be reflected in the expression "structural analysis." It can mean either analysis of a thematic structure or of a nonthematic, content-neutral structure. The former analysis is thematic; it is none other than what has been known as thematic analysis. But the latter analysis, being purely structural, is structural analysis in its technical sense and in distinction from thematic analysis. The ternary analysis in the demonstration proper is purely structural, while the one in the recapitulation is thematic. The former claims a purely structural antinomy, while the latter claims a thematic antinomy and its resolution.

Let us now consider the validity of these two versions of the ternary analysis. Our authors have characterized the thematic antinomy between the two quatrains as the opposition between passivity and activity. They have argued that the lovers and the scholars of the first quatrain embody the theme of passivity by virtue of their susceptibility to passivity, and that the theme of activity in the second quatrain is expressed by the power of Erebus. This argument cannot be validated by the text of the poem, which neither mentions the powers of Erebus nor implies the passivity of the lovers and the scholars. On the contrary, the lovers and the scholars are represented as agents who love (aiment), and this active role is reinforced by two adjectives fervents and austères. The two adjectives frileux and sédentaires may imply their inactivity, but the attribute of being inactive is quite different from that of being passive. Nor is it the case that Erebus is depicted as an agent any more active than the lovers and the scholars. He is the subject of a verb in its subjunctive mood; his implied power fails to achieve his goal. Thus the alleged thematic opposition between passivity and activity cannot be given textual justification.

The purely structural antinomy that our authors have claimed in the rhyme scheme appears to be an equally dubious one. This claim is based on a numerical ground: the two quatrains have two rhymes each, while the sestet has three rhymes. This numerical difference does not seem to be strong enough to be called an opposition or antinomy. Insofar as the rhyme structure is purely formal structure, its antinomy should be defined in structural rather than numerical terms. In structural terms, an antinomy or opposition can be found between the rhyme structure of the first quatrain and that of the second quatrain; the structure of one is exactly the opposite of the other in the sequence of masculine and feminine rhymes. In this case, a structural antinomy means a structural opposition. This sort of structural opposition cannot be found between the octave and the sestet; the difference in their rhyme structures is a matter of binary distinction rather than opposition. Hence there is no structural justification for the alleged antinomy in the rhyme scheme of the sonnet.

The antinomies or oppositions which have been claimed in both versions of the ternary analysis thus turn out to be no antinomies or oppositions at all. If there is no antinomy or opposition, there can be no resolution either. Consequently, both versions end up in negative results. This is the only point of agreement for the two versions of the ternary analysis, beside its initial ternary framework. Beyond these two points of departure and final result, the two versions are systematically different. One is a purely structural analysis; the other is a thematic one. One is supposed only to pose an antinomy; the other is supposed not only to pose but also resolve one. One is meant to be progressional; the other is not. However, all these differences do not add up to anything because the alleged antinomies have no ground to stand on.

BINARY ANALYSIS

In the demonstration proper, our authors present first a syntactic version of their binary analysis and then its semantic version. The syntactic version is to demonstrate a syntactic resemblance between the first quatrain and the first tercet, and between the second quatrain and the second tercet.[6] The first quatrain consists of two clauses, one of which is a subordinate clause and begins with the relative pronoun *qui*. The construction of the first tercet is a clear parallel to this; it also consists of two clauses, one of which is a subordinate clause and begins with the same relative pronoun. The second quatrain consists of two independent clauses; so does the second tercet. In both stanzas, the second independent clause takes up two lines. So the construction of the second quatrain parallels that of the second tercet.

The semantic version of the binary analysis is much more complex than the syntactic version. It consists of the following three types of semantic correspondence. (1) the horizontal correspondences between the first quatrain and the first tercet and between the second quatrain and the second tercet, (2) the vertical correspondences between the two quatrains as a whole and the two tercets as a whole, and (3) the diagonal correspondences between the first quatrain and the second tercet and between the second quatrain and the first tercet.[7] Of these correspondences, the first one is said to reinforce the syntactic resemblances our authors have established in their syntactic analysis. The other two are presumably detectable on semantic grounds alone.

The argument given in support of the horizontal correspondences concerns the semantic nature of grammatical subjects. All grammatical subjects in the first quatrain and the first tercet are animate terms, whereas one of the two subjects in the second quatrain and all subjects of the second tercet are inanimate substantives (*l'Érèbe, leurs reins, des parcelles, un sable*). This semantic argument turns on the distinction between animate and inanimate nouns. In some languages, I understand, this distinction is indicated by some grammatical devices, just as the distinction between masculine and feminine nouns is indicated by different articles. Since French has no grammatical device for demarcating animate from inanimate nouns, our authors must be using some informal criterion for this distinction. But they do not explain the nature of their informal criterion.

When the distinction between animate and inanimate terms is informally or nongrammatically employed, it is generally treated as the distinction between living and nonliving (or lifeless). By this semantic convention, the first two of the four expressions our authors classify as inanimate seem to be animate. *Leurs reins* (the loins of the cats) should be classified as animate rather than inanimate. If the cats are alive, their loins must also be alive. Of course, if the cats are dead, their loins must be dead. Obviously our poet is talking about the living cats and their living loins; *leurs reins* is qualified by the adjective *féconds*, which represents an attribute of living.

The question whether *l'Érèbe* should be classified as animate or inanimate is a more complex issue than the question of *leurs reins*, because we can take two different semantic attitudes toward it, namely, the intratextual and extratextual. Within the text of the poem, *l'Érèbe* is clearly assumed to be a living agent, who is capable of entertaining desires and executing actions. Intratextually, it makes no sense to say that this is an inanimate word; to say so would destroy the meaningfulness of the second stanza. However, extratextually, it is possible to regard *l'Érèbe* as a nonexistent mythological being. On this ground of nonexistence, one may be tempted to classify it as inanimate (what does not exist does not live either). But that classification is semantically invalid.

As a semantic device, the animate-inanimate distinction concerns solely the semantic nature of linguistic terms, that is, the meaning of those terms. But the question of existence or nonexistence is extrasemantic; it goes well beyond the meaning of linguistic terms. Hence the question of existence or nonexistence is irrelevant to the animate-inanimate distinction of linguistic terms. Let us take the case of dinosaurs. The semantic classification of the word "dinosaur" as animate or inanimate cannot be affected by the extrasemantic fact that dinosaurs are extinct. That word is an animate term because the attribute of living is included in its meaning. For the same reason, *l'Érèbe* should be classified as an animate term.

By the informal semantic standard, both subject terms of the second quatrain turn out to be animate, only two of the three subject terms in the second tercet remain inanimate. In fact, they are the only inanimate subject terms in the entire sonnet. Consequently, the horizontal correspondences stand on an ill-founded semantic distinction.

The argument in support of the vertical correspondences concerns the semantic nature of grammatical objects. Our authors claim a semantic resemblance of the two tercets on the ground that all their object terms are inanimate substantives (*les nobles attitudes, leur prunelles*). This semantic argument is as faulty as to claim that *leur reins* is inanimate; *leur prunelles* must be as alive as the cats. Our authors do recognize the semantic heterogeneity of object terms in the two quatrains. The only object word *les chats* in the first quatrain is animate. Two of the three direct objects in the second quatrain are inanimate (*le silence et l'horreur*), while one of them (*les*) is a pronoun standing for animate objects (*les chats*). Thus the semantic foundation in support of the vertical correspondences is just as dubious as the one in support of the horizontal correspondences.

The argument used in claiming the diagonal correspondences concerns the semantic relation of subject and object terms. The exterior stanzas are said to be alike in having both subject and object terms in the same semantic category of either animate or inanimate. In the first stanza, both subject and object terms belong to the animate class (*amoureux, savants—chats*); in the last stanza, both of them belong to the inanimate class (*reins, parcelles—prunelles*).[8] In the interior stanzas, conversely, subject and object terms are said to belong to opposite categories. In the second stanza, an animate subject (*ils* = *les chats*) is opposed to inanimate objects (*silence, horreur*), and an inanimate subject (*l'Érèbe*) is opposed to an animate object (*les* = *les chats*). In the third stanza, an animate subject (*ils* = *les chats*) is opposed to an inanimate object (*attitudes*). These elaborate claims are semantically faulty, because there is no semantic justification for classifying *l'Érèbe* and *prunelles* as inanimate.

None of the three semantic corespondences has a sound semantic justification. In this regard, the syntactic correspondence is a much more solid claim than the semantic correspondences. Hence the syntactic correspondence alone turns out to be an acceptable result of the binary analysis in the demonstration proper. In the recapitulation, the binary analysis is given a completely different format. Our authors altogether drop their syntactic and semantic arguments, nor do they mention the syntactic and semantic correspondences. They simply claim one thematic opposition between the octave and the sestet, and describe the nature of this opposition by saying that the sestet dispenses with the point of view of the observer (*amoureux, savants, puissance de l'Érèbe*), and situates the being of the cats beyond all spatiotemporal limits.[9] Presumably, in the octave, the cats are situated within spatial and temporal limits, and described from the point of view of an observer. This is a fairly accurate characterization of the difference between the octave and the sestet.

Within this overall structure of binary opposition, our authors recognize a close relation (*relation étroite*) between the first quatrain and the first tercet, and between the second quatrain and the second tercet. The first quatrain introduces the spatiotemporal limits (*maison, saison*); the first tercet abolishes them (*au fond des solitudes, rêve sans fin*). The second quatrain defines the cats in terms of the darkness in which they are placed; the second tercet in terms of the light they radiate (*étincelles, étoiles*). These observations are fundamentally correct.[10] Although our authors do not use the term "opposition" in referring to these "close relations," these relations can be regarded as secondary or subsidiary oppositions which articulate the thematic content of the primary opposition.

This binary analysis in the recapitulation shows some coincidence with the binary analysis of the demonstration proper. The thematic opposition between the octave and the sestet coincides with the vertical correspondence of the demonstration proper, which opposes the two quatrains to the two tercets. Both of them stand on the same binary division of the sonnet. The secondary thematic oppositions resemble the horizontal correspondences; they stand on the same pairing of the four stanzas. To be sure, the horizontal correspondences are relations of resemblance, while the secondary thematic oppositions are relations of oppositions. Nevertheless, the latter can be regarded as an adaptation of the former. In fact, the entire binary analysis in the recapitulation can be regarded as an adaptation of the vertical and horizontal correspondences. In that case, only the diagonal correspondences have not been used in constructing the binary analysis of the recapitulation. Perhaps for this reason, our authors give a separate account of the diagonal correspondences under a new label "a third division."

This third division is established by regrouping the two exterior (the first and the last) stanzas as one unit, and the two interior (the second and the third) stanzas as the other. This division is now said to be superimposed on the second division, but the nature of this superimposition is not explained. What our authors mean to say may be no more than that the third division is another version of their binary analysis. The unique feature of this version is its use of Jakobson's favorite distinction between metaphor and metonym. According to him, all rhetorical figures operate on either one of two principles: resemblance or contiguity. The principle of resemblance is exemplified by the operation of metaphors (the lion as a metaphor of courage), and the principle of contiguity by the operation of metonyms (the scepter as a metonym of kingship). The relation of resemblance is called the metaphoric relation; the relation of contiguity is called the metonymic relation. The structural analysis based on these relations may be called the rhetorical analysis or version, because they concern the operation of rhetorical figures.[11]

In the first and the last stanzas, our authors argue, the relations of contiguity develop into the relations of resemblance, or alternatively, the metonymic relations evolve into the metaphoric relations. In the first stanza, the contiguity of the cats to the lovers and the scholars evolves into the resemblance of the cats to the lovers and the scholars. In the last stanza, the cats cannot be placed in any metonymic relations with anything outside them, because they constitute the whole cosmos there and can have no external relation of contiguity with anything else. Hence, our authors argue, the external relation of contiguity is interiorized in the fourth stanza, and metonym is replaced by synecdoche. By this rhetorical device, our authors hold, the parts of the cat's body (reins, prunelles) prepare the metaphoric evocation of the astral and cosmic cat. Thus the same progression from the metonymic to the metaphoric relations is said to be observable in both the exterior stanzas, although the progression is internal in one and external in the other.

This is an ingenious argument and its ingenuity lies in the notion that synecdoche is an interiorized form of metonymy, which in its normal form presumably stands on the external relation of contiguity. Though ingenious, this argument cannot stand because the last stanza contains no synecdoche. Synecdoche is a rhetorical device for using a part for the representation of the whole, or the whole for the representation of a part. The last stanza does not use parts of the cats (reins, prunelles) to represent the whole cats; the function of these two words is to be the grammatical subjects for partial descriptions of the cats. Hence our authors' analysis of the rhetorical figures is incorrect as far as the last stanza is concerned, although it is quite accurate and useful for the understanding of the first stanza.

Our authors' account of the rhetorical figures in the two interior stanzas begins with a notion of equivalence: the equivalence of the cats and the *coursiers funèbres* in the second stanza, and that of the cats and the *sphinx* in the third stanza. These equivalences are metaphoric relations. The first one is rejected; the second one is accepted. The rejection of the former equivalence leads to the rejection of the contiguity between the cats and *l'Érèbe*; the acceptance of the latter equivalence leads to the settlement of the cats in *au fond des solitudes*. On these grounds, our authors hold that the construction of the two interior stanzas alike relies on the transition from the metaphoric to the metonymic relations. This transition is, in their words, the inverse of the transition they have claimed in the two exterior stanzas. Hence the exterior stanzas are said to be opposed to the interior stanzas.[12]

The second stanza indeed sets up a metaphoric resemblance between the cats and the *coursiers funèbres*, and rejects that resemblance. But it is difficult to argue that this rejection leads to the rejection of the contiguity between the cats and Erebus. In the second stanza, *l'Érèbe* is introduced right after the second line which asserts the cats' search for the silence and the horror of darkness (*ténèbres*). *L'Érèbe* can be regarded as the personification of *ténèbres*. The former is the last word of the second line; the latter is the first word of the third line. This syntactic contiguity of these two words is meant to reinforce the identity of their references, and this identity is further reinforced by the phonic similarity of *ténèbres* and *l'Érèbe*, which is correctedly observed by our authors.

Through the close referential relation of these two words, the second stanza establishes a close contiguity of *les chats* with *l'Érèbe* via *ténèbres*, whose silence and horror are the objects of search by the cats. This close contiguity can naturally lead us to expect that the cats can be harnessed to Erebus' funeral chariot. This natural expectation is rejected by the last two lines of the second quatrain. This is indeed the rejection of a metaphoric relation between *les chats* and *les coursiers funèbres*, but is not meant to affect the contiguity or metonymic relation of *les chats* to *l'Érèbe*. This contiguity is meant to be accepted as long as the silence and the horror of darkness remain the objects of the cats' search. Therefore the rhetorical structure of the second stanza involves no transition from metaphoric to metonymic relations.

Our authors' description of the rhetorical figures in the third stanza is substantially correct. This stanza indeed asserts a metaphoric relation between the cats and the sphinxes, which is developed by using the metonymic relation or contiguity of the sphinx to *the fond des solitudes*. This contiguity echoes back to the contiguity of *les chats* to *l'Érèbe* via *ténèbres*. The former contiguity represents the attainment of the goal which is represented as the object of search in the latter. These two contiguities are thus two stages in the development of one contiguity. This is an additional argument in support of the claim that the second stanza does not repudiate but affirms the contiguity of the cats to Erebus. Thus our authors' rhetorical analysis of the second stanza is unacceptable, although it is acceptable for the third stanza.

With these disappointing results of the rhetorical analysis, we come to the end of the binary analysis in the recapitulation. The binary analysis has altogether resulted in four versions, two each in the demonstration and recapitulation. The syntactic and the semantic versions of the demonstration proper are clearly pure structural analyses; they involve content-neutral grammatical or linguistic structures. The first version of the binary analysis in the recapitulation is a thematic analysis. The second version of the binary analysis in the recapitulation is the rhetorical one, and it is not easy to determine whether this version belongs to the thematic analysis or the purely structural analysis.

Roman Jakobson would regard it as a purely structural analysis because it relies on his two central linguistic categories of contiguity (metonym) and resemblance (metaphor), which constitute his syntactic and semantic principles. But some may dispute this view of the rhetorical analysis and classify it as thematic on the ground that metaphors and metonyms are not content-neutral and that the operation of those rhetorical figures cannot be understood without knowing their meaning or content. This objection stands on the apparent inseparability between the structure of rhetorical figures and their meaning-content. I am inclined to agree with this view and regard the rhetorical analysis as a thematic one. To put it alternatively, the rhetorical analysis seems to involve the thematic content of the sonnet just as much as does the first version of the binary analysis in the recapitulation, which we have already classified as a thematic analysis.

If we add these four versions of the binary analysis to the two versions of the ternary analysis, we have altogether six versions. Our authors recognize one singularly striking feature that is shared by all these six versions, namely, that none of them has produced a perfectly balanced binary division of the sonnet ("an equilibrium of isometric parts").[13] This recognition reveals that the binary principle and its operation constitute the central concern of our authors throughout their structural analysis, whether they operate with the binary or the ternary division of the sonnet. They seem to be distressed over the fact that the sonnet has invariably turned out to be an asymmetrical binary system, whether it is analyzed as the opposition of the octave to the sestet or of quatrains to tercets. This perpetual imbalance in a binary schema is a highly abnormal state of affairs in Lévi-Strauss' structuralism.

The equilibrium of two equal or isometric parts, or their

perfect balance, is the normal state of affairs in the operation of Lévi-Strauss' binary principle. This binary equilibrium can be disturbed by contingent forces which can render the two parts unequal. The resulting disequilibrium is always regarded as the disturbance of normality.[14] By this structural standard of normality, the structure of "Les Chats" as revealed by the ternary and the binary analysis turns out to be consistently abnormal. Our authors have seen that this consistent abnormality cannot be avoided as long as they operate with the natural division of the sonnet into four stanzas. Consequently they have devised a drastic procedure of ignoring its natural division and dividing it into two equal parts. This drastic procedure leads to their isometric analysis.

ISOMETRIC ANALYSIS

Our authors first divide the sonnet into two equal parts by using the seventh and the eighth lines as the boundary: "the seventh line would end the first half of the poem, and the eighth line would mark the beginning of the second half."[15] Since these two lines perform this special function of isometric division, our authors hold, they display a set of special features that are not shared by the other lines of the sonnet. These two lines contain the only proper name (*l'Érèbe*) and the only singular verb used in the sonnet. These two lines do not use the present tense, which is used in the rest of the sonnet. Since these and other special features make those lines stand out as a special unit or couplet, our authors argue, they should be called the median couplet or distich.

If those two lines constitute a special segment, however, they cannot perform the function of bisecting the sonnet into two equal halves, because this special segment becomes a third unit in its own right. This triadic result goes against the original

intention of our authors, which was to divide the poem into
two equal parts of seven lines each. They have now divided it
into two parts of six lines each and a third part of two lines.
Our authors duly recognize this triadic result of their attempted
isometric division: "Actually, in more than one respect, the
poem falls into three parts: the middle two lines and two isometric groups, that is to say, the six lines which precede the
two lines and the six which follow them."[16]

The isometric analysis in the demonstration proper falls
into two stages: to exhibit the unique, salient features of the
median distich; and to manifest the hidden symmetry between
the two isometric parts of the sonnet. Our authors' attempt to
exhibit the unique features of the median distich degenerates
into an extended discussion on the special characteristics of
the second quatrain as a whole. For example, they studiously
explain how the rhyme texture of the second quatrain is quite
different from that of other stanzas.[17] For another example, the
nasal vowels are used sparingly in the second stanza, but lav-
ishly in other stanzas; the second stanza has an excessive number of the liquid phonemes in comparison with other stanzas.[18]
These and other special features of the second stanza render
that stanza so different from others that they are called "the
aberrant character of this quatrain."[19]

These observations about the second quatrain are indeed
correct, but their correctness forces us to demarcate the entire
second stanza rather than its last two lines as the special unit
for the bisection of the sonnet. Our authors, however, do not
consider the structural consequence of using this special unit
for the division of the sonnet; it can oppose the first quatrain
to the two tercets. Whether this division is considered as the
binary opposition of one (stanza) against two, or as that of four
(lines) against six, it turns out to be a far more unbalanced, less
isometric, than any other division attempted by our authors.

In the second stage of their isometric analysis, our authors
first try to establish a structural unity of the first six lines on

the ground that the composition of those lines extensively employs coordinate phrases, whose symmetrical structures are established by the conjunctive *et*, for example, *les amoureux fervents et les savants austères*. The first quatrain contains three such phrases, and the first two lines of the second quatrain two such phrases. Because of this structural unity, our authors now argue, those six lines can be regarded as a sestet and be opposed to the last six lines.[20] The sonnet can now be regarded as a construction of two sestets demarcated by a median distich.

Our authors then try to establish a symmetrical balance between this newly formed sestet and the original sestet. To this end, they propose to divide the newly formed sestet into two tercets, and try to justify the division by appealing to the different grammatical roles *les chats* plays in these two new tercets. In the first of them, it is the grammatical object of a verb. In the second, it becomes the grammatical subject of verbs via the pronouns *qui* and *ils*. This grammatical difference neatly divides the newly formed sestet into two tercets, which can be considered a congruent counterpart to the two tercets in the original sestet. The sonnet is thus shown to be a congruent binary structure which has two tercets on both sides of the median distich.

Our authors then show another way of articulating the balance or congruence between the original and newly formed sestets. This is to respect the natural boundary of the first quatrain and regard the first two lines of the second quatrain as a couplet, and then reorganize the last two tercets into one couplet and one quatrain. For this purpose, they separate line eleven from the first tercet and attach it to the second tercet, thereby creating "an imaginary quatrain."[21] This imaginary quatrain is now claimed to be a mirror image of the first quatrain; the same relative pronoun *qui* marks the beginning of the last line of the first quatrain and of the first line of the imaginary quatrain. The lines nine and ten of the first tercet are now claimed as a couplet that can be balanced with the first two lines of the second quatrain. The sonnet is now shown to have the balanced structure of one quatrain and one couplet on each side of the median distich.

These isometric divisions of the sonnet point to one inherent danger of aprioristic structuralism. There is an inherent temptation to disregard the original structure of a poem and replace it with an artificial one in order to secure the preconceived structural results. This preoccupation with preconceived results goes directly against the spirit of scientific analysis, which can be called empirical or phenomenological. The spirit of empirical analysis is not to impose a preconceived structure on the object of analysis, but to let it reveal its own structure whether it be binary or ternary. This spirit of phenomenological inquiry is flouted by every structural apriorism, and the so-called structural analysis of a poem becomes its structural dismemberment.

Our authors do not terminate their isometric analysis with the binary symmetry they have carved out between the first and the last six lines, but turn their attention to an entirely different issue. This is the thematic issue of how the cats are transformed or transfigured throughout the sonnet. As long as the isometric analysis was concerned with the problem of structural symmetry between the first and the last six lines, it was a purely structural analysis, especially because structural symmetry was claimed on the basis of grammatical structure alone. As soon as the analysis is redirected toward the thematic issue of transfiguration, it appears to become a thematic analysis. Hence the isometric analysis appears to be a mixed mode. However, this impression is misleading; there is no real connection between the two analyses.

That there is complete independence between the two can be shown by the following considerations. Our authors have tried to establish the isometric symmetry between the two halves of the sonnet without appealing to their thematic content. They do not even think of using the isometric division of the sonnet as a framework for describing the transfiguration of the cats. For this thematic description, they rely on the sonnet's natural division between octave and sestet: "The two quatrains objectively present the nature of the cat, whereas the two tercets bring about its transfiguration."[22]

The objective presentation of the cats in the two quatrains is said to be given in two stages. In the first quatrain, *les chats* is presented as the unifier of two antinomic attributes, sensuality and intellectuality, whose binary opposition is represented by the juxtaposition of *les amoureux fervents* and *les savants austères* in the first line. Although *les chats* is the object of the verb *aiment*, our authors claim, it implicitly assumes the role of subject, that is, the subject of the two antinomic attributes. In the second quatrain, the cats are formally elevated to the position of subject for the verb *cherchent*, and retain the original antinomy of lovers and scholars in their capacity as *amis de la science et de la volupté*. This antinomy of attributes is sustained, our authors hold, not only in the objective presentation of the cats' nature given in the octave, but also in their transfiguration that takes place in the sestet.

The transfiguration of the cats in the two tercets is said to consist in giving some miraculous quality to the cats which were initially presented as ordinary objects in the two quatrains. The first tercet is said to achieve this operation by linking the cats to the image of the sphinxes and taking them from the everyday household environment to the depth of the infinite deserts. Our authors regard the second tercet only as an epilogue to this great transformation. The function of this epilogue is to take up the original theme of lovers and scholars stated in the first quatrain and to restate the notion of the cats being *amis de la science et de la volupté* asserted in the second quatrain.

They conclude this thematic analysis by noting a striking conformity between the transfiguration of the cats and the horizontal parallelism which they used in the binary analysis. The transformation achieved by the first tercet corresponds to the opposition of the first to the third stanza; the narrow limits of space and time (*maison, saison*) imposed by the first stanza are opposed by the removal or suppression of boundaries (*fond des solitudes, rêve sans fin*). Similarly, the transformation achieved by the second tercet corresponds to the opposition of the second to the last stanza: the magic of the light radiating from the cats in the second tercet triumphs over *l'horreur des ténèbres*, from which the second quatrain has almost drawn misleading conclusions.[23]

These are the two versions of the isometric analysis in the demonstration proper, the first purely structural and the second thematic. In the recapitulation, our authors make some startling claims for their isometric analysis. (1) this analysis alone gives the sonnet "the appearance of an open system in dynamic progression from beginning to end," while the binary and the ternary analyses give it the appearance of a closed system; and (2) they had provisionally set aside their isometric analysis when they recognized this unique feature of it.[24] In the demonstration proper, they had given no indication whatsoever that they were even provisionally leaving their isometric analysis unfinished, or that they had recognized anything unique about it.

Whether their claims are justifiable is not an important question, in and of itself; their importance lies in the implication that the isometric analysis has a unique capacity shared by neither the binary nor the ternary analysis, namely, it alone can give the poem the appearance of an open, dynamic system. As we have seen, the isometric analysis in the demonstration proper produced nothing but a static symmetry as long as it was confined to the grammatical structure of the poem. Only when our authors turned their attention to thematic content did their isometric analysis take on the aura of a dynamic progression. That is, not the isometric analysis per se but the thematic approach has given the analysis of the poem its dynamic progression. This is an obvious conclusion dictated by the nature of a thematic development, whose dynamic character cannot be contained in a closed system.

In the isometric analysis of the recapitulation, our authors ignore their earlier notion of the elaborate structural symmetry between the first and the last six lines, and only retain the notion of the median distich. The function of this median distich is said to resemble the functions of modulation in a musical composition, and is described in the following rhetorical terms:

> The objective of this modulation [of the median distich] is to resolve the opposition, implicit or explicit from the beginning of the poem, between the metaphoric and the metonymic approaches. The solution achieved by the final sestet consists in transferring this opposition to the very heart of the metonymy, while expressing it by metaphoric means.[25]

Comprehension of this obscure passage largely depends on understanding what is meant by the opposition between the metaphoric and the metonymic approaches. Our authors did not mention such an opposition in their previous rhetorical analysis of the sonnet. On the contrary, they gave us the impression that there was a close cooperation between the two rhetorical figures. The very notion of an opposition between the metaphoric and the metonymic relations defies our understanding. Our authors' description of the resolution of this opposition is equally incomprehensible; it is said to consist in transferring the opposition to the very heart of the metonymy, while expressing it by metaphoric means. This is simply an opaque metaphor. Consequently, we can make nothing of this whole passage.

Our authors themselves immediately drop their pretense for rhetorical analysis and describe the dynamic progression of the sonnet in plain thematic terms. At the same time, they also completely abandon the mediational function of the median distich. Thus their final thematic account reverts to the notion of the transformation of the cats achieved by the two tercets. In the first tercet, the cats originally enclosed in the house are said to be taken outside in order to expand spatially and temporally in infinite deserts and a dream without end. In the second tercet, the suppression of frontiers becomes interiorized by the cats' attaining cosmic proportions, since they conceal in certain parts of their bodies (*reins* and *prunelles*) the sand of the desert and the stars of the sky.

The common goal of these two transformations is the elimination of spatiotemporal limits ("the suppression of the frontiers"), but this common goal is achieved externally in the first tercet and internally ("interiorized") in the second tercet. Hence there is a certain parallel between the two transformations, but our authors recognize no exact "equilibrium" between them: "the first still owes something to appearance and to dream, whereas in the second case the character of the transformation is affirmed as truly achieved. In the first, the cats close their eyes to sleep; in the second, they keep them open."[26] This characterization of the two transformations is quite different from the one our authors gave in the demonstration proper, which regarded the second transformation as the epilogue to the first.

As long as the second tercet was placed in such a subordinate relation to the first, there was no reason to consider their equilibrium or disequilibrium. But our authors are now interested in the binary contrast between the two; they are giving equal weight to the two transformations. This binary outlook leads our authors to rename the disequilibrium between the two transformations as a binary opposition: "the dilation of the cats in time and space [in the first tercet] vs. the constriction of time and space into the being of the cats [in the second tercet]."[27] This opposition is said to evoke the original opposition set up by the juxtaposition of lovers and scholars in the first line of the sonnet, which is sustained throughout the poem and retained in its last stanza: "the *reins féconds* recall the *volupté* of the *amoureux*, as do the *prunelles* the *science* of the

savants."[28] In the words of our authors, the thematic opposition
of the sonnet is never resolved, but only transposed. They try
to reinforce this conclusion by appealing to Baudelaire's other
poems and writings, which reveal the poet's perpetual concern
with the theme of androgyny, the duality and opposition of
male and female. Our authors now claim that this thematic
duality underlies the various oppositions presented by "Les
Chats." In support of this claim, they quote Michel Butor's
observation that for Baudelaire "these two aspects: femininity
and supervirility, far from being exclusive, are bound together."[29]

Our authors' claim that the thematic opposition of the sonnet is never resolved but only transposed is disputable. This
claim clearly goes against the quoted observation by Michel
Butor, which stresses the union of the opposite attributes rather
than their opposition. It also goes against the image of an androgyne, which usually stands for a resolved opposition rather
than an unresolved one. Most of the extratextual arguments
and evidence that our authors have produced seem to be in
support of the sonnet's thematic resolution. But these extratextual considerations can be dismissed, since our authors'
analysis of the sonnet is meant to be exclusively textual. What
cannot be so easily dismissed is our authors' claim that there
is an opposition between the two transformations of the cats
achieved by the two tercets. For this claim is based on their
textual analysis and reflects their strange view of the sonnet's
thematic development.

If the two transformations are really opposed to each other,
they have to be regarded as two separate thematic developments
rather than as two phases of one continuous thematic development. Each of these transformations is supposed to present
"an inverse image of the cats"—presumably inverse to the
image of the cats projected by the octave.[30] This initial image
of the cats is presumably contained within the spatiotemporal
limits, whose suppression is achieved in two different ways in
the two tercets—one internally and the other externally. In that

case, the thematic progression of the sonnet is seen as taking two different directions in the sestet, and the two transformations are viewed as parallel developments, which may be called a binary thematic development. This is indeed an unusual form for a thematic development.

A thematic development is generally regarded as one continuous progression—a unitary development. Such a unitary thematic account was achieved in the isometric analysis of the demonstration proper by assuming a subordinate relation of the second to the first tercet and by stressing continuity of the thematic development ("The metamorphosis unfolds itself right up to the end of the sonnet").[31] In the recapitulation, however, our authors have stressed the opposition of the two transformations in place of their continuity. Thus they have given two different thematic conclusions, while using the same thematic materials. Consequently, the two isometric thematic accounts may be regarded either as two versions of one thematic analysis or as two different thematic analyses. At any rate, it may be fair to conclude that the isometric analysis has resulted in three versions: one structural and two thematic ones.

STRUCTURAL ANALYSIS VS. THEMATIC ANALYSIS

When we add these three versions to the two versions of the ternary analysis and the four versions of the binary analysis, we can count altogether nine different versions of our authors' structural analysis of the sonnet. An immediate question that arises in confrontation of these nine versions is the question of their mutual relation. To answer this question of mutual relation vis-à-vis the five versions of the demonstration proper was our authors' original motive for composing the recapitulation, that is, to show how these five versions "blend, complement, and combine with each other, thereby giving the poem the character of an absolute object."[32] Instead of giving such an explanation, they produced four more versions in the recapitulation. So we are compelled to give our own account of the mutual relation of these nine versions.

Five of the nine are thematic accounts, while four of them are purely structural. Three of the four thematic versions have turned out to be acceptable, and these three are the one binary thematic account and the two isometric thematic accounts. Only one of the four purely structural accounts has turned out to be acceptable, and that one is the syntactic version of the binary analysis. Moreover, the three thematic accounts appear to be three different ways of stating the same thematic development. As we have seen, the identity of thematic content in the two isometric thematic accounts is obvious. The identity of thematic content in the isometric and the binary thematic accounts is already indicated by the striking similarity that our authors have recognized between the two transformations of the cats achieved by the two tercets and the horizontal correspondences.

The relation between the isometric and the binary thematic accounts can be stated as follows. The isometric thematic version shows how the image of the cats is transformed from the octave to the sestet. Now this transformation is achieved by transforming the framework of description and reference, and this latter transformation is the essence of the binary thematic version. That is, the octave provides the description of the cats in terms of their relation to other entities and within spatio-temporal boundaries, whereas the sestet does it without using such a framework of description and reference. Insofar as the binary thematic analysis is concerned with the frameworks of description and reference used in the projection of the image of the cats, it is no more than a preliminary or provisional statement of the thematic progression that is finally captured in the isometric thematic analysis. Thus we can reduce the three thematic versions to one thematic version and reach our final count of two acceptable versions: one purely structural and one thematic.

These two represent the two different approaches our authors have employed in their structural analysis: the purely structural and the thematic one.[33] These two approaches produce two fundamentally different ways of reading the sonnet: as an open or as a closed system, in the words of our authors. A thematic development is a dynamic progression which requires an open system. Hence a thematic approach is incompatible with a closed system. On the other hand, a purely structural approach, which produces a static structural symmetry or asymmetry devoid of thematic content, requires a closed system rather than an open one. By this general requirement of the two approaches, all thematic versions should read the sonnet as an open system, while all the purely structural versions should read it as a closed one. This expected result is, however, in conflict with our authors' own verdict; they have branded only one of the thematic versions as an open system and the other thematic versions as closed systems along with the purely structural versions.

This discrepancy may reflect our authors' misjudgment induced by their excessive reliance on their binary principle in their thematic analyses. To be sure, the binary schema can be useful in the analysis of a thematic development; the first half of the development can be contrasted with its second half. But this binary procedure can conceal the dynamic character of the development by presenting it in the static schema of binary symmetry or asymmetry. Take, for example, our authors' binary thematic account, which establishes a binary contrast between the octave and the sestet. Because they assume it to be a static contrast, they fail to perceive the dynamic character of a thematic development which underlies that binary contrast. Hence they conclude that their binary analysis produces a reading of the sonnet as a closed system.

The schema of binary contrast can have one more adverse

effect on the thematic approach. By constricting a thematic account to a binary contrast, the binary principle can conceal the continuity of a thematic development. The thematic development of a poem is one continuous movement from its first to its last line; it cannot be confined to any binary contrast or demarcation. Let us again take the example of our authors' binary thematic account, which is limited to the thematic transition from the octave to the sestet. Constrained by their binary schema, they cannot recognize the thematic transition from the first to the second quatrain, and from the first to the second tercet. Instead of these thematic contrasts and transitions, they provide the contrasts and transitions from the first quatrain to the first tercet, and from the second quatrain to the second tercet, both of which are confined within the framework of the primary contrast and transition from the octave to the sestet.

Our authors could have accounted for the thematic contrast or transition between the two quatrains and between the two tercets by applying their binary principle respectively to the octave and the sestet and by establishing a binary opposition within each of those two sections. In the isometric thematic analysis, they do claim a thematic opposition between the two tercets although they do not claim a corresponding contrast between the two quatrains. Preoccupied with this notion of contrast, however, they claim a thematic opposition between the two tercets rather than their thematic continuity. Consequently, as we have seen, they have concluded their isometric thematic version with the bizarre implication that the two tercets achieve two parallel thematic developments. They have not been able to recognize the continuity of a thematic movement even within one sestet, which incidentally constitutes only one compound sentence.

In the last chapter, we saw that the Lévi-Straussian structural analysis is limited to synchronic approaches and that it is incapable of handling diachronic problems. The binary contrast or symmetry in a static system is its synchronic feature;

the thematic development of a poem is its diachronic feature. Now we can see that the binary analysis is limited to the synchronic approaches precisely because the binary principle is a principle of static opposition and equilibrium. To say that it cannot cope with the diachronic problems is to understate its shortcomings. The truth of the matter is that it has the inherent tendency to distort or misrepresent even the dynamic progression as no more than a binary opposition within a static system.

THEMATIC RECONSTRUCTION

What sort of thematic account of "Les Chats" could our authors have rendered, if they had not been constrained by their binary bias? This is the intriguing question I propose for consideration in order to determine the extent of the distortion their binary bias has imposed on their thematic account. The objective of this endeavor is to free their thematic account of their self-imposed binary constraints so that it can give us one continuous thematic development of the sonnet. Hence the proposed attempt is largely a matter of restructuring our authors' thematic account on the basis of the textual data and observations they themselves have used.

We may begin this hypothetical reconstruction by accepting their observation that the first line of the sonnet poses a bipolar opposition by the juxtaposition of *les amoureux* vs. *les savants*, and of *fervents* vs. *austères*. As our authors claim, these juxtapositions may represent bipolar oppositions of a far more pervasive scope, such as male vs. female, intellect vs. sensuality, or even powerfulness vs. tenderness. The first stanza, we can now see, presents *les chats* as the union of these polarities: it is the grammatical object of the single verb (*aiment*) of the main clause, which operates, with its single adverb (*également*), on the two juxtaposed subjects. This function of *les chats* as the medium of union is further reinforced by the binary conjunction of four adjectives into two pairs, one of which (*puissants et doux*) qualifies *les chats* directly, and the other of which (*frileux et sédentaires*) qualifies the same grammatical object through the relative pronoun *qui*.

The union of bipolar attributes in the cats is not additive; the bipolar attributes do not retain their separate identity in this union. Although the two pairs of attributes assigned to the cats (*puissants et doux, frileux et sédentaires*) still resonate with the original juxtaposition of *les amoureux* vs. *les savants* through the conjunctive phrase "comme eux . . . et comme eux," there is no way of setting up a neat parallel between either of the two pairs with the pair of *les amoureux* and *les savants*. For example, it is impossible to say that *frileux* reflects the nature of *les amoureux*, while *sédentaires* reflects the nature of *les savants*. For both adjectives are jointly applicable to either of them. Hence the cats represent a true union or fusion of the original bipolar attributes.

This idea of fusion is also manifested through the punctuation scheme of the first quatrain. The binary opposition of the attributes in question appears to be represented by the bisection of the two interior lines by the medial caesuras, and their union by the enclosure of those two broken lines within the two unbroken exterior lines. This graphic or auditory manifestation of the union of the bipolar attributes may be further reinforced by the conjunction of the "masculine" rhymes with the "feminine" substantives, as our authors have maintained. At any rate, this notion of union permeates the construction of the entire first stanza.

The second quatrain opens with the reaffirmation of the role of *les chats* as the unifier of bipolar attributes (*amis de la science et de la volupté*). This role of *les chats* is further substantiated by its single verb (*cherchent*) and by the conjunction of its objects *silence* and *horreur* in their common source *ténèbres*. The silence of darkness is so intimately connected with the horror of darkness that it becomes impossible to tell whether they refer to two aspects of the same thing or they are two ways of referring to the same thing. Thus the union established and reaffirmed in *les chats* is now extended even to the objects of its verb.

The transition from the first to the second stanza involves a change in the role of *les chats* from the grammatical object to the grammatical subject. This change has already begun in the last line of the first stanza, in which *les chats* functions as the de facto subject through the relative pronoun *qui*. In the second stanza, this relative pronoun is replaced by the pronoun *ils*. Since a relative pronoun also performs the grammatical role of a pronoun, the successive use of *qui* and ils renders smooth and gentle the change in the grammatical role of *les chats*—as gentle as the cats are said to be (*doux*) in the first stanza.

The really important change that takes place in the role of *les chats* is not the fact that it formally becomes the subject of a main verb, but that it becomes the subject of an action verb (*cherchent*). In the last line of the first stanza, *les chats* is the de facto subject of two predicates (*sont frileux et . . . sédentaires*), both of which seem to indicate inactivity rather than activity. In the second line of the second stanza, *les chats* clearly becomes an active subject. In fact, the second stanza has more action verbs than any other stanza. The emergence of activity as the central theme of the second stanza seems to be highlighted by the excessive use of the liquid phonemes (/l/, /r/) in the second stanza. Our authors have correctly observed that the second stanza employs a far greater number of those liquid phonemes than any other stanza, and that those phonemes give the limpid impression of flowing and gliding.[34] This limpid impression effectively actualizes the notion of the cats as *puissants et doux*. The association of this power of flowing and gliding with the cats is further accentuated by the recurrence of the hushing phoneme /ʃ/ as the first consonant of both the verb *cherchent* and its subject *les chats*.

The fact that *les chats* is the subject of the activity *cher-chent* is liable to make them the slaves of the objects they love and seek. This tendency to become enslaved to the objects of love and search is always inherent in the very power of longing. If *les chats* were to succumb to this tendency, they would become enslaved to *l'Érèbe* as his *coursiers funèbres*. The second stanza establishes the identity of *ténèbres* and *l'Érèbe* through the contiguity of the two words; it also establishes the close affinity of *ténèbres* and *funèbres* through their phonic similarity. But *les chats* cannot be forced into that slavish role, because of *leur fierté*. Since the love of pleasure harbors far greater danger of enslavement than the love of knowledge, the control of *volupté* is much more important than that of *science*. That the former control is especially maintained by *fierté* is indicated by pairing this word with *volupté* in the common rhyme. *Leur fierte* assures the lordship of *les chats* over the objects of their love and search.

Leur fierté also echoes back to the phrase *orgueil de la maison* in the first stanza. As an appositive of *les chats*, this phrase makes *les chats* the semantic object of *orgueil de la maison*.[35] Hence the role of *les chats* in the third line of the first stanza is doubly that of an object, that is, the semantic object of *orgueil* as well as the syntactic object of *aiment*. In the second stanza, *les chats* is presented as the semantic subject of *fierté* by joining it to the possessive pronoun *leur* (whereas *orgueil* is possessively joined to *la maison* through the preposition *de*), and by making it the syntactic object of the cats' own action verb *incliner*. Thus the second stanza doubly assures the role of *les chats* as the subject of their passion as well as their action.

In more than one sense, the second stanza demonstrates the lordship of *les chats*—the lordship over the object of their search as well as over the activity of search itself, over the passion and pleasure of search as well as over the knowledge of it. With the lordship of *les chats* thus securely established, the third stanza opens with the cats as the sole subject in their own world. In the transition from the second to the third stanza, the character of *les chats* as subject undergoes considerable transformation. In the second stanza, *les chats* is depicted as a subject in search of an object; in the third stanza, it is portrayed as a self-contained subject in need of no object. This reversal in the role of *les chats* is not real but only apparent; it is already prepared for in the second stanza.

In the second stanza, the objects of the cats' search are said to be *le silence et l'horreur des ténèbres*, and these are no ordinary objects. They are nonentities (*néants*). Consequently, to be in search of them is to be in search of nothingness. Those nonentities are all that is needed for enclosing the self-containedness of *les chats*. By the time the cats are compared to the self-contained sphinxes, the latter are placed in *au fond des solitudes*, which echoes back to *le silence et l'horreur des ténèbres*. The cats of the second stanza are in search of the domain of nothingness; the cats of the third stanza are installed in that domain as the lords of their own self-contained being. In this regard, the cats are like the lovers and the scholars at the height of their maturity; the objects of their love and knowledge are contained in their own being.

The self-containedness that the cats achieve in the third stanza is a fruition of the theme of androgyny. Male and female are in search of each other because of their separation from each other. An androgyne is in need of no one outside itself, because it is a union of male and female. It is a self-contained being. As the unifier of bipolar attributes, *les chats* is a dual symbol of androgyny and self-containedness. The third stanza portrays these two features of the cats by the imagery of great sphinxes. The theme of androgyny is represented by the union of animal and human features in the sphinxes' bodies. On the cosmic level, the duality of male and female stands for all dualities, and the duality of human and animal is only one of them. The theme of self-containedness is represented by the great sphinxes' endless dream; to be self-contained is to be free of limits and boundaries.

The self-containedness of the sphinxes and the cats is, however, seen only from the perspective of an external observer in the third stanza. The lordliness of the cats is shown only through their *nobles attitudes*, and the attitudes in general are external relations one takes toward someone else. Likewise, the word *semblent* makes the last line of the third stanza an external description of the sphinxes, that is, a description of them as they appear to external observers rather than as they truly are in and of themselves. This barrier of external perception and description is broken by the final stanza, which describes the cats and the sphinxes as they truly are in and of themselves. Hence the transition from the third to the final stanza is a shift in perspective, which our authors have tried to capture with their notion of interiorization.

This perspectival shift is accompanied by a corresponding shift in the modes of description. The first tercet describes the whole cats and the whole sphinxes; the second tercet describes not the whole animals but only some of their parts (*leurs reins, leurs prunelles*). The descriptions of those whole animals seem to presuppose an observer who can command an overview of those animals from the vantage point of external perception. The description of their parts implies an observer who goes beyond this level of an external overview and gains an inner view of what lies beneath it. This perspectival advance is also reflected in the transition from the metaphoric to the literal language. The metaphoric language inevitably involves external relations, because it relies on the comparison of the objects described to some other objects. This element of externality is avoided by replacing the metaphoric language of the third stanza with the literal language of the final stanza. By describing even the magical and the mystical in one literal language, this stanza fully realizes the unity of all languages and all experiences.

Our authors have claimed that the original opposition of *les amoureux* vs. *les savants* is retained throughout the sonnet and restated in the binary opposition of *leurs reins* vs. *leurs prunelles* in the final stanza. This claim can be supported only by demonstrating that the conjunctive *et* of the last stanza performs the same function of establishing a binary contrast as it does in the first line of the sonnet. But the function of the conjunctive *et* is radically different in these two cases. Whereas it establishes a symmetrical contrast between the two phrases of the first line, it cannot do the same for the two clauses it connects in the last stanza, because the two clauses are grammatically asymmetrical. One of them takes up only one line; the other takes up two lines. One of them has a transitive verb; the other one has an intransitive verb.

Whereas *les amoureux fervents* and *les savants austères* are presented side by side in a single line, *leurs reins féconds* and *leurs prunelles mystiques* constitute the first and the last phrases of the last stanza. The function of this last stanza is to show the continuity of these two terms via a series of linking terms. *Leurs reins* is first linked to *d'étincelles magiques*, which is then linked to *des parcelles d'or*, which is finally linked to *leurs prunelles mystiques*. Of these three links, the first and the last are obvious, because they are syntactically given. But the middle one cannot so obviously spelled out in syntactic terms. The two phrases *d'étincelles magiques* and *des parcelles d'or* belong to two independent clauses; the conjunctive *et* which connects these two clauses provides no syntactic connection between the two phrases. As our authors point out, however, the two words *etinCELLES* and *parCELLES* have close semantic and phonological affinities. These affinities are further reinforced by the contiguity of these two words in the final stanza.

The relation of these two words is much similar to that of *ténèbres* and *l'Érèbe* in the second stanza, which reinforces the continuity and unity of their references initially established by their semantic and phonological affinity. This grammatical device is used in the last stanza in conjunction with the poetic device which was used to reinforce the union of the opposites in the first stanza. The middle line of the last stanza is broken by a medial caesura, and this broken line is enclosed by two unbroken exterior lines. As in the first stanza, this enclosure of broken lines by unbroken lines gives a graphic impression of bringing about the fusion of a fissured world. Moreover, the joint use of these two devices presents unity and continuity as two features of one common theme.

The unity and continuity of *leurs reins* and *leurs prunelles* were prepared by the androgynous image of the great sphinxes in the third stanza. Just as their animal bodies and human heads fuse into each other, so *leurs reins* and *leurs prunelles* become contiguous and continuous. This is why the last stanza can be regarded as a literal description of what was presented metaphorically in the third stanza. The last stanza accomplishes one more elaboration on the theme of androgyny. In the third stanza, this theme is still confined to the sphinxes and the cats; in the last stanza, it is extended to the whole universe. This extension is achieved through the use of the binary contrast between sand and stars that is implied by the last two lines of the last stanza. This binary opposition can be taken to represent the cosmic opposition between the earthly and the heavenly, the corporeal and the spiritual, the natural and the supernatural, the temporal and the eternal.

Our authors do claim that the last stanza does not resolve but only crystallize these cosmic polarities. Contrary to this view, these polarities are absorbed into the continuity and unity of *leurs reins* and *leurs prunelles* by an ingenious grammatical device. This is the device of using the word *sable* as a part of the adverbial phrase *ainsi qu'un sable fin*, which qualifies the verb *étoilent*, which has its root in the word *étoile*. By this grammatical device, the words *sable* and *étoile* both become parts of one predication, which affirms the unity of two natures reprsented by the sphinxes and the cats.

This predication also achieves the poetic effect of converting the inanimate entities such as sand and stars into the living organs of the cats and the sphinxes. This poetic effect is diametrically opposed to the implication of our authors' claim that all the grammatical subjects and objects are inanimate terms in the last stanza, whereas they are all animate terms in the first stanza. This grammatical fact, if true, would imply that the sonnet starts out with a world of animate beings in its first stanza and converts it into a world of inanimate beings by the end of the last stanza. On the contrary, the thematic development of "Los Chats" achieves a pantheistic conclusion, in which even the inanimate objects of the universe such as sand and stars become alive through the magic power of the cats and the sphinxes. By the end of the sonnet, the cats represent the androgyny of the whole universe; they represent the overcoming of the cosmic demarcation between the living and the dead. For this reason, they are entitled to the label our authors give them, "the cosmic cats."

This brings us to the end of our venture for reconstructing our authors' thematic analysis by eliminating its binary distortions. Our reconstruction has shown that the thematic development of the sonnet is continuous, or that it is not confined to binary segmentations. Furthermore, it has also shown that the central theme of the sonnet is not the binary opposition of attributes but their union. Even the first stanza puts forward not the opposition of *les amoureux* and *les savants*, but their unity, that is, the idea that they are really alike in their maturity and hence equally love the cats who are like them. The thematic development of the sonnet is to articulate, elaborate, expand, and elevate this theme of union to the cosmic scale. By their dogmatic adherence to the binary principle, our authors have misconstrued this theme of union as one of binary opposition.

Now we have to face our final question: How is this thematic analysis related to the purely structural analysis of the sonnet? Our authors did not have to face this question, because they failed to see the distinction between the thematic and the purely structural approaches. Once we recognize this distinction, we cannot evade this question because it concerns one of the central problems in poetics, namely, the relation between form and content in a poem. What is the relation between the thematic content of a poem and its purely formal structure (which should not be confused with its thematic structure)? As to this question, it is possible to entertain three answers: (1) the purely formal structure of a poem has its own autonomy and ultimacy, and need not have any connection with its thematic content; (2) it contributes to the structural beauty of the poem; and (3) it is one of the means used for its thematic development.

Let us now consider how these three answers can be applied to the syntactic analysis of the sonnet. Our authors have pointed out the syntactic correspondence between the first and the third stanza, and between the second and the fourth stanza. In the last chapter, we saw that Lévi-Strauss appears to assume the ultimacy of structures, that is, they are not subservient to any function or purpose. Our authors may take this view of structural ultimacy toward the syntactic correspondence in question, that is, it serves no other function than being itself. This is a radical view, since it does not even allow the possibility of poetic functions for the syntactic correspondence. For that reason, the syntactic and other results of our authors' purely structural analysis can be dismissed or condemned as irrelevant to the understanding of "Les Chats" as a poem.[36]

Our authors can avoid this charge of irrelevance only by recognizing and justifying the poetic function of their purely structural results. For example, they can say that the syntactic correspondence in question enhances the beauty of the sonnet's pure structure. That is, the syntactic resemblance between the first and the third stanzas, and between the second and the last

stanzas, is an element of structural beauty in the same manner
as are the rhymes, the rhythms, or the number of syllables in
every line. Since this function of enhancing structural beauty
is not subservient to the function of aiding thematic development, this view of poetic structure can be taken as a modified
version of structural ultimacy, an aesthetic version that asserts
the aesthetic independence of formal structure.

This second position inevitably implies the absence of intimate union between formal structure and thematic content,
which is quite unsatisfactory for those who accept the traditional notion of poetic unity, which means, above all, the unity
of form and content. This unsatisfactory implication can be
avoided by demonstrating that the purely formal structure of
a poem is a medium for its thematic development, for example,
by showing that the syntactic correspondence in question participates in the thematic development of the sonnet. This is to
demonstrate that syntactic structures are integral features of
thematic development.

Let us consider the relative pronoun qui at the beginning
of the last line of the first and the third stanza, by virtue of
which our authors have claimed a syntactic correspondence
between those two stanzas. We have seen that the function of
this relative pronoun in the first stanza is to facilitate the transition in the grammatical role of les chats from the object of a
verb in the first stanza to the subject of a verb in the second
stanza. But a similar function of transition cannot be attributed
to the relative pronoun qui in the third stanza. The third stanza
does not present les chats as the object of a verb; it opens with
les chats as the subject through the pronoun ils. In the last
stanza, les chats continues to be the subject of descriptive verbs
through the pronoun leurs. Since the cats begin and end as the
subjects of descriptive verbs in the sestet, there is no way for
the relative pronoun qui to play any transitional role.

Our authors have also claimed a syntactic resemblance
between the second and the last stanzas on the ground that

each of them is composed of two coordinate clauses. We have seen that the two coordinate clauses of the last stanza constitute one chain of predication. But the same cannot be said about the two coordinate clauses of the second stanza. The second of these two clauses is a negative qualification of what is asserted by the first of them, whereas the second clause of the last stanza constitutes the second segment of one assertion that is jointly made by its two clauses. This difference is reflected in further details of grammatical structure which are not taken into account by our authors. Whereas the two clauses of the second stanza have different tenses and moods, the two clauses of the last stanza have the same tense and mood. Whereas the two clauses of the second stanza are connected with a semicolon, the two clauses of the final stanza are connected with a comma and the connective *et*.

From these two examples, we may draw the following conclusions. No syntactic resemblance between any two units of a poem can ever be complete unless one of them is a repetition of the other. Hence the structural problem of syntactic resemblance always involves the problem of determining the degree of resemblance, which takes into account the points of difference as well. Even when two poetic passages show a relatively high degree of syntactic resemblance, the two similar syntactic structures involved may perform quite different thematic functions. Hence the notion of syntactic resemblance is of little value for thematic understanding, as long as it is taken as a notion of content-free structure.

CHAPTER FIVE

Structuralist Marxism

LOUIS ALTHUSSER'S INTERPRETATION of Marx has been called structuralist Marxism. If Lévi-Strauss' binary structure is applicable only to primitive cultures, it is most unlikely to be applicable to such a complex system of thought as Marxism. In what sense, then, can Althusser's Marxism be regarded as structuralist? To be sure, the word "structure" prominently figures in his interpretation of Karl Marx's writings, for example, "the economic structure," "the social structure," "the structure in dominance," "the effectivity of structure," "the centered structure," "the decentered structure," "the different structured levels," etc. Althusser's Marxism can be properly regarded as structuralist, if the word "structure" in his extensive usage retains the unique meaning it is given in Lévi-Strauss' structuralism, namely, the binary structure. Hence our question boils down to the semantic issue: What is the meaning of the word "structure" in Althusser's interpretation of Marxism? As a preliminary to settling this issue, we have to clarify the logical structure of Hegel's dialectic, not only because Marx's idea of dialectic was derived from it but also because Lévi-Strauss' structuralism has sometimes been discussed in dialectical terms by himself and others.

THE LOGICAL STRUCTURE OF HEGEL'S DIALECTIC

The logic of Hegel's dialectic is triadic. It consists of three moments: thesis, antithesis, and synthesis. The first two moments establish the dialectical conflict or opposition to be resolved in the third moment. Let us now compare this triadic schema with Lévi-Strauss' culinary triangle.[1] This triangle also consists of three nodes, which represent *raw*, *cooked*, and *rotten*. However, the triangular relation of these three nodes is established not by a resolution of any conflict but by the intersection of two binary oppositions.

The first binary opposition in the constitution of Lévi-Strauss' culinary triangle is the distinction between the food which is fresh and raw and the food which is no longer fresh and raw. This opposition can be conjoined to the binary opposition between nature and culture. By this conjunction, the first binary opposition can assume two different forms because fresh, raw food can lose these qualities through natural or cultural processes. Through natural processes, it can become rotten; through cultural processes, it can become cooked.

The main function of the culinary triangle is to establish two different ways of distinguishing food which is fresh and raw from food which is no longer fresh and raw. This requires two schemata of binary distinction. Neither of the binary schemata embodies any conflict; nor does the culinary triangle represent any reconciliation or mediation. In Lévi-Strauss' structuralism, the function of binary opposition is not to represent conflict but to establish distinction and equilibrium, which require no reconciliation. Hence the triadic schema of the culinary triangle performs an entirely different function from the function of Hegel's triadic schema. In the culinary triangle, the notion of triadic relation can be reduced to the notion of dyadic relation; but the same reduction cannot be made in Hegel's dialectical logic.

For a further illustration of this fundamental difference between Hegel's and Lévi-Strauss' triads, let us compare the culinary triangle with the traffic-signal triangle.[2] This triangle is also composed of three elements: green (go), red (stop), and yellow (caution). It is obvious that this triangle is not constituted by the intersection of two binary oppositions. It starts out with one binary opposition, the one between red and green, and then introduces yellow as the third term to indicate the transition between the first two terms. Since the third term is not reducible to either of the first two, the traffic-signal triangle is irreducibly triadic. Its logic is fundamentally the same as the triadic logic of Hegelian dialectic, and different from the dyadic logic of Lévi-Strauss' structuralism.

Let us now consider Lévi-Strauss' favorite dyad, nature vs. culture. We have already seen his distinction between the natural and cultural processes for transforming fresh and raw food. This is a dyadic distinction. As such, it operates with the same dyadic logic that underlies Lévi-Strauss' other binary oppositions such as above vs. below, light vs. dark, and this world vs. the other world. In its own right, the opposition between nature and culture involves no notion of conflict or opposition in its ordinary sense, because it is mainly a matter of contrast and distinction. This binary opposition can become the ground for disorder and conflict only when its demarcation is overstepped or when its equilibrium is disturbed.

This brings us to one of the most fundamental differences between Lévi-Strauss' dyadic logic and Hegel's triadic logic. In Hegel's triadic schema, the opposition of thesis and antithesis is by its nature a dialectical conflict. The first two moments of Hegel's triad cannot withstand each other without the mediation of the third moment. On the other hand, the two moments of Lévi-Strauss' dyad can maintain their own equilibrium; they do not need the intervention of a third term.

In Hegel's dialectic, nature and culture are related not in

a dyadic but a triadic schema. In Hegel's system, nature is never directly related to culture. Nature is the second moment in Hegel's most comprehensive triad: the logical idea (the idea in itself), nature (the idea outside itself), and spirit (the idea in and for itself). Each of these three moments is a triad in itself, and the triad of spirit is composed of subjective spirit, objective spirit, and absolute spirit. In Hegel's system, the notion of culture can be construed in two different ways, that is, in its narrow and broad sense. In its broad sense, culture can mean the entire triad of spirit; in its narrow sense, it can mean only objective spirit. In its broad sense, culture can be regarded as the synthesis of the logical idea and nature. In its narrow sense, it is opposed to subjective spirit. In neither sense is culture directly opposed to nature.

I have given this comparison for one special reason. On some occasions, Lévi-Strauss has used the Hegelian language of conflict (or contradiction) and its resolution, and this has misled some commentators to assume that his binary logic performs a function similar to that of Hegel's dialectic. For example, he says that "the purpose of myth is to provide a logical model capable of overcoming a contradiction (an impossible achievement if, as it happens, the contradiction is real). . . ."[3] This parenthetical remark is revealing. In Hegel's dialectical logic, the opposition of thesis and antithesis is claimed to be not an apparent but a real contradiction. Since it is a real contradiction, it generates a logically inevitable conflict.

Undeterred, K. O. L. Burridge makes an honest attempt to give a Hegelian form to structural analysis.[4] His attempt begins with the following short New Guinean myth.

Once upon a time the leading man of the village was fishing by the light of his bamboo torch in Cipenderp stream when it came on to rain. The leading man and all the other men and women of the village took shelter under the lee of a large stone. The last to come were a boy and his sister, orphans. They were dirty, unwashed, and smelly.

'Hey! You two can't come in here!' exclaimed the leading
man. 'You smell too much!'

The storm increased in intensity, the rain poured down, the
two orphans sought shelter in a hollow tree.

Seeing what had happened, the Great One on High sym-
pathized with the orphans. He caused the stone to envelope the
villagers.

The orphans returned to the village, mourning their fellows.
Later they tried to crack open the stone. It was no use. They
killed all the pigs in the village, collected piles of foodstuffs
and, with the help of neighbours, put all the meat and tubers by
the stone.

It was no good. The villagers died of hunger inside the stone.

For this myth, Burridge provides the following Lévi-Straussian
structural analysis:

The initial situation may be broken down into the 'contraries' 'light' and 'darkness', which may be said to be mediated by
'stream'. For, since a stream flows on in the same way whether
it is light or dark, it is unaffected by the contraries and so resolves
them. But a stream is water, water is rain, and rain is the source
of the stream: we get the contraries 'in the rain' and 'out of the
rain'. This pair is resolved in the notion of 'shelter' which is
itself broken down into 'good' people in one kind of shelter and
'smelly'—or, as is the case if we take note of the cultural content
of the vernacular terms—'bad' people, the orphans, in another
kind of shelter: stone, which makes cultural tools, as opposed
to hollow tree, a wild or non-cultural place. If these contraries
are mediated by more rain, the latter introduces the Great One
who, in two contexts, further separates the orphans from the
'good' people. We are left with the shadowy presence of the
Great One, and the orphans who, one may presume, restart community life through an incestuous union. As between 'good'
people and 'bad' people, or the Great One and community, or
the Great One and the orphans, or incest and non-incest, or
perhaps dual origin and single origin (orphans, Great One),
which is the main contradiction that the myth is attempting to
overcome by the positing of a logical model?

If the initial contrary of light and darkness is really mediated by "stream" as Burridge claims, his structural analysis

of this myth clearly takes on a Hegelian flavor because mediation is a typically Hegelian way of handling binary oppositions. But this claim of mediation is quite unconvincing: "stream" is alleged to resolve the conflict of light and darkness simply because it is unaffected by the conflict. To say that one thing is not affected by another can imply no more than that those two things have nothing to do with each other, or that their relation is completely external and incidental. The claim that "stream" functions as an agent of mediation requires in this myth a much stronger argument; it must show a much more intimate relation.

It may be more accurate to describe the structural development of the myth as a succession of contraries: the first contrary or polarity of light and darkness is succeeded by the second one ("water in the rain" vs. "water out of the rain"), which is in turn succeeded by the third (good people vs. smelly people), which is in turn succeeded by the fourth (shelter under a stone vs. shelter in a hollow tree). This succession or conjunction of polarities is consistent with the logic of binary opposition; it is also reminiscent of Lévi-Strauss' use of polarities in his structural analysis of the Theban myths. Of course, the conflict of one polarity cannot be resolved by conjoining or replacing it with another polarity. In fact, the conjunction and succession of polarities in this myth only intensify and complicate its original conflict to such an extent that it becomes hard to tell, as Burridge observes, "which is the main contradiction that the myth is attempting to overcome by the positing of a logical model?"

Eventually, the Great One brings the conflict to an end. However, he does not belong to any one of the polarities which have constituted and complicated the original conflict. In Hegel's system, the agent of mediation and reconciliation is never meant to be introduced as an external agent of intervention. The Great One has no internal connection with the conflict. Consequently, he cannot be accepted as a Hegelian agent of mediation. In fact, the myth ends with the elimination of one of the two contending parties. This type of ending cannot be regarded as reconciliation.

For these and other reasons, Burridge's Hegelian rendition of Lévi-Strauss' structuralism comes to a negative conclusion: "Given the dialectics, and given that the purpose of myth is to provide a logical model capable of overcoming a real contradiction, it is not clear—at least to me—in what sense real contradictions are overcome."[5] Burridge's whole trouble stems from his initial premise ("Given the dialectics"); Hegelian dialectics can never be given by the dyadic logic of Lévi-Strauss' structuralism. No doubt, Burridge was misled to this initial premise by Lévi-Strauss' careless, unwarranted use of Hegelian language.

In all fairness, we should concede Lévi-Strauss' right to use the word "dialectic" to describe the workings of his dyadic logic. In fact, the operation of any logical system can be called dialectic; there is no reason to presuppose that Hegel has established a monopoly on this magic word. Throughout his *Savage Mind*, Lévi-Strauss tries to demonstrate the dynamism of his dyadic logic, that is, its function of establishing and maintaining binary social equilibrium. Sometimes he does use the word "dialectic" in referring to this dynamism. But that should not mislead us into assuming that his dialectic is the same kind as Hegel's. Since their logical systems are fundamentally different, the difference between their dialectics must be equally fundamental.

There is one more basic difference between Lévi-Strauss' binary and Hegel's triadic logic. The former is a system of co-ordination; the latter is a system of subordination. There are many triads in Hegel's system, but none of them belongs to the same level as another. All his triads are organized into an architectonic system. In contrast to this, the many polarities in Lévi-Strauss' structuralism are related to each other through their homological equivalences on the same level. Furthermore,

Hegel's system of subordination is progressional, while Lévi-Strauss' system of coordination is nonprogressional. These two systems take on different modes of temporality.

This outline of Hegel's system is essential for understanding the structural characteristics of Marxism, for Marx claims to have derived his dialectical materialism through a systematic inversion of Hegel's dialectical idealism: with Hegel, the dialectic "is standing on its head. It must be turned right side up again."[6] In this inversion, Marx shifts the primacy of dialectic from ideas to people and the material conditions of their existence. In Hegel's system, ideas and concepts are the primary agencies for dialectical movement. If any other things, such as persons and institutions, happen to serve as dialectical agencies, they do so not in their own right but as the bearers of certain ideas, since ideas alone have dialectical powers. Marx rejects the primacy of ideas; in his view, people and their interests are the only dynamic agencies that can generate and sustain dialectical movement. Furthermore, their interests are determined by the class structure of their society. Hence the primary dialectical conflict is the contradiction between the exploiting and the exploited class. If anything else participates in this dialectic of class struggle, it does so not in its own right but as an instrument of the contending classes.

This inversion of Hegel's system into Marxism does not reject Hegel's triadic logic but dictates a different use of it. Marx takes seriously Hegel's claim that the conflict of thesis and antithesis is a contradiction and that the contradiction is not apparent but real. If the contradiction of thesis and antithesis is logically real, even God cannot bring about their reconciliation because what is logically contradictory is impossible in every possible world. Hence Marx claims that the contradiction of class struggle can be resolved only by the elimination of the exploiting class by the exploited class. When two things are logically incompatible, their conflict can be resolved only by eliminating one of them. It is theoretically possible to resolve the contradiction of class struggle by eliminating the exploited class rather than the exploiting one. But this resolution would be sought neither by the exploited, nor even by the exploiting class, because the exploiting class would cease to be the exploiting class and would terminate all its class privileges with the elimination of the exploited.

Since Marxism systematically refuses to admit a third class as an agent of mediation in class struggle, and since it recognizes only the two contending classes and the conflict of their interests, it may appear to be operating with a dyadic logic. However, this is only an appearance. In Lévi-Strauss' structuralism, as we have seen, the dyadic logic is essentially the primitive format for establishing social equilibrium and cooperation. In Marxism, the dyadic relation of the exploiting and exploited classes is always the social framework for exploitation and contradiction. Whereas the Lévi-Straussian dyad is a relation of complements, the Marxian dyad is a relation of conflict. The former is a self-sufficient relation which can be theoretically perpetuated without introducing a third term. The latter is a self-destructive relation destined to be transformed into another, and this necessary transformation requires the introduction of a third term.

In the transformation of a dyad into a monad or another dyad, the monad or the new dyad functions as a third term for the original dyad. For example, when the class struggle of capitalism is resolved through the establishment of a socialist state, the latter stands as a third term for the dyadic relation of the bourgeoisie and the proletariat. The socialist state combines the functions of the bourgeoisie and the proletariat by taking over the former's capital as the state capital and by reemploying the latter as the state employees. Hence the logic of Marxian dialectic is essentially triadic and progressional; it is a system of progressional subordination rather than nonprogressional coordination. Unlike Lévi-Strauss' dyad, Marx's dyad can never find stable equilibrium within itself; it is perpetually driven by its own inner conflict, which can never be resolved except through the advent of the next dialectical stage.

Moreover, the Marxian triad is ultimately historical, where the Hegelian triad is primarily logical and secondarily historical. Hegel's system embodies two modes of progression: the logical and the historical. In the logical progression, one simple idea of *pure being* develops into a whole system of more and more complex ideas. This logical progression was not known either in Plato's or in Aristotle's system of subordination. The historical progression of Hegel's system is only the temporal manifestation of its logical progression. Marx cannot accept the very notion of logical progression because he rejects the primacy of ideas and the notion of their dynamism. Consequently, the progression of Marx's dialectical materialism is limited to the historical mode.

THE DIALECTICAL STRUCTURE
OF OVERDETERMINATION

This is a brief sketch of Marx's inversion of Hegel's system. This inversion preserves many Hegelian features by retaining the logic of triads, the system of subordination, and the notion of historical progression. In these respects, Marxism is as systematically opposed to Lévi-Strauss' structuralism as is Hegelianism. But Louis Althusser maintains that Marx's notion of dialectic has been misunderstood by taking Marx's metaphor of inversion in its pure and simple mode. He devotes his entire essay, "Contradiction and Overdetermination," to the task of explaining how the problematic metaphor of inversion is to be understood.[7] In this essay, Althusser maintains that the contradiction in Marxian dialectic is "overdetermined," whereas such is not the case with Hegelian dialectic.

The word "overdetermination" means that something is determined not by one factor but by many. A contradiction is overdetermined when it is determined not by one but by many conflicts. For the sake of convenience, we may as well introduce the expression "simple-determination": a contradiction is simple-determined when it is determined by one dialectical conflict alone. Althusser rightly claims that contradiction in Hegel's system is always simple determined. Hegel may recognize many factors or levels of historical movement, but the nature of every historical contradiction is claimed to be determined by the dialectic of ideas which constitute the "inner essence" of that contradiction.[8] All other levels or features of history are no more than the epiphenomena that "express" this essential dialectic of ideas. Hence Althusser calls Hegel's monistic view of historical dialectic "the global expressive causality of a universal inner essence immanent in its phenomena."[9]

As long as Marxism is viewed as a simple inversion of Hegel's system, the former must be assumed to be a dialectical system of simple-determination just like the latter. In fact, this has been the way Marx has been understood among the so-called orthodox Marxists. For example, they have declared that the most fundamental level of Marxian dialectic is the economic level of society (its base or infrastructure), and that the dialectic of this level determines the dialectic of the whole society (its infrastructure and superstructure). This interpretation of Marx has been known as his economic determinism, and it is a clear case of simple-determination. Louis Althusser regards it too simpleminded and too Hegelian. He maintains that Marx's real view of social causation is much more sophisticated. In Marx's dialectical scheme, he holds, there are many levels of social causation and dialectical determination, and each of them has its own tempo and relative autonomy. In his view, this is the great insight of Marx, which has been distorted by the orthodox Marxists and which he is trying to restore with his doctrine of overdetermination.

Althusser argues that his notion of overdetermination is consistent with Lenin's reading of Marx.[10] In this argument, he converts Lenin's metaphor of the weakest link in a chain ("A chain is as strong as its weakest link") into that of a rope made by braiding together many strands of fiber. Lenin uses the former metaphor in describing the position of Tsarist Russia in the chain of imperialist states: she was the weakest link in the chain. However, the latter metaphor is implicitly operative in Althusser's understanding of Lenin's words, "the accumulation and exacerbation of all the historical contradictions then possible in a single State."[11] By these words, Althusser claims, Lenin means to say that the revolutionary situation in a given state is determined not by one simple contradiction but by the accumulation and exacerbation of a number of contradictions. That is, a revolutionary situation emerges only when contradictions break out in all social levels at the same moment. Althusser calls this joint occurrence of contradictions a "ruptural unity"; social revolution is like the breaking of a rope which requires "the unity of rupture" in all the strands of that rope.[12]

The doctrine of overdetermination should not be confused with the doctrine of reciprocal determination, which has been advocated by Georg Lukács, Karl Korsch, and the various members of the Frankfurt school in general.[13] Reciprocal determination, which has also been proposed in opposition to the economic determinism of orthodox Marxists, is the claim that the superstructure of a society is not always determined by its infrastructure (economic structure), and that there is a reciprocal interaction between the two. The doctrine of reciprocal determination is a doctrine of interaction; it is meant to explain how the different levels of society interact with one another. On the other hand, Althusser's doctrine of overdetermination is a doctrine of self-determination and autonomy; it is meant to explain how each level of society acts on itself and maintains a measure of its own autonomy.

Those Marxists who have advocated the doctrine of reciprocal determination may very well have presupposed relative autonomy and self-determination for the different levels of society, because any social level may be presumed to have the power to act upon itself if it has the power to act upon other levels. Conversely, Althusser's doctrine of relative autonomy may imply the doctrine of reciprocal determination, because the notion of relative independence may entail the notion of relative dependence. Hence these two doctrines can be considered logical complements, although each of them can be asserted independently. Nevertheless, the credit for having advocated the doctrine of relative self-determination, in its own right, clearly belongs to Louis Althusser.

Since Althusser is convinced that each level of society has its own relative autonomy, he tries to distinguish Marx's view of social totality emphatically from Hegel's monistic view:

> We know that the Marxist whole cannot possibly be confused with the Hegelian whole: it is a whole whose unity, far from being the expressive or 'spiritual' unity of Leibniz's or Hegel's whole, is constituted by a certain type of complexity, the unity of a structured whole containing what can be called levels or instances which are distinct and 'relatively autonomous', and co-exist within this complex structural unity, articulated with one another according to specific determinations, fixed in the last instance by the level or instance of economy.[14]

In general, Althusser recognizes three levels of society: the economic, the political, and the ideological (sometimes he adds the fourth level called the level of theoretical practice). In Hegel's expressive totality, he says, all these different levels express one essential dialectic and constitute one stream of history. In the language of time, they are "contemporaneous" with one another ("the contemporaneity of the present"), or rather their time is "continuous and homogeneous."[15] In Marxian pluralistic totality, he claims, each of "the different structured levels" maintains its own rhythm of dialectic and its own tempo of historical development:

> This is the principle on which is based the possibility and

necessity of different *histories* corresponding respectively to each of the 'levels'. This principle justifies our speaking of an economic history, a political history, a history of religions, a history of ideologies, a history of philosophy, a history of art and a history of the sciences, without thereby evading, but on the contrary, necessarily accepting, the relative independence of each of these histories in the specific dependence which articulates each of the different levels of the social whole with the others.[16]

Since the dialectics of these different social levels may have different rhythms and tempos, their contradictions may become "active" at different historical moments. However, when their contradictions become active at the same moment, they eventuate in a "ruptural unity."

This is a rough outline of the pluralistic conception of dialectic which Althusser advocates explicitly against Hegel's monistic view and implicitly against the monistic interpretation of Marx's view. In order to avoid some confusion, we had better distinguish the overdetermination from its component determinations. The latter belong to the different levels of a society; the former belongs to the society as a whole. The former is overdetermined, whereas each of its component contradictions is simple-determined. The structure of a component contradiction can be described by a binary opposition, because it involves one dialectic and because each dialectic can be regarded as a binary opposition. On that supposition, the structure of an overdetermined contradiction can be viewed as an assemblage of binary oppositions, because an overdetermined contradiction is composed of its simple-determined components. An assemblage or a cluster of binary oppositions is structurally similar to the structure of primitive mentality as delineated in Lévi-Strauss' psychological structuralism. This structural similarity may appear to be a solid ground for calling Althusser's Marxism structuralist.

This structural similarity appears to be enhanced by Althusser's tendency to emphasize the structural invariants in Marxism. For example, he gives the impression that the three structured levels (the economic, the political, and the ideological) are structural invariants of all societies. This tendency for seeking out structural invariants is even more pronounced in Althusser's colleague Étienne Balibar. Whereas Althusser's use of structural invariants is rather informal, Balibar tries to make a formal tabulation of them.[17] For example, he claims that the mode of production in every society is constituted by the combination of five elements: the laborer, the means of production, and the nonlaborer are combined by two relational elements, the property connection and the appropriation connection.[18] No doubt, the notion of structural invariants is also a salient feature of Lévi-Strauss' structuralism.

In spite of these surface resemblances, the structure of Althusser's Marxism is fundamentally different from that of Lévi-Strauss' structuralism. All the constituent binary oppositions of the latter are equal and equivalent to one another. This equality and equivalence do not obtain in Althusser's Marxism. The relative independence of the different social levels is at the same time their relative dependence on one another. Furthermore, the measure of dependence and independence is not uniform for all social levels. Although the economic level does not always dominate other social levels, it is still the most basic level ("the determination in the last instance" belongs to the economic level).[19] The different social levels constitute one hierarchy of domination; Althusser's Marxism is ultimately a system of subordination rather than that of coordination, despite the relative autonomy of each social level.

Furthermore, it is incorrect to view the dialectical structure of a component contradiction simply as binary. As we have shown, the logic of binary opposition is the logic of equilibrium; in and of itself, it is incapable of generating any conflict or its resolution. In contrast to this, every component contradiction embodies a potential or actual conflict or "rupture," whose resolution requires a triadic schema. As long as Marxism is to be construed as a doctrine of historical dialectic and contradiction, it cannot dispense with triadic logic. Althusser may indeed be right in holding that each level has its own dialectic rhythm and tempo. However, the structure of this pluralistic dialectic cannot be correctly represented as a cluster of binary oppositions, because it is a cluster of triads.

Finally, Althusser's Marxism is progressional, whereas Lévi-Strauss' structuralism is nonprogressional. In Marxism, even the so-called structural invariants, such as the elements and modes of production, take on cumulative significance because they have different qualities and textures depending on the different historical stages in which they are situated. As Althusser points out, the fundamental feature of Marx's criticism of classical economics is his claim that its conception of economic categories is ahistorical and that those categories must be historicized to reveal their historical relativity.[20] Althusser clearly recognizes historicity as a fundamental difference between Marxism and Lévi-Strauss' structuralism.[21] Marxism in any version is as inexorably historicistic as it is triadic.

These considerations show that Althusser's Marxism is a progressional system of subordination. In this regard, there is no fundamental difference between it and Hegelianism or orthodox Marxism. Structurally, all these systems are diametrically opposed to Lévi-Strauss' structuralism, which is a nonprogressional system of coordination. The word "structure" in Althusser's writings does not retain the unique meaning it has in Lévi-Strauss' structuralism (the binary structure), but has the general meaning that is equivalent to the meaning of "system" or "whole."[22] Consequently, the structural machinery of Lévi-Strauss' structuralism is useless for understanding the logical structure of Althusser's Marxism.

CHAPTER SIX

Semiology and Grammatology

BEYOND AND AFTER Lévi-Strauss, linguistic structuralism has shown a much greater vitality than psychological structuralism. Expecially in the field of literary criticism, it has spawned many unusual projects and experiments, which shall engage our attention on another occasion.[1] All these projects and experiments are confined within the linguistic dimension of human culture. In that regard, they do not truly fulfill Lévi-Strauss' original ambition of using the structure of language to analyze the structure of human culture in its entirety, thereby making the scope of linguistic structuralism coextensive with the scope of culture itself. Roland Barthes has tried to recapture this original spirit of linguistic structuralism in his *Elements of Semiology*. For this enterprise, he relies on semiology rather than linguistics; hence his program may be called semiological structuralism.

BARTHES' SEMIOLOGY

Barthes' program is to analyze the structure of all cultural complexes by treating them as systems of signs, which express or convey meanings. For example, a certain system of garments or foods can express or convey a set of meanings; they are coded systems of signs for expression or communication by vestimentary or alimentary means.[2] Defined in this broad sense, signs constitute the entire fabric of human culture, and language is only one special type of sign system. The study of signs in this broad sense should be called universal semiology or semiotics, which can provide a structural account of the entire human culture.

This grand conception of semiology was one of the scientific dreams Ferdinand de Saussure had entertained for future generations:

> A science that studies the life of signs within society is conceivable. . . . I shall call it semiology (from Greek sēmîon 'sign'). Semiology should show what constitutes signs, what laws govern them. Since the science does not yet exist, no one can say what it would be. . . . Linguistics is only a part of the general science of semiology.[3]

Saussure then predicts that the study of social conventions and cultural institutions shall be included in this future science: "By studying rites, customs, etc. as signs, I believe that we shall throw new light on the facts and point up the need for including them in a science of semiology and explaining them by its laws."[4]

Following Lévi-Strauss' procedure, Barthes accepts certain categories already established in the science of linguistics and tries to extend them to the nonlinguistic dimensions of human culture. He begins with Saussure's distinction between langue and parole. Langue is language considered as a system of signs or codes; parole is language considered as a series of actual utterances and statements. The latter is event; the former is structure. Barthes applies this Saussurian distinction to the food system. The sequence of particular courses in a given meal is a parole; the general convention governing the meal is a langue. The langue of alimentary language is the general system of possibilities of selecting and combining different courses into a meal; its *parole* is any actuality realized out of those possibilities.

The Saussurian distinction between *langue* and *parole* can also be applied to the furniture, the garment, and the car systems.[5] The actual array of furniture in any given room is a *parole*; the possibilities of selecting and combining different pieces into that array or any other arrangement constitute a *langue*. The various pieces of clothes one wears for any given occasion is a *parole*; the possibilities of selecting and combining those and any other pieces into an acceptable form of attire belong to the *langue* of vestimentary language. Every car can be considered as a *parole*; it is produced by selecting and combining different parts. The possibilities of their selection and combination belong to the *langue* of the automobile industry as a coded system.

This procedure of investigating all cultural complexes as systems of signs is called the universal semantization, and Barthes' universal semiology is a program for universal semantization.[6] It is a program for decoding the meaning of any cultural complex, linguistic or nonlinguistic. In Barthes' view, there is no reason to delimit the notion of sign to the domain of linguistic signs; all cultural complexes can and do function as signs insofar as they have or express meanings. The program of universal semantization logically follows from the obvious premise that all sectors of human culture are pervaded by meanings, that is, signification is the universal feature of all cultural complexes.

The claim that even the nonlinguistic features of human culture have meanings appears to be indisputable, because every cultural complex is a meaning complex. But do they have the sort of meanings which semantic systems have? This is the critical question for Barthes' program of universal semantization. Meals and garments seem to have no more than the meanings of conventional associations. For example, a turkey dinner can be said to mean Thanksgiving, because the former has been associated with the latter. Some linguists have claimed that the meanings of words are established by conventional associations; for example, the word "tree" has its meaning through its conventional association with the real trees in the domain of objects. On this view of linguistic meanings, a turkey dinner has the same mode of signification that linguistic signs have.

However, there are a few points of difference between these two modes of signification. Whenever one uses the word "tree," one means a tree or trees. But not every turkey dinner means Thanksgiving; some turkey dinners can be had on some other occasions. Moreover, there are many other kinds of dinner which do not have the sort of conventional association that a turkey dinner has; for example, a chicken, a steak, or a pork dinner has no special association with any particular event or occasion. In fact, the vast majority of our food is devoid of any conventionally established meanings. If any of our food is to be regarded as signs because of their conventional meanings, the category of sign can apply only to a very small fraction of it. No doubt, this is true of our clothes, our furniture, and any other features of human culture. That is, it is not a general rule but a rare exception that some elements of culture can be regarded as sign systems by virtue of their conventionally established meanings.

On what ground, then, can Roland Barthes claim the semantization of cultural objects as a general rule? He says:

> This semantization is inevitable: *as soon as there is a society, every usage is converted into a sign of itself;* the use of a raincoat is to give protection from the rain, but this use cannot be dissociated from the very signs of an atmospheric situation. Since our society produces only standardized, normalized objects, these objects are unavoidably realization of a model, the speech [*parole*] of a language [*langue*], the substances of a significant form.[7]

In this passage, Barthes is giving two reasons for his doctrine of universal semantization. First, every cultural object has a set of conventionally established relations and associations. Second, it is a *parole* of a *langue*. Although these two reasons may be related, they can be examined separately.

No doubt, a raincoat is associated with rainy weather conditions; one may say that the wearing of a raincoat *means* rainy weather conditions. However, a raincoat is not always worn on a rainy day; it can also be worn on a sunny day. But this objection can be handled with a linguistic analogy: a raincoat can be used inappropriately or unconventionally, just as much as a word or a sign can. Hence a raincoat seems to have its own meaning of conventional associations, just as the word "raincoat" has. If this conventional association between a raincoat and weather conditions is sufficient to call a raincoat a sign, every meal can be called a sign whether it is a meal of special occasion or that of everyday variety. While a special meal is associated with a special occasion, a common meal is associated with a common occasion. One association cannot be any stronger or weaker than the other. This seems to justify Roland Barthes' doctrine of universal semantization.

However, this principle of universal semantization cannot be contained within the domain of culture. For not only every cultural object, but also every natural object has a set of established associations. The natural phenomenon of rain is generally associated with cloud, humid air, muddy fields, wet clothes, just in the same way the cultural object of a raincoat is associated with weather conditions. If a raincoat is to be regarded as a sign, rain itself must be so regarded. As long as the meaning of a sign is assumed to be no more than its association with other things, there is no way to deny the function of signification to natural objects and give it only to cultural objects. Barthes can limit the function of signification to cultural objects by stipulating that the meaning of a sign is a set of associations established by culture and not by nature. But that will be an arbitrary measure of stipulation and discrimination.

This arbitrary measure would place an unnecessary obstacle against the obvious extension of semiology from the domain of culture to that of nature. If it is desirable to extend the scope of semiology to the entire domain of culture, it should be even more desirable to extend it to that of nature. The broader scope a science gains, the greater power it commands. If the entire domain of nature as well as culture can be conceived and analyzed as a coded system or systems, the dominion of Barthes' semiology can become truly universal. Nothing in heaven or on earth can ever be left out of it. But what is to be gained by this grand universal science except for the fancy doctrine of universal semantization, a fancy label for the familiar notion that every object has a set of established associations?

Roland Barthes' second reason for regarding cultural objects as signs is the applicability of the distinction between *langue* and *parole* to them. This distinction is a special version of the old metaphysical distinction between universal and particular, that is, its application to the domain of linguistics. Every occurrence of the sound /r/ in speech is a particular manifestation of the phoneme /r/ as a universal; every utterance of the word "raincoat" in speech is a particular instantiation of the sememe "raincoat" as a universal. Likewise, every statement or utterance as a whole is a particular realization or actualization of a universal formula. For example, the statement "Roland is wearing a raincoat," is a particular instantiation or manifestation of many universals on phonological, syntactic, and semantic levels. These universals constitute a *langue*, while their particular manifestations become *paroles*.[8]

This distinction between universal and particular is sometimes known as the one between type and token, between a universal and its instances or realizations, or between possibles and actuals. Since a *langue* is a system of possibles, it can offer the possibilities of selection and combination in the production of *paroles*. A universal is a model or paradigm of possibilities to be realized in particular instances. This relation of universal and particular implicitly underlies Barthes' own characterization of cultural objects we have just quoted: "these objects are unavoidably realization of a model, the speech [parole] of a language [langue], the substances of a significant form."

In his doctrine of semantization, Barthes has made the langue/parole distinction coextensive with the universal/particular distinction. Hence the categories of langue and parole have become applicable to objects of not only culture but also nature, because the universal/particular distinction applies to all things. Thus the second reason Barthes has given for regarding cultural objects as signs also dictates that natural objects must also be so regarded. If this dictate is to be followed, his semiology will become a truly universal science, whose scope will be coextensive with the whole universe.

Roland Barthes has given his semiology the appearance of being a universal science of culture by overextending the linguistic categories to the entire domain of culture. This categorial extension is an inherent tendency in any version of linguistic structuralism, because its central motivation is to regard nonlinguistic entities as extensions of language or as different kinds of language. In other words, language is accepted as the ultimate model of analysis and understanding in linguistic structuralism; everything else is investigated and interpreted through this universal model. Consequently, the science of linguistics becomes the arch-science whose sphere of control and influence cannot be delimited. This is the common tendency we have observed in Lévi-Strauss and Barthes.

But there is some difference between Lévi-Strauss' version of linguistic structuralism and Barthes' version. Lévi-Strauss employs the structure of language (e.g., binary opposition) in his structural analysis of cultural phenomena; Barthes uses the categories of linguistics (e.g., langue and parole) in his semiology. Unlike the structure of language, linguistic categories are structurally neutral. Hence Barthes is not committed, in his semiology, to any a priori structure of language. Nor does he employ any particular structure of language in his structural analysis of nonlinguistic sign systems. The structure of those systems is to be discovered by empirical investigations, whether it be the system of furniture or that of clothing. Barthes' semiology can be no more than a heuristic device for suggesting and implementing those empirical investigations.

In one regard, Barthes' semiology falls short of Saussure's ideal of universal semiology. Saussure said, "Semiology should show what constitutes signs, what laws govern them." That is, the necessary preliminary to the construction of universal semiology is to discover the universal properties of signs and the universal laws of their operation. This discovery can be made by investigating all the different types of signs, whether they are linguistic or nonlinguistic. Barthes has not performed this general investigation; instead he has tried to use the properties and laws of linguistic signs as substitutes for the universal properties and laws of all types of signs. Nor has he thought of justifying this substitution. For that reason, Barthes' attempt for constructing a universal semiology turns out to be careless and thoughtless. He has tried to construct his ambitious edifice without even recognizing the necessity of preparing its foundation.

This charge of carelessness and thoughtlessness may be too harsh by the prevailing standard in French structuralism. Even Lévi-Strauss has never considered the necessity of mapping out all the structures of language in advocating and practicing his linguistic structuralism. Instead he has taken the easy path of adopting the binary principle as the all-encompassing linguistic structure. None of his followers have gone through the laborious chore of determining the totality of linguistic structures as a preliminary stage for the implementation of linguistic structuralism. As a matter of fact, the entire movement of linguistic structuralism has thrived on the assumption that the structure of language has been discovered and delineated by the science of language, especially by structural linguistics. This assumption has in turn been reinforced by another assumption that we have a privileged access to language, which is never available in our access to other objects of cognition.

Let us compare our language of stars and quarks, worms and germs, with these objects themselves. These objects are extramental, whereas our language of these objects is mental. We can gain access to these objects by locating them outside our minds, but there is no need for us to take this empirical detour to get our access to our language of those objects. Although we can never be certain about what a star or a germ is really like, we can always be sure of what we mean by the word "star" or "germ," or the structure of a sentence in which it appears. Our access to our language appears to be nonempirical or a priori. It is this seemingly a priori, therefore privileged, access to our language and its structure that may have underlaid the a priori tendency in Lévi-Strauss' and other linguistic structuralism.

The examination and rejection of these aprioristic assumptions may be said to mark the transition from structuralism to post-structuralism. Jacques Derrida has been one of the pivotal figures in this transition. He has refused to follow the simple-minded move of identifying the structure of language with the binary principle or the syntactic structure. For him, the structure of language means the structure of signification, because language is a system of signification. Any other features of linguistic structure should be understood as an integral element of the structure of signification, that is, part of the overall pattern for the performance of signification. This function is, he has maintained, most eminently embodied in a written sign (grammé) or writing (écriture). Hence semiology (a general theory of signs) is reducible to grammatology (a theory of written signs).[9]

DERRIDA'S GRAMMATOLOGY

In the West, Derrida says, spoken language has always been taken as primary, and written language as secondary. The latter has been regarded only as a supplement or substitute for the former. This traditional belief of the West has Derrida labeled as phonocentrism; it is a debasement and repression of writing, which has been dictated by a metaphysical conspiracy or dogmatism, called the "metaphysics of presence." His grammatology is to expose the error of this metaphysical dogma and demonstrate the ultimacy of written signs; that is, even spoken words can discharge their function of signification only as written signs.

What, then, is the unique feature of written signs? Although Derrida has given various descriptions of it, they can be summed up as semiotic independence. The existence and operation of written signs are independent of any agents, whether they be called writers or authors, or readers or receivers. On the other hand, spoken words are not presumed to enjoy this kind of independence. Derrida has used extensively the Husserlian category of "absence" in elucidating the semiotic independence of written signs. They can exist and function in the absence of or in separation from their authors. Spoken words can neither be separated from their authors, nor be encountered in their absence. A script "does not exhaust itself in the moment of its inscription," whereas an utterance cannot endure beyond the moment of its being uttered.[10]

To be sure, physical independence is not quite the same as semiotic independence. Despite the physical independence or separation of written signs from their authors, it is still possible that those signs may be semiotically dependent. Hence Derrida's ultimate emphasis falls on the independence of their semiotic function; that is, they can act and function as signs in complete independence of their authors. "To write is to produce a mark that will constitute a sort of machine which is productive in turn, and which my future disappearance will not, in principle, hinder in its functioning."[11] Every script is an autonomous machine.

The autonomy of this machine is not limited to its relation

to its author; it is equally independent of its receiver. A written message has its meaning before and after it is read by its receiver. It must be able to *act* in the absence of both its author and receiver.[12] Finally, Derrida claims its independence from the object of its signification, the signified or its referent. The inscribed sentence "The sky is blue" means whatever it means whether the sky is blue or not; its meaning does not change with the condition of the sky.[13] Likewise, the meaning of the inscribed word "unicorn" does not depend on the existence of unicorns. There is nothing that can compromise the semiotic independence of writing. It is total and complete.

Although spoken words are physically dependent, Derrida maintains, they are semiotically as independent as written words. Let us now suppose that a speaker utters the words, "The sky is blue." Through the utterance of these words, the speaker can mean whatever he wants to mean, because those words mean what they mean in their own right. If those words have no independent meaning, nothing can ever be expressed or conveyed by any speaker through their use. The process of understanding the meaning of "The sky is blue" as spoken words cannot be any different from that of understanding the same words as a written message. Whether I encounter these words in a talk or text, I must understand its meaning as an independent function of those words. To look upon them as an act or product of a subject does not change the picture, because a verbal act or product can be understood only by virtue of their semiotic independence. Since semiotic independence is a necessary and essential feature of spoken words as well as of written words, Derrida extends the name of "writing" or "text" to what has been known as oral or natural language.[14]

The word "writing" (*écriture*) is Derrida's technical term for what has been generally known as a sign; it is "the common name for signs which function despite the total absence of the subject."[15] If any sign cannot function in such a total absence of human subjects, it cannot properly be called a sign. Hence the two words "writing" and "sign" in Derrida's vocabulary are coextensive; his grammatology (the science of writing) is his semiology (the science of signs). His elevation of the word "writing" as his central semiotic term is his tactic of expediency for highlighting his thesis that semiotic independence is the defining characteristic of all signs. This maneuver of expediency rests on the contingent fact that the physical independence of written signs is obvious and that this obvious fact can be exploited in demonstrating their semiotic independence. This expediency, however, tends inherently to cause confusion between physical independence and semiotic independence. Thus Derrida can be misunderstood to uphold the semiotic independence of written words only and not spoken words. In that event, his grammatology might appear to be an attempt to reverse the traditional primacy of spoken over written language.[16]

Derrida's notion of sign is not limited to the domain of linguistic signs; likewise, his notion of writing covers all signs, linguistic or nonlinguistic:

> And thus we say "writing" for all that gives rise to an inscription in general, whether it is literal or not and even if what it distributes in space is alien to the order of voice: cinematography, choreography, of course, but also pictorial, musical, sculptural "writing." One might also speak of military or political writing in view of the techniques that govern those domains today.[17]

Not only a set of conventions or techniques but also an entire age or culture is called a "text" or "writing" by Derrida. For example, the life of Rousseau is a text; so is the age in which he lived. From this extension of the words "writing" and "text," there naturally follows his seemingly startling statement that there is nothing outside the text (il n'y a rien hors du texte). But there is nothing startling about it, for the word "text" has been fantastically expanded to cover the whole universe. This Derridean verbal maneuver may be called "textualization" in analogy to the Barthesian maneuver of semantization.[18]

As synonyms of "sign," "writing" and "text" are quite confusing. But Derrida has given us a series of less confusing synonyms: "mark," "trace," "supplement," etc. Although this battery of synonyms may imply different points of emphasis and different nuances, all of them share at least one common notion, the idea of semiotic independence as the essential mark of all signs. This notion appears to be an adaptation of Saussure's conception of *langue* as an independent system of signification. Derrida often compares the semiotic independence of signs or writing to that of a code, and sometimes illustrates the nature of the former with the working of the latter. He has repeatedly claimed that, like a code, a mark or writing can never be enclosed in any given context, and that it can be repeated and iterated in countless other contexts.[19] A code is a system of signs; as such it fulfills Saussure's definition of *langue*.

In comparing *langue* with *parole*, Saussure has stressed the independence of the former and the dependence of the latter: "*langue* is not a function of the speaker," whereas *parole* is such a function (an individual act).[20] The existence and operation of *langue* do not depend on any individual subjects, whereas *parole* is inseparable from them. Furthermore, the semiotic independence of *langue* is a necessary condition for the possibility of *parole*; individual subjects can say what they mean to say only by virtue of the fact that *langue* is a system of signs whose meanings are independent of any individual speakers and hearers. To that extent, Saussure has implicitly admitted the semiotic dependence of *parole* on *langue*, and this dependence can be construed as the independence of *parole* from the individual subjects.[21] If the signification function of *parole* is derived from *langue*, it cannot be regarded as a function of an individual subject, either. Hence Derrida seems to have the right to extend the semiotic independence of *langue* to the domain of *parole*, and elevate it as the universal characteristic of signs whether they occur as constituents of *langue* or *parole*.

Derrida's thesis of semiotic independence is, however, not merely an extension of Saussure's idea; the former contains one radical element not present in the latter. This element is the total independence of all signs from both individual and collective subjects. Saussure has never taken this extreme position; he has denied only the dependence of *langue* on any individual subjects, not on all subjects. His conception of *langue* always presupposes a collective subject or intersubjectivity; for example, English as a *langue* can exist and operate only in English-speaking communities. Sometimes he tries to spell out this inseparable relation between a *langue* and its speaking community in concrete terms:

> *Langue* exists in the form of a sum of impressions deposited in the brain of each member of community, almost like a dictionary of which identical copies have been distributed to each individual. Language exists in each individual, yet is common to all. Nor is it affected by the will of the depositories.[22]

The total independence of signs from all subjects, individual and collective, appears to be an implausible thesis. It appears to be impossible even to entertain the notion of a sign that can, all by itself, discharge its function of signification. Perhaps we may gain a better grasp of this difficult thesis in Derrida's critique of Edmund Husserl's theory of signs, in which Derrida made one of his first attempts to formulate his own theory of signification.[23]

HUSSERL'S THEORY OF SIGNS

In his *Logical Investigations*, Edmund Husserl opens his inquiry into the nature of signs by taking note of the fact that the term "sign" (*Zeichen*) has a double meaning (*Doppelsinn*). It can mean either an expression (*Ausdruck*) or an indication

(*Anzeichen*).[24] The function of an expression or expressive sign is to express meaning (*Bedeutung*), which is an ideal content rather than a factual entity.[25] For example, the notion of a triangle as a plane figure consisting of three straight lines and three angles is an ideal content; any particular triangle is a factual entity. Whereas the factual entities are subject to contingency and mutability, ideal entities like the essence of triangles or horses are always self-identical and invariant. The ideal content is called the eidetic essence. Husserl's theory of eidetic essences is a revival of Plato's theory of Forms or Ideas, and the medieval doctrine of common nature or essence, which has been known as essentialism or realism.

Eidetic essence should be distinguished from the objective correlate of an expression, or its objective reference or referent.[26] Any particular horse that can be referred to by the use of the word "horse" is an objective reference of that signifier. Two names which differ in the ideal content of their meanings can have the same objective reference. For example, "the victor at Jena" and "the vanquished at Waterloo" name the same referent, Napoleon, although the ideal content of one is different from that of the other. The objective reference of a signifier has also been known as its extension, and its ideal content as its intension. Although the ideal content of meaning is invariant, Husserl observes, its objective reference is variant. He illustrates this point with the example of the word "horse." In spite of its fixed ideal content (eidetic essence), the objective reference (extension) of this word perpetually changes as new horses are born and old horses die.

Whereas the objective correlate of an expressive sign is a real object, it may appear, its ideal content or essence is only a mental entity, which has no existence outside the human mind. But Husserl emphatically insists on the extramental existence of eidetic essences. Their existence is also transtemporal; the essence of triangularity can never change or perish with time. Husserl maintains that human minds can perceive eidetic essences, and the perception of those essences is called eidetic intuition or meaning-intuition. This intuition is the semantic basis for the meaning of an expressive sign. This does not mean that everyone who uses the word "horse" correctly intuits or understands its meaning; meaning-intention may not coincide with meaning-intuition. When an expressive sign is used with a correct understanding of its meaning or eidetic essence, however, there is an intimate unity of meaning-intention and meaning-intuition.

The function of indication is quite different from that of expression. Husserl's examples of an indication are a brand as the sign of a slave, a flag as the sign of a nation, and especially all marks (Merkmale) of various kinds.[27] None of them involves the notion of an ideal content or eidetic essence, which is an abstract entity. What is signified by an indicative sign is not an abstract but a concrete entity, not a universal but a particular. What is signified by the sign of a slave is a particular (a slave); what is signified by the sign of slavehood is a universal (slavehood). Particulars can be pointed at or indicated, whereas universals cannot. This function of pointing at something is the indicative function; it may be called the indexical function, the function of indices in general. All indexicals, which are sometimes known as demonstratives ("this," "that," "here," "there," etc.), are indicative signs.

The indicative function is not preserved only for human beings and their indexical gestures. It can be performed by marks of all kinds. The footprint of an animal indicates the animal; the track of a snake indicates the snake; smoke indicates fire. For the same reason, our facial expressions and the tone of our voice are also indicative signs. The indicative relation can obtain between any two things, whether they are human or inhuman, animate or inanimate. But it is not a simple two-term relation; it always involves a third term, a thinking subject, for whom an indicative sign indicates something beyond itself. In Husserl's words, anything can be called an indication, "if and where it in fact serves to indicate something to some think-ing being."[28] Hence indicative relations belong to what has generally been known as the association of ideas. But the as-sociation of ideas should not be confused with eidetic intuition. The former is situated in the contingent domain of particulars, and the latter in the timeless domain of universals.

This is an outline of Husserl's theory of signs, and Derrida's critique of it is twofold: (1) Husserl has not given a theory of a sign in general, because his theories of expressive and indic-ative signs do not add up to a unified theory of signification, and (2) they do not add up to anything because they are in-consistent. These negative assertions do not, however, consti-tute the ultimate objective of his critique; they are only prelim-inaries for his attempt to construct a general theory of signs.

Derrida first considers Husserl's characterization of ex-pressive signs, and points out one of its strange features, namely, the fact that they are never to be encountered in the context of communication. The connection betweeen an ex-pressive sign and its ideal meaning-content can be seen only by the speaking subject, who establishes that connection through his eidetic intuition and meaning-intention. When I use the word "horse" to express the eidetic essence of horses, I can be sure of the connection between what I want to say and what I really say. Nobody else can intuitively perceive this connection in my mind, and my word "horse" is no more than an indicative sign for anyone but myself. It indicates what is in my mind. Hence Husserl says, "All speech inasmuch as it is engaged in communication and manifests lived experience operates as indication."[29]

Husserl's expressions can exist only in the interior domain of soliloquy. This is a paradoxical notion of an expression, according to Derrida. The word "expression" (Ausdruck) means exteriorization (Äusserung), but Husserl's expressions are functions of interiorization.[30] Husserl's expressions are not expressive; they are devoid of exteriority. This paradoxical conception of expressions goes against Husserl's own definition of a word as a bodily entity animated by its soul, which is its meaning.[31] It is a soul without body; it is a voice without sound ("the voice that keeps silence").[32] This is the phenomenological voice, the voice of the transcendental subject, the subject that still remains after the phenomenological reduction of the real world.[33] In Derrida's view, Husserl's later notion of transcendental subjectivity is already operative in his definition of expressive signs.[34]

The phenomenological voice is the voice of immediate presence; it is immediately present to what is perceived in an eidetic intuition. When one says the word "horse" in his inner voice, he can immediately see the connection between the word and its meaning. The meaning is fully and immediately present to the inner voice. This privileged position of inner voice (*voix* or *phone*) is the foundation of phonocentrism that has prevailed in the West. Phonocentrism has also been logocentrism, because the *phone* of inner voice is inseparable from the *logos*, the object of eidetic intuition. Both logocentrism and phonocentrism extol the primacy of immediate presence or the plenitude of intuition—the metaphysics of presence.

Even inner speech cannot, Derrida says, guarantee the immediate unity between an expressive sign and its ideal meaning, unless the utterance of the sign and the intuition of its ideal content are made in the same instant.[35] Any time interval between the two breaks up the immediate presence of an expression to its meaning. Suppose someone who utters the word "horse" in his inner speech an instant after his intuition of the equine essence. The time interval between his meaning-intuition and his meaning-intention makes it impossible to assure that what he means to say is perfectly the same as what he perceived in his eidetic intuition an instant earlier. For this assurance, he has to rely on his memory, but his memory is always subject to contingency and fallibility. For these reasons, Derrida concludes, the act of expression cannot retain the certainty of eidetic intuition.

Fully aware of this inevitable contingency of any time interval, Husserl tried to secure the intuitive certainty of an expression by conceiving it as an instantaneous act. Only through its instantaneity can an act of expression release itself from the chain of time and constitute itself as an act of pure auto-affection or subjectivity, which is completely independent of everything contingent.[36] But this notion of an instantaneous act has, Derrida shows, been rendered illegitimate by Husserl's own theory of internal time-consciousness. Husserl has demonstrated that time is never experienced simply as a succession of discrete moments, and that the awareness of the present moment is inseparably connected with the past through *retention* and with the future through *protention*.[37] If our experience of temporality itself can never be the experience of the instantaneous, Derrida argues, we can never perform an instantaneous act. As long as a human subject is situated in the temporal flux, it can never attain the self-evident certainty of pure auto-affection.

Husserl developed his theory of internal time-consciousness after abandoning his prephenomenological position. He had come to realize that his doctrine of eidetic essences involves a metaphysical dogmatism. The eidetic essence is a metaphysical entity, and any assertion about it is a metaphysical dogma. The recognition of this dogmatism undermined his theory of eidetic intuition, because any dogmatism is incompatible with the notion of self-evident intuition. In order to find the truths of self-evident intuition absolutely free from any tinge of dogmatism, Husserl initiated his program of phenomenology, which brackets off everything that lies outside the sphere of pure self-consciousness.[38] Thus he confined the domain of self-evident intuition to the domain of transcendental consciousness. What can be truly and fully present to our awareness is not any extramental entities such as eidetic essences but our own awareness itself. This phenomenological turn has not only produced the notion of temporality that is incompatible with the notion of an expression as an instantaneous act, but also rejected the doctrine of eidetic intuition, which is the foundation of every expressive sign. If there are no eidetic intuitions, there can be no expressive signs.

These are Derrida's carefully considered reasons for rejecting Husserl's theory. Since expressive signs as conceived by Husserl cannot exist even in the domain of interior monologue, Derrida concludes that all signs, expressive or indicative, operate as indications. But he cannot accept Husserl's characterization of indicative signs either. According to Husserl, an indicative sign has no ideal content; it has no *meaning* in its strict sense. For example, the indicative sign "this" can be used to indicate a horse, a tree, a triangle, or anything else, whereas the expressive sign "horse" can mean only horses. Since an indicative sign has no ideal content, its meaning is always its referent. The referent of an indicative sign is generally given through perception. Just as the meaning of an expressive sign is given through the presence of an eidetic essence, the meaning of an indicative sign is determined through the presence of perceptual object.

Derrida finds this theory of indication faulty on two counts. He holds that the meaning of an indicative sign is as much an ideal content as that of an expressive sign, and that this ideal content is not given or determined by the presence of any objects. He tries to demonstrate these two points with the example of the most familiar indexical term "I." According to Husserl, this word has no meaning unless its indicative function is fixed through perceptual presence; it is impossible to tell who is meant by this word without perceiving who is using it. Against this view, Derrida bluntly maintains that the word "I" has an ideal content, and that it can be known without perceiving who is using the word. Its ideal content is the notion of someone who is speaking, and this ideal content does not depend on the presence of any speakers. If it were to depend on such presence, the sentence "I am dead" can never have any meaning, because a dead speaker can never be present. The meaning of "I am dead" is never dependent on the fact that I am dead. *Gegen-standslosigkeit* (the absence of objects) is never the same as *Bedeutungslosigkeit* (the absence of meaning).[39]

The upshot of Derrida's critique of Husserl's indication is that indicative signs behave exactly the same way as expressive signs do. So Derrida rejects Husserl's distinction between expressive and indicative signs and affirms their essential unity.[40] Husserl has introduced their distinction to cope with the problem of double meaning (*Doppelsinn*), that is, to explain why the word "sign" has two meanings. But Derrida's critique has shown that it is a wrong way to cope with that problem. Instead of holding that the double meaning of the word "sign" is due to the existence and operation of two kinds of signs, it should be said that the word has two meanings because every sign has two features, namely, its ideal content and its indicative function. How can these two features of a sign be explained without appealing to the presence of either eidetic essences or perceptual objects? This is the central question that constitutes the constructive phase of Derrida's critique.

HUSSERL'S *SIGN* VS. DERRIDA'S *TRACE*

Derrida tries to accomplish this phase of his critique by capitalizing on Husserl's theory of time. As we have seen, Husserl has shown that the present moment is experienced in the context of retention and protention, memory and expectation. This may be called the Husserlian structure of temporality or temporalization, and it is opposed to the Aristotelian or traditional view of time. According to this view, the experience of time is ultimately the experience of the present moment; the past is constituted by the continuous passage of present moments and the future by the anticipation of present moments to come. The present generates the past and the future. This presumed ultimacy of the present leads to the metaphysics of presence.

Contrary to this view, Husserl's theory of temporal structure means that the presence of the present moment is made possible by the structure of retention and protention. The presence of the present is not ultimate but derivative.

The dependence of the presence on retention and protention means that the experience of the present becomes possible through the re-presentation of what is no longer or not yet present. Hence, Derrida points out, Husserl has recognized the irreducibility of re-presentation to presentation.[41] Derrida holds that the structure of re-presentation is the structure of retention, and that a trace is constituted by this structure of retention. A trace is a mark or a remainder (restance) of something that has already become absent; it performs "this function of substitution or supplementation (suppléance) in general, the 'in the place of' (für etwas) structure which belongs to every sign in general."[42] The track of a snake performs the function of standing for the snake, which is no longer there. This substitution function is, for Derrida, the essence of signification function, and the substitution function ultimately depends on the function of retention.

Derrida does not want to limit the function of retention to personal memory, because the notion of retention is more fundamental than that of memory. Memory is based on the retentional function of traces. Hence Derrida calls the trace "the arch-phenomenon of memory."[43] For the same reason, he calls the traces the arch-writing (archi-écriture). The function of writing as sign depends on the retentional function of traces. Writing in general is better suited for the function of retention than speaking, and Derrida's emphasis on writing as the most eminent example of signs is to accentuate its retentional function. But the retentional function of a trace or sign is never complete; it is only one side of its temporalization. The other side of it is its effacement; every trace is perpetually effaced. Effacement brings about the pastness of past; to be past is to be effaced. Effacement and retention are two equally essential features of a trace; "effacement belongs to the very structure of the trace. Effacement must always be able to overtake the trace; otherwise it would not be a trace but an indestructible and monumental substance."[44]

In his theory of writing, Derrida has himself done some injustice to this integral relation of retention and effacement. He has placed so much emphasis on the retentional function of written signs that their durability may appear to be their only essential feature. For this reason, John Searle has misunderstood Derrida's thesis to be that permanence is the essential property of writing.[45] The notion of permanence is obviously incompatible with the notion of effacement. The notion of effacement can be more effectively illustrated by the metaphor of voice than that of writing, and the metaphor of voice is almost visible in the following description of trace: "In presenting itself it [trace] becomes effaced; in being sounded, it dies away."[46]

In its retention and effacement, the notion of trace cannot be fully defined in terms of absence alone any more than in terms of presence, although Derrida's occasional rhetorical emphases may give the misleading impression that a trace is solely a function of absence. As a retention of past, a trace must be situated in the present moment and at the same time refer to the past. Likewise, the effacement of a trace also involves the present and the past; it is a temporal process that cannot be contained in any single present moment. The present and the past are two necessary elements for the constitution of a trace. Hence Derrida says that a trace or mark "is neither present nor absent," that is, it transcends the opposition of presence and absence.[47]

What emerges as central in Derrida's conception of trace is the importance of temporality. The relation of a trace and its original is the relation of what is present and what is past, and this temporal relation is the foundation for the relation of a signifier and its signified. The concept of temporality that is operative in Derrida's conception of trace is a legacy from the later Husserl. During his phenomenological days, Husserl tried to establish the foundation of knowledge within the domain of our consciousness. Unlike the domain of eidetic essences, the domain of consciousness is a field of temporal flux (the stream of consciousness). To secure an unshakable foundation for our knowledge in such a flux was a far more awesome challenge than to find one in the immutable domain of eidetic essences. One of his ingenious moves in meeting this challenge was his doctrine of phenomenological constitution, namely, the theory that all the noematic structures intuited by the transcendental consciousness have been constituted by the transcendental consciousness itself. The transcendental consciousness can have absolute certainty of its cognition, because the domain of its cognition is coextensive with that of its constitution. One can be sure of knowing what one constitutes in one's own consciousness.

Husserl extends the notion of phenomenological constitution even to the structure of temporality. The structure of our awareness of time has three moments, past, present, and future. These three temporal moments reflect the three moments of intentionality; the retention of the past, the perception of the present, and the protention for the future. This triadic structure is the ultimate form for transcendental synthesis, that is, the constitution of the temporal world by the transcendental subject. Martin Heidegger has accepted this temporal structure of subjectivity for the construction of his fundamental ontology, the ontology of *Dasein* (human existence).

Heidegger characterizes the structure of Dasein as the structure of Care (*Sorge*) on the ground that its ultimate nature is to care for its own being. Dasein cares for its own being as situated in the present, as thrown (*geworfen*) there from the past, and as projecting itself into the future.[48] Through this Care-structure, the being of Dasein is spread over the three moments of temporality; it can never be confined within any particular moment. Heidegger presents this notion of being and temporality as a deliberate attack on the traditional notion of reality as being present, namely, the view that whatever truly exists is located in the present moment.[49]

It is uncertain and immaterial whether the centrality of temporalization in Derrida's conception of trace is derived from Husserl's phenomenology or Heidegger's fundamental ontology. When Derrida characterizes the traces as *differance* (see the next section), he himself recognizes its closeness to Heidegger's notion of temporalization: "I shall note that between differance as temporalizing-temporalization and what Heidegger says about temporalization in *Sein und Zeit*—between these two there is a close, if not exhaustive and irreducibly necessary, interconnection."[50] But Heidegger's notion of temporality is a continuation of Husserl's theory of temporal synthesis. Once this notion of temporality is accepted, Derrida holds, the notion of immediate or full presence shows itself as impossible, because the present moment is inseparably connected with what is not present.

There is one element in Derrida's conception of temporality that is prominent neither in Husserl's nor in Heidegger's conception. That is the importance of space and spatialization. Derrida claims the inseparability of temporalization from spatialization. Hence the constitution of a trace or sign is described as "time's becoming spatial or space's becoming temporal."[51] This linking of time and space as the matrix of traces makes it doubly impossible for the notion of immediate presence to function as the foundation of signification. The immediacy of the present moment is always mediated by the process of temporalization and that of spatialization. These two mediation processes are fully exemplified in writing, whereas they can be easily suppressed and overlooked in spoken words, especially in their inner enunciation. Their suppression has produced the illusion of immediacy and immediate presence, the transparency of the self to itself. This is the vocal illusion, the illusion of immediate presence inevitable in the voice of speaking, that has fostered the metaphysics of presence, logocentrism, and phonocentrism.[52]

Derrida's theory of sign as a trace or mark may appear to be his reformulation of Husserl's theory of indicative signs; Husserl has regarded marks or traces as eminent examples of indication. For this reason, Derrida's theory is liable to be taken for another version of nominalism.[53] For Husserl's theories of indicative and expressive signs are his restatement of the two contending theories of verbal meaning: nominalism and essentialism. Derrida's theory is obviously incompatible with essentialism, but it is equally incompatible with nominalism. Although nominalism rejects the presence of universals as the foundation for the meaning of signs, it does not question the presence of particulars as its semantic foundation. But the presence of particulars is as unacceptable within Derrida's framework of temporality as the presence of universals. Therefore any metaphysical doctrine that claims the immediate presence and encounter of perceptual objects is also condemned as a metaphysics of presence, the illusion of immediacy.

Derrida states the impossibility of encountering particulars in the plenitude of their presence in various ways. For example, he says, "There never was any 'perception'; and 'presentation' is always a representation of the representation that yearns for itself therein as for its own birth or its death."[54] This is his way of saying that perceptual objects are encountered never in their naked presence, but always through their representation or conceptual mediation. For this reason, he rejects the notion of proper (propre) name or proper (literal) meaning.[55] Proper names and literal meanings are presumably derived from the immediate presence of objects. Since that is impossible, Derrida holds, every name or meaning is metaphorical or analogical; "language never escapes analogy."[56]

The impossibility of encountering perceptual objects in their immediate presence constitutes the singular feature of the

Derridian trace. The ordinary notion of a trace contains the notion of its original which can be encountered in perception. But this ordinary notion of the original and its encounter is categorically dissociated from Derrida's notion of trace: "It is a trace of something that can never present itself; it is itself a trace that can never be presented, that is, can never appear and manifest itself as such in its phenomenon."[57] Therefore, every Derridian trace is a trace of a trace of a trace ad infinitum; there is no "originary trace."[58] The absence of the original or referent is not simply a structural *possibility* as Derrida claims in moments of moderation and concession, but its structural *necessity* dictated by his doctrine of *archi-trace* and *archi-écriture*.[59]

The Derridian trace has no original. This is the enigma that lies in the center of Derrida's grammatology. How can we understand a theory of signification that does not rely on the presence of any objects, whether they be perceptual or eidetic? This is the enigma we have run into in the course of our attempt to resolve our original enigma: How can any sign operate in complete independence of both individual and collective subjects? Our attempt has turned out to be a clumsy maneuver of compounding one enigma with another. Perhaps we can unravel this compounded Derridian enigma by tracing it back to Saussure's theory of language, which appears to be the main source of Derrida's semiotic inspiration.

The singular feature of Saussure's theory is his assertion that language cannot be reduced to a simple naming process.[60] The notion of language as a naming process is one premise that has never been contested by either nominalists or essentialists. Their dispute has been limited to the question of what objects are named by language. Nominalists have maintained that language derives its meaning as names of particulars; essentialists have maintained that language derives its meaning as names of universals. The naming function of language presupposes that reality contains all the distinctions and differences to be named by language. Saussure cannot accept the existence of such prelinguistic distinctions, for he believes that all the distinctions and differences in reality are introduced by language. In his view, therefore, a correct theory of language should explain not how language names or captures the prelinguistic distinctions of reality, but how language introduces linguistic distinctions into reality. He has tried to provide such a theory of language with his notion of linguistic articulation, that is, how language generates its own system of distinctions and differences.

SAUSSURE'S *DIFFERENCE* VS. DERRIDA'S *DIFFÉRANCE*

Saussure says, "The linguistic sign unites, not a thing and a name [a naming-process], but a concept and a sound-image."[61] For example, the word "tree" unites the concept of trees and the sound-image consisting of three phonemes. Then he notes that both concepts and sound-images are psychological entities. This leads to what may be called the Saussurian paradox.[62] Sound-images cannot be discriminated from each other without using concepts, but concepts can neither exist nor be used until they are embodied in sound-images. Saussure tries to resolve this paradox by postulating that language is a generator of distinctions and differences. On the conceptual side, it generates a system of ideas, whose values can be determined solely in relation or opposition to one another. On the material side, it generates a system of sound-images or phonemes, whose values can be determined solely in relation or opposition to one another. These two are not separate processes, but two inseparable features of one process. As the generator of self-differentiating systems, language takes on the awesome appearance of the Neoplatonic One.[63]

The distinctions and differences generated by language are self-contained; their values cannot be determined by their relation to extralinguistic entities. This is the ultimate point of Saussure's characterization of *langue* as a self-contained whole. These distinctions are sometimes called negative distinctions, because they are "purely differential and defined not by their positive content but negatively by their relations with the other terms of the system."[64] They are also called "differences without positive terms":

> Everything that has been said up to this point boils down to this: in language there are only differences. Even more important: a difference generally implies positive terms between which the difference is set up; but in language there are only differences *without positive terms*. Whether we take the signified or the signifier, language has neither ideas nor sounds that existed before the linguistic system, but only conceptual and phonic differences that have issued from the system.[65]

Saussure's view of language can be called linguistic conceptualism, and as such it is a descendant of Kant's conceptualism. Kant's conceptualism was proposed as a mediation of continental rationalism and British empiricism. Since continental rationalism was a continuation of medieval essentialism and since British empiricism was that of medieval nominalism, Kant's conceptualism was meant to supersede the claims of both the essentialist and the nominalist traditions. These claims were analogous to the one rejected by Saussure in his advocation of linguistic conceptualism, namely, the claim that language is a naming function.

Continental rationalism and British empiricism had operated on two common premises, namely, that our language is an expression of our ideas and that our ideas reflect the objective nature of reality. As expression of ideas, language is performing the function of mirroring the nature of reality, which is another version of naming function. The doctrinal difference between rationalists and empiricists does not concern this function of our ideas or language; it revolves around the question of how the objective nature of reality happens to be reflected in the subjective domain of ideas. British empiricists tried to resolve this problem with their genetic account of ideas, that is, all our ideas arise from sense impressions or perceptions of external reality. If they do arise from impressions of reality, they should naturally reflect the nature of reality.

This empiricist account was unacceptable to rationalists for two reasons. First, it stands on a naïve but implausible assumption that the sense impressions of reality can be compared with reality itself. But this comparison is impossible, because reality is, unlike its impressions, inaccessible to us. We encounter reality only through its impressions. The impressions of reality are like the Derridian traces, whose originals forever escape our grasp. Second, rationalists believed in the existence of innate ideas whose genesis could not be explained by the empiricist account, such as the idea of causality or necessity. But these ideas presented an embarrassing problem to rationalists themselves. If those ideas are innate to our subjective mind, there is no reason for them to reflect the nature of reality. Even if they do reflect it by some chance, there seems to be no way to find out that such is the case.

Kant resolved this baffling problem by his revolutionary claim that our a priori concepts do constitute the order of empirical reality. Prior to our conceptual constitution and distinction, Kant holds, there is no order in the world of our experience. With Kant, the function of concepts was transformed from the role of cognition to that of constitution. Fully aware of the radical character of this move, Kant called it his Copernican revolution. By and large, the development of continental philosophy in general and of German idealism in particular after Kant can be characterized as a series of elaborations on this Copernican revolution. Saussure's linguistic conceptualism is a linguistic reaffirmation of this Kantian revolution.

We may gain a clearer understanding of Saussure's linguistic conceptualism by discriminating various versions of conceptualism. We can begin with the distinction between the static and the dynamic versions. Static versions hold that a conceptual system is permanently fixed. Kant's theory of a priori concepts is the most eminent example of this version.[66] Although those a priori concepts are the fountainhead of all distinctions, they are not generated by any process of differentiation. The dynamic versions hold that a conceptual system is never fixed but perpetually changes. Hegel's theory of conceptual or logical dialectic is the most articulate representative of this version.[67] It is the dialectical process of generating the entire Hegelian conceptual system. In this process, the simplest of all concepts (the pure concept of being) differentiates and multiplies itself into a whole system of concepts. This conceptual dialectic can be regarded as a conceptual restatement of Neoplatonic "emanation."

Although Hegel's conceptualism involves a dynamic process, it is not any more contingent or historical than Kant's a priori conceptual system. Hegel's dialectic is primarily logical and conceptual, and only secondarily historical and empirical; his historical dialectic is said to be only a temporal manifestation of his logical, conceptual dialectic. Hence both Kant's and Hegel's conceptualisms are a priori versions. In contrast to these a priori versions, it is possible to conceive of an a posteriori or empirical version: the generation of conceptual distinctions is regarded as an empirical and contingent process. This empirical or historical version is Saussure's linguistic conceptualism.

The contingency of Saussure's linguistic conceptualism is not limited to the historical transformation of language; it is also concerned with the point of departure and that of arrival. It does not accept any privileged point of origin, like Kant's a priori concepts or Hegel's simplest concept, for the initiation of conceptual distinctions. Nor does it assume any teleological destiny for the transformation of language. Although Saussure often uses the word "evolution," he has no intention of implying that there is any teleological direction for linguistic evolutions. His "evolution" is always dictated by fortuitous historical circumstances; it is a contingent result of historical processes. In Derrida's favorite expression, Saussure's linguistic conceptualism has no closure either at its beginning or at its end.

Despite its historical contingency, Saussure holds, language can be studied from two different perspectives: the synchronic and the diachronic. The synchronic perspective produces "synchronic linguistics," which gives a description and analysis of language as it is at any given historical moment. The diachronic perspective delivers "diachronic linguistics," which describes and analyzes the historical transformation of language between any two historical moments.[68] Of these two perspectives, the synchronic one has often received the main emphasis in Saussure's reflections on language. For example, his description of *langue* as a self-contained whole is synchronic. His method of structural analysis in general has been conducive to the synchronic approach, because the very notion of structure is primarily the notion of synchronic structure.[69] For this reason, Saussure has given the impression that his structural linguistics has ignored the diachronic dimension of language. Jacques Derrida's purpose is to revitalize this neglected dimension of Saussure's linguistic conceptualism, and his category of "differance" is to accomplish this purpose by accentuating the temporal dimension of signification.[70]

Derrida calls the Saussurian operation of generating the linguistic and conceptual distinctions "the play of differences."[71] "Differance" is meant to capture the essence of this play, which consists of two features. One of them is conceptual and the other is temporal. The conceptual feature is the conceptual relation and opposition of all elements in a linguistic system, and this conceptual relation per se is not a temporal relation. But Derrida is emphatic in claiming that the production of conceptual distinctions and their relations is always a temporal process. Hence every process of signification involves these two features of conceptual operation. In order to incorporate these two features into his category of differance, he defines it as the conjunction of the notion of difference and that of deferment.[72] The former is a conceptual notion, and the latter is a temporal one. Derrida places his primary emphasis clearly on the latter by declaring that his differance is irreducibly a process of temporalization.

What consequences can follow from this emphasis on the temporal dimension of signification? This is the central question for understanding the difference of Derrida's theory from Saussure's and any other linguistic theories. One of these consequences is the notion of deferring, that is, the meaning of any sign is perpetually deferred, or the signified concept can never be fully present to the signifier. Derrida believes that this notion of perpetual deferment is already contained in Saussure's notion of *langue*; the first consequence to be drawn from it is said to be

> that the signified concept is never present in itself, in an adequate presence that would refer only to itself. Every concept is necessarily and essentially inscribed in a chain or a system, within which it refers to another and to other concepts, by the systematic play of differences. Such a play, then—differance—is no longer simply a concept, but the possibility of conceptuality, of the conceptual system and process in general.[73]

This passage can be given two different readings, depending on whether "the systematic play of differences" is taken as a conceptual or a temporal operation. As far as Saussure was concerned, it was a conceptual operation. Because of this conceptual operation, the meaning of a word can never be directly given by hooking it up with its concept. The articulation of a concept inevitably involves the mediation of the entire conceptual system. For example, the concept of a tree can be determined only through its relation to the concepts of soil, water, air, grass, plants, animals, etc., each of which can also be determined through its relation and opposition to other concepts, and so forth ad infinitum. This necessity of conceptual mediation makes it impossible for any signifier to be in conceptual immediacy with its signified concept.

But this impossibility of conceptual immediacy is not the same as that of temporal immediacy, which Derrida asserts in his denial of immediate or adequate presence. He can assure the impossibility of immediacy between the signifier and its signified concept only by taking "the systematic play of differences" as a temporal operation or process. This is why he calls this play, differance, a "process in general." If the play of conceptual articulation is taken as a temporal process, then the signified concept can never be fully present to its signifier, because every conceptual process is a temporal one and because the articulation of every concept is potentially an infinite process.

The primacy of temporal process over conceptual process is the heart and soul of Derrida's theory of signification. Expressed in alternative terms, conceptual process is only an effect or manifestation of temporal process. This is a reversal of Hegel's position, in which temporal process was regarded as a manifestation of conceptual process. This reversal almost completes Derrida's systematic reversal of the entire gestalt of Hegelianism. Derrida admits that his differance is a sort of displacement of Hegel's system, or its scattering.[74] As he points out, it is highly misleading to use the word "differentiation" to describe his differance; this word implies "some organic unity, some primordial and homogeneous unity, that would eventually come to be divided up and take on difference as an event."[75] Derrida's differance is not the genesis of *many* from *one*; it is a Neoplatonic play without the One, or a perpetual flux of irreducible multiplicity. It has neither an origin nor a destiny; it knows neither a procedural rule nor a performative norm. It is a "bottomless chessboard where being is set in play."[76]

Derrida tries to justify his primary emphasis on the temporal dimension of *langue* by highlighting its inseparable connection to *parole*. He quotes the following statement of Saussure on the relation between *langue* and *parole*:

> *Langue* is necessary in order for *parole* to be intelligible and to produce all of its effects; but *parole* is necessary in order for *langue* to be established; historically, the fact of *parole* always comes first.[77]

This statement claims *parole* as a factual entity or a primary (first) actuality. It also implies that *langue* is only an abstraction from this factual entity. Whereas *langue* is a structure, *parole* is an event. As an event in time, it fulfills one of the essential conditions for belonging to the domain of actuality. Being not an event in its own right, *langue* cannot fulfill this condition. Hence it must be regarded as no more than an abstraction from the temporal world of concrete reality. When we lose sight of this relation between *langue* and *parole*, Derrida seems to say, we erroneously attribute conceptual independence or self-containedness to *langue*. As soon as we recognize *langue* as an abstraction from *parole*, on the other hand, we can readily see the dependence of conceptual relation and process in *langue* on the temporal relation and process that governs the domain of *parole*.

Derrida finally rounds out his temporal conception of signification by claiming that the distinction of *langue* from *parole* is itself a product of differance:

> If, by hypothesis, we maintain the strict opposition between *parole* and *langue*, then differance will be not only the play of differences within *langue* but the relation of *parole* to *langue*, the detour by which I must also pass in order to speak, the silent token I must give, which holds just as well for linguistics in the

strict sense as it does for general semiology; it dictates all the
relations between usage and the formal schema, between the
message and the particular code, etc.[78]

The strict opposition between *langue* and *parole* is only a hypothesis, and it is no more than a silent token for the concrete
act of speaking. If differance establishes the relation of *parole*
to *langue*, it should also establish all other relations between
the concrete and the abstract, such as usage and formal schema,
because the relation of the abstract to the concrete is ultimately
the relation of structure to event or process. Any conceptual
or linguistic structure is only a moment in the endless process
of differance. Hence Derrida's differance is to reverse the primacy of *langue* over *parole* in the Saussurian structural
linguistics.

Derrida's concern on the ontological relation of structure
and process did not emerge with his reflections on Saussure's
linguistic conceptualism. This ontological concern began with
his struggle with Edmund Husserl. Derrida correctly perceived
the ontological relation of structure and process as the central
question that had guided Husserl's checkered philosophical
career. Derrida characterizes Husserl's career as a series of relentless attempts to reconcile the structuralist demand with the
genetic demand. The former is the demand for a comprehensive
articulation of structure; the latter is the demand for the determination of its genesis or origin.[79] Structuralism is the belief
that structure can never be reduced to its genesis; geneticism
is the belief that structure can be explained by its genesis.

In his first major philosophical work *Philosophie der Ar-
ithmetik*, Derrida observes, Husserl took a genetic stand and
tried to explain the structure of arithmetic as a psychological
genesis. But this genetic account was invalidated by Frege's
criticism of psychologism, and Husserl became convinced of
the impossibility of giving a genetic account of normative or
ideal entities such as mathematical objects. So he launched

his own relentless attack on psychologism and historicism, and advocated the eternal structure of eidetic essences in his *Logical Investigations*. But he came to realize that this Platonic position was a metaphysical dogmatism and proposed his phenomenological program, in which everything outside the domain of indubitable consciousness was to be bracketed off.

Derrida says that the first phase of Husserl's phenomenology was as structuralistic as his *Logical Investigations*; the invariant structures of noemata were assumed to be as immune to the temporal process of generation and destruction as the eternal structures of eidetic essences. Their only difference was their locations. The eidetic essences were located in the Platonic heaven, and the noemata in the transcendental consciousness. Only later did Husserl come to see the need to explain the genesis of noematic structures, and tried to fulfill this need by instituting his genetic phenomenology. At the same time, Derrida notes, Husserl came to shift his interests from the bracketed world of phenomenological investigations to the *Lebenswelt*.[80]

This transition from the structural to the genetic phenomenology has brought Husserl all the way back to the genetic position with which he had begun his philosophical career. But Husserl could not bring himself to reaffirm his original position, because he could not accept all the consequences of geneticism and historicism. Hence his later geneticism is tightly controlled by his structuralism. He indeed admits the genetic constitution of noematic structures by the transcendental consciousness. But this genetic view is qualified by his claim that all genetic constitutions are governed by the structure of transcendental temporality, which is neither contingent nor temporal. Constrained by this structuralist prejudice, Derrida holds, Husserl eventually failed to accept fully the openness of the world. Derrida means to overcome this Husserlian failure by acknowledging the absolute contingency and primacy of temporality in his doctrine of trace and differance.

To accept Husserl's doctrine that the structure of temporal synthesis is constituted by the transcendental subject is to subject the process of synthesis to its immutable structure. The primacy of temporal process can be secured only by recognizing the dependence of subjectivity itself on the temporal power of differance. So Derrida maintains that consciousness and self-consciousness become possible only through differance, that the unity and the self-presence of the self are made possible through the system of linguistic distinctions, and that even the subject's power of synthesis is derived from the retentional and the protentional nexuses of traces.[81] In short, the constitution of subjectivity and its operation depend on the constitution and operation of traces.

The traditional belief that the existence and function of signs depend on the intentionality of subjects, individual or collective, has had everything upside down. It is not man who makes sign. It is through sign that human beings become the thinking, speaking, and writing subjects. As to the domain of objects, we have no access to it except through our signs; they are the sole agents for introducing distinctions into the seamless domain of reality. Our signs cannot perform this function if they must derive their power of signification from the domain of objects. Thus our signs must be independent of their objects as well as of their subjects. This dual independence of signs or traces resolves the two enigmas or the compound enigma we have encountered in our exposition of Derrida's grammatology.

CHAPTER SEVEN

Cultural Diversity and Historical Relativity

IN ASSESSING THE value of Derrida's grammatology, it is advisable to be aware of the difference between two issues: its validity as a theory of signification, and its function as a critique of the general premises for structuralist or formalist programs. In this chapter, I will set aside the first issue and consider only the second. The second issue is mainly concerned with Derrida's emphatic emphasis on the primacy of temporality over any linguistic or semiotic structures. If linguistic structures are generated and transformed through the play of *differance*, they can never be invariant in all ages and cultures. The contingency of those structures means their diversity, and this goes directly against the most fundamental assumption of linguistic structuralism and other formalist programs.

Linguistic structuralism has operated on the assumption that the structure of language is invariant. Thus the scope of its structural universals has been assumed to be unlimited; for example, the principle of binary opposition has been assumed to be applicable to all ages and cultures. That is, the scope of its validity is transhistorical and transcultural. This assumption of structural invariance has been a common premise for all formalist programs. Hence most formalists have failed to recognize the historical contingency of their formal or structural universals, and ignored historical perspectives. In their analysis, one does not feel that a historically situated subject is confronting a historically situated object. Instead, one gets the impression that a timeless subject is analyzing a timeless object in a timeless perspective.

If this sense of timeless vision and understanding is well founded, it can be taken as concrete evidence that formalists have succeeded in elevating their programs of human studies to the majestic level of natural science. The Pythagoreans, the fountainhead of all formalist schools from ancient Greece down to our own world, are said to have experienced a mystical vision in contemplating the truth of the Pythagorean theorem. That theorem was perhaps the first fruit of formal-structural analysis; by contemplating it, the Pythagoreans may have felt that they were seeing through to one of the timeless secrets governing the nature of all physical shapes and sizes. The true devotees of natural science can find and reexperience this Pythagorean mysticism on a far grander scale in their contemplation of Newton's theory of gravitation or Einstein's general theory of relativity. Their ecstatic experience is rooted in the eternal verities of natural science.

It is in imitation of natural science that formalists have adopted their nonhistorical approaches. Only by presuming the transhistorical and transcultural universality of their formal structures, they may have thought, could they carry out their programs of human studies as truly scientific enterprises, which could produce timeless truths just like natural science. But this presumption has turned out to be vulnerable. Lévi-Strauss discovered his structural universal of binary opposition in his investigation of totemism and kinship in certain primitive societies; there was no guarantee that the validity of the same structural universal was not to be limited to the locus of its discovery. The New Critics assembled their structural universals for literary analysis through their investigation of modern European poetry; there was no guarantee that those universals would be valid and useful in analyzing the poetic structure of other ages and other cultures.

In spite of the provincial bases for the discovery of their formal structures, most formalists hoped and assumed that those formal structures would be valid for all ages and cultures. In making this hopeful assumption, they also assumed that they were following a well-established practice of the natural scientists. When a natural scientist dissects a snake and examines the structure of its heart, he seems to assume that all other snakes have the same kind of heart, whether they live in America, Asia, or Africa. In Hume's words, they assume the uniformity of nature. In an analogy to this presumption in natural science, formalists assumed the uniformity of human nature and culture as an essential premise for elevating their programs of human studies to the truly scientific level. Freudians assumed the uniformity of human psychological structure; the New Critics assumed the uniformity of poetic structure.

However, to presuppose the uniformity of nature is only one half of the scientific procedure in the formation of scientific concepts and in the determination of their scope. Scientists recognize the diversity of nature as well. When a zoologist finds a two-chambered heart in a snake, he cannot assume outright that the same heart structure can be found in all species of snakes. Any one of the possibilities that the two-chambered heart structure can be found in only one species of snake, or in all species of snakes, or even in all species of reptiles or animals, is compatible with the uniformity of nature as well as its diversity. The doctrine of the uniformity of nature does not by itself set the boundaries of scientific universals. The scope of those universals can be determined only by empirical investigations.

Beside this empirical method, there is only one other way to determine the scope of a scientific universal. That is the method of definition. For example, if the property of having a two-chambered heart is to be accepted as one of the defining characteristics of all snakes, the scope of this universal can be conclusively determined by this definition. However, the structural universals of formalist programs have never been proposed as definitional essences. For example, the New Critical universals of paradox and irony have never been proposed as the defining properties of poetry. Hence the transcultural and transhistorical validity of structural universals can be established only by empirical investigations. Let us now see how well some of these universals beside those of Lévi-Strauss' structuralism can stand the empirical tests of their boundaries.

UNIVERSALISM VS. PROVINCIALISM

The New Critics have contended that paradox and irony constitute the formal structure of all poetry; that is, they are the structural universals for organizing a poem into an artistic whole in every age and in every culture. Against this presumed universality of paradox and irony, I have shown that they constitute not the essential structure of all poetry but the provincial character of modern European poetry.[1] I have further shown that modern European poetry acquired these provincial traits by reflecting the unique character of modern European sensibility.

Modern European sensibility developed in the transition from the medieval concern with the other world to the Renaissance concern with this world. But the transition was not an easy one to make, for it was as difficult to forget the old religious concerns which had governed European life for over a millennium as it was to remain faithful to them in the face of rising concern with the secular world. This difficulty induced an acute sense of ambivalence and ambiguity into the Renaissance ethos. Many Renaissance figures tried to resolve this ambivalence by a bold attempt to realize the medieval religious ideals in their secular world. They hoped that this would enable them to remain faithful to both their old and their new concerns, since they were transferring the old concerns to a new domain of realization.

However, the attempt to realize the old religious ideals in the secular world involved an inherent contradiction. The medieval religious ideals had been developed as the ideals of infinite perfection, which could be realized even in the eternal kingdom of God only with the aid of his infinite power. These ideals could not easily be accommodated within the mutable kingdom of finite human beings. Thus the bold Renaissance attempt resulted in a series of irresolvable dialectical conflicts between the finite and the infinite, the eternal and the temporal, the human and the divine. This inevitable conflict between old ideals and their new realm of realization produced the unique Renaissance spiritual epidemic called *paradoxia epidemica*.[2] Thus the Renaissance sensibility came to be permeated by a pervasive sense of paradox and irony.

Modern European poetry has reflected the same sense of ambivalence, ambiguity, and paradox because it is a product of modern European sensibility. Since the New Critics have developed their structural universals mainly through their formal analysis of modern European poetry, they have come to assume the universality of paradox and irony. But the provinciality of these universals becomes obvious as soon as they are extended beyond the province of modern European poetry. For example, they are usually inapplicable to medieval didactic works. Since those works are meant to convey straightforward teachings, they cannot leave much room for paradox and irony. The New Critics have tried to save the validity and sanctity of their structural universals by advocating their notion of didactic heresy: true works of literature or great poems must be free of didactic simplicity.

This radical move amounts to exalting their structural universals as the defining characteristics of all good poetry and literature, if not all poetry and literature. This is to secure the validity of those universals by a fiat of definition, insuring their applicability to all good poetry and literature. But this insurance can be obtained at the extraordinary price of relegating the Bible, Milton, and Dante to the province of bad poetry, as Herbert Muller has pointed out.[3] In order to avoid this embarrassment, Cleanth Brooks sets out to find some streaks of paradox and irony in Dante's *Commedia*. But all he can find to his purpose is Dante's condemnation of one or two popes in Hell. On this scant evidence, Brooks tries to exempt Dante from the didactic heresy: "Indeed, I should say that Dante was willing to expose his preachment to something very like 'ironical contemplation'."[4]

Brooks' reading of Dante is a little too ingenious. Dante places a couple of popes in his Hell not for any "ironic contemplation" but for outright condemnation. He wants to convey the simple orthodox teaching that every unrepentant sinner is subject to condemnation whether he has occupied an exalted position or a humble station on earth. There is nothing ironical about it. As a matter of fact, the entire *Commedia* is permeated with the spirit of clarity and simplicity rather than that of paradox and irony.

Dante reserves paradox as a special device for stating the two dogmas of Christian mystery, the Incarnation and the Trinity. A good example of this is the opening line of Saint Bernard's prayer to the Queen of Heaven on Dante's behalf: "Virgin mother, daughter of thy son" (*Par*.33.1). This line consists of two oxymora that are indeed paradoxical in human terms. The first of them (her being a virgin and a mother at the same time) manifests the mystery of the Incarnation; the second (her being the daughter of her own son) expresses the mystery of the Trinity. These paradoxes are surely devoid of any sense of irony; on the contrary, they are presented in the aura of devotion and reverence.

All this is not meant to convey the impression that the

rhetorical devices of paradox and irony are not used in the poetry of other cultures than that of modern Europe, or even that the use of those devices is not important outside the cultural context of modern Europe. What is unique about modern European poetry is that paradox and irony are not merely local rhetorical devices controlling a few passages of a poem, but the central, pervasive principles for the organization of its entire body of theme and imagery. This is the reason for labeling them the formal universals of modern European poetry. They are culture-bound because they are manifesting a rather unique feature of modern European sensibility.

Sigmund Freud's psychoanalysis is also a structural program. His interpretation of dreams and other psychological phenomena is governed by his preoumed notion of psychological structure, as much as the New Critics' interpretation of poetry is guided by their presumed notion of poetic structure. But it is much more difficult to determine the scope of his structural universals than that of the New Critics'. In the first place, Freud kept revising his conception of human psychological structure. In the second place, his structural universals are given in many different strata. In this discussion, we shall focus our attention on what may be called the core of the Freudian psychological structure, which endured and retained its identity to the end of his checkered career.

The binary distinction between the conscious and the unconscious is the structural universal that appears in the first layer of Freud's psychoanalysis. The scope of this universal may be unlimited. The triadic distinction of ego, superego, and id is the structural universal that emerges in the second layer of the same analysis. Even this universal may be applicable to all human beings, and it is not even a new structural model. Freud's triadic schema is a reformulation of Plato's tripartite division of the human soul, namely, intellect, spirited element (feeling), and appetites (desires). This theory has been the ultimate paradigm for the various Western conceptions of the human soul from ancient Greece through medieval Christianity down to our own day.

Although Freud's theory of psychological structure is a reformulation of this traditional tripartite theory, its novelty lies in relocating the center of the human psyche in sexuality. According to him, the central force of human instinct is the libido, which goes through three stages of development, the oral, anal, and Oedipal stages. These three stages of sexuality constitute the main framework for the development of the whole psyche.[5] At this third stage of Freud's analysis, the universal validity of his structural universals seems to become problematic.

What is obviously disputable is Freud's claim for the centrality of sexual instinct in the human psyche. Beginning with Plato and Aristotle, many philosphers and psychologists have assumed that the appetite for food is a more fundamental instinct in human beings than sexual appetite. However, it is quite possible that the sexual instinct was the main source of psychological problems for the neurotic patients Freud drew from the Viennese leisure class, because they never had to cope with the onerous problems of providing the necessities of their daily existence. In the world of scarcity, where the supply of daily food is precarious, it is quite possible that sexual instinct may take the second place to the instinct for food, and the survival instinct may function as the primary cause of neuroses.[6] Hence Freud's theory of sexuality may be valid only within the relatively opulent bourgeois societies. In the world of highly competitive aggression, it is also conceivable that aggressive instinct may be the primary cause of psychological problems.[7]

It is one thing to recognize the sexual instinct as one of the universal human instincts and another thing to claim it to be the dominant force of the id. Every human being, as a member of the animal species, is born with the sexual instinct; it is one of the phylogenetic universals given by nature. But our way of coping with it may very well be a matter of habit and custom perpetuated by culture. The fact that the sexual instinct had become the dominant force of the unconscious among Freud's patients may have merely reflected the nature of their culture. That is, the centrality of sexuality in Freud's theory may belong not to the invariant underlying structure of instinctual forces, but to the variant cultural forms of their manifestation. This difficult question on the relation between nature and culture has aroused the interest of many psychologists and anthropologists and engaged their efforts in one of the most controversial disputes of this century.

The disputants have been divided roughly into two groups: one may be called the psychological universalists, and the other, the cultural contextualists. The former have claimed the primacy of psychological forces and universals over cultural forces and universals, while the latter have argued for the opposite view. Freud himself took the lead in advocating not only the transcultural universality of his psychological structure but also its primacy over social structure. He maintained that the structure of the totemic social order was instituted by projection of the psychological structure, and that the institution of its social or political authority was established by externalization of the inner authority of the superego. As the superego of an individual is formed by the resolution of his Oedipus complex, so was the first totemic authority established by the resolution of the Oedipus complex of the primal horde.[8]

In opposition to Freud's psychological universalism, Bronislaw Malinowski, Margaret Mead, and Abram Kardiner championed cultural contextualism.[9] They maintained that the phylogenetically given psychological forces are no more than the basic forces to be molded, directed, and controlled by culture, and that psychological universals such as Freud's are determined by the cultural context. In their view, the structural universals of the human psyche are culture-bound; in the view of their opponents, those universals are transcultural.

The Oedipus complex was the focal issue in this dispute between the psychological universalists and the cultural contextualists. The psychological universalists tried to prove the transcultural universality of the Oedipus complex by detecting its manifestations outside Europe, that is, in some African and American tribes.[10] In most of these tribes, the exact duplication of the Oedipus complex could not be found, because they lacked the necessary social and cultural conditions for the formation of that complex (e.g., the European form of the father-son relation). At best, they manifested some equivalents of that complex, that is, psychological phenomena more or less similar to it (e.g., the defiant attitude of a boy against his maternal uncle in a matriarchal tribe, where boys receive their discipline mainly from their maternal uncles). In most cases, however, the so-called equivalents of the Oedipus complex seemed to lack some of its essential features, such as the desire to kill the father figure or the desire to marry the mother. Hence cultural contextualists claimed that these could not be regarded as manifestations of the Oedipus complex or their equivalents, and that the controversial complex was uniquely a European or even a modern European psychological phenomenon.

I should mention some recent developments in the continuation of this dispute. Jacques Lacan rejects the naïve view that the Freudian unconscious is situated beyond the domain of human culture and language. According to him, every child goes through two stages of psychical development. The first stage is the imaginary (imaginaire) order, in which the child is aware of the images of its own body and its mother's in their prelinguistic immediacy. The second stage is the symbolic (symbolique) order, in which the child becomes, through the mediation of language, acquainted with the symbolic meanings of its physical organs (such as the phallus) and its social milieu. When the human psyche passes from the first to the second stage, its original prelinguistic structure is replaced by a linguistic structure. In this linguistic stage, the human psyche becomes truly human, and the structure of its id becomes identical with the structure of language.[11] The Oedipus complex marks this critical transition of a child from the imaginary to the symbolic order.

Since every language is culture-bound, Lacan's view of the id may imply that not only the existence of Oedipus complex but its manifestation is culture-dependent. Gilles Deleuze and Felix Guattari have pursued this line of thought in proposing their Marxian thesis that the Oedipus complex is a unique product of the capitalist family system. Outside the countries of European capitalism, they have claimed, this complex has been found only in those African and other primitive tribes which have been infected by the repressive ethos of European imperialism and colonialism: "Oedipus is always colonization pursued by other means, it is the interior colony, and we shall see that even here at home, where Europeans are concerned, it is our intimate colonial education."[12]

Operating without the influence of either Lacan or Marx, Harold Bloom has demonstrated that the agony of Oedipus complex has long been the common fate of modern European poets. Their Oedipus complex has taken the form of immense anxiety of indebtedness and influence they feel toward their precursors, their literary father figures. They have tried to resolve this literary form of Oedipus complex by deliberately misinterpreting those father figures, which is the literary version of patricide. Bloom says "Every poem is a misinterpretation of a parent poem. A poem is not an overcoming of anxiety, but is that anxiety."[13]

Bloom recognizes that even in Western culture this anxiety of indebtedness and influence is a recent syndrome, which has been inflicted on many poets since the Renaissance. When he examines the attitude of poets toward their precursors prior to the onset of this syndrome, he is struck with the gracious manner in which the achievements of the earlier poets were received as gifts by the later poets: "At the height of this matrix of generous influence is Dante and his relation to his precursor Virgil, who moved his ephebe only to love and emulation and not to anxiety."[14]

This glaring difference in the attitudes of poets toward their precursors before and after the Renaissance appears to reflect the cultural transformation of the West. Before the Renaissance, poets lived in a communal world where the members of the community perpetuated their identity in sharing their heritage with one another. After the Renaissance, poets had to work in an individualistic world, where all individuals had to establish and protect their individuality through their own unique achievements. In the former, tradition and influence were indispensable to one's identity; in the latter, they were detrimental to one's individuality.

This is a radical transformation in the entire fabric of human relations, which has taken root in every level of community from the nuclear family and personal friendship, through political and social organizations, to religious and world orders. Within the family, the son is set against the father; in society, a citizen is set against other citizens; in the church, a believer is set against other believers. Whereas in ancient and medieval Europe the son sought his identity in his continuity with the father, in modern Europe he tries to establish his identity by severing that familial continuity. The so-called Oedipal wish to kill one's own father is no more than a neurotic manifestation of this individualistic compulsion for independent self-identity.

In ancient and medieval Europe, the individual rights of citizens were assumed to be derived from the communal nexus of the political and social order. In modern Europe, the individual rights of citizens have been assumed to be the ultimate value, for whose protection and enjoyment the political and social orders have been fabricated. This is the transition from the doctrine of natural law to that of natural rights. The doctrine of natural law presupposed the ontological priority of a community over its members; the doctrine of natural rights has reversed this order of priority.

The modern notion of natural rights can perhaps best display its drastic novelty when it is contrasted with the medieval notion of grace. In medieval Christendom, the individual gratefully accepted whatever he or she had, as a gift or favor (gratia) from a higher power or authority. Most political and economic rights were also regarded as such favors or privileges. Of course, the ultimate source of all grace was believed to be God the Almighty. In contrast to this, the modern notion of natural rights is to claim that there are certain basic things in human life which must not be looked upon as gifts or favors but be demanded as an essential, minimal feature of being an individual.

As long as the individual was assumed to have essential being primarily as a member of a community, he or she sought self-identity in the communal nexus. Operating under the modern notion of individuality, however, individuals must establish their self-identity beyond the domain of communal nexuses, that is, through their own accomplishments and achievements. But these accomplishments and achievements cannot be made without presupposing the cultural legacy and heritage of the community. To that extent, the individual is bound to depend on the community even in struggling to achieve a unique individuality. This inevitable dependence is bound to contaminate the sense of self-identity that is supposedly grounded on one's own achievements and accomplishments. Consequently, cultural legacy and heritage have become a source of perpetual anxiety in our modern world, whereas they had been objects of gratitude and source of security in ancient and medieval Europe.[15] The Oedipus complex is not the cause of this anxiety in self-identity but only one of its syndromes. Hence the trauma of modern poetry as portrayed in Bloom's *The Anxiety of Influence* emphatically attests to the culture-boundness of that complex.

Jacques Derrida is correct in observing that one of the central concerns in phenomenology has been to safeguard the structural demand against the genetic one. Edmund Husserl had tried to accomplish this by bracketing off the whole mundane world of empirical reality and confining his phenomenological analysis to the domain of pure self-consciousness. But this had the unsatisfactory tendency to constrict the domain of phenomenological analysis and impoverish its content. Many of his followers, such as Martin Heidegger or Maurice Merleau-Ponty, have made bold attempts to extend the scope of phenomenological analysis to the contingent world of our daily existence or perception, and still fully meet the original structural demand of phenomenology by demonstrating the structural invariance of human existence or perception. We shall briefly consider the result of Heidegger's attempt.

In *Being and Time*, Heidegger performs his *Daseinanalysis*, a phenomenological analysis of the structure of human existence (*Dasein*). In this phenomenological analysis, he employs a system of structural universals called *existentialia*. They are presented in a more elaborate schema than Freud's structural universals. The first layer of existentialia is Being-in-the-world, that is, to be in the world is the most basic feature of human existence. Being-in-the-world is further analyzed into Being-situatedness (*Befindlichkeit*), Understanding (*Verstehen*), and Discourse (*Rede*).[16] Being-situatedness is the mode of being concerned with what one is and has been; Understanding is the mode of being concerned with what one can and wills to be. The former is one's "thrownness" (*Geworfenheit*) into the world, the nexus of contingent circumstances in which one finds oneself, whether one likes it or not. The latter is one's "projection" into the future, into the set of possibilities which one can choose and realize. Understanding belongs to the domain of possibilities, while being-situatedness belongs to the domain of actualities.

Discourse is the third moment of Being-in-the-world, in which the thrownness and the projection of human existence are meaningfully articulated and disclosed. Unfortunately, discourse can easily degenerate into the everyday talk (*Gerede*) of the anonymous crowd (*das Man*), which is saddled with generality and ambiguity. Caught in this inauthentic mode of articulation and disclosure, Dasein cannot grasp the unique character of its own situation and possibilities, and fails to realize its authentic existence. This type of conformity to *das Man* is called inauthentic existence, which is Dasein's Fall (*Verfallen*) or Fallenness (*Verfallenheit*).

Being-in-the-world can be accepted as a truly universal existentiale for the whole human race, because one cannot conceive of human existence apart from the existential world. The three moments of Being-in-the-world (Being-situatedness, Understanding, and Discourse) can also be accepted as structural universals for all human existence, insofar as every human being is thrown into this world and is forced to make something of himself or herself in it, and insofar as his or her self-understanding and self-projection are possible through discourse and communication. Even Fallenness can be regarded as an existential universal, insofar as every society or culture provides a set of ideals to be achieved and insofar as every human being may fall away from those ideals. All these existentialia can be admitted as structural universals of human existence, if they are taken in their generality. In that generality, however, they belong to the definitional essence of being human.

However, Heidegger does not leave his existentialia on the level of definitional necessity and generality but provides them with concrete features, whose universality is questionable. Fallenness is described not simply as the failure to be one's ideal being, but as becoming a victim of conformity to the anonymous crowd (*das Man*). This specification can be true only in those societies where the ideal of becoming a unique individual is already operative as the compelling principle of motivation. But such individualistic societies are recent products of the modern West. In many other parts of the world, conformity is regarded as a ground of virtue rather than vice, while the desire to be a unique self is assumed to be a temptation to the sin of deviation. Even in the West, conformity used to be seen as the assured path to virtue. In medieval Europe, to be a virtuous Christian was to conform with the standards established by the recorded lives of the saints. This ethos of conformity was perhaps most devoutly expressed in the medieval ideal of governing one's life by imitation of Christ.

The basic feature of Being-situatedness is said to be anxiety (*Angst*), which is analyzed as the recognition of one's own nothingness. Heidegger says that a human being becomes a unique individual through this existential anxiety.[17] In moments of anxiety, one realizes that one's unique being cannot be determined by any of one's social positions or relations. Apart from those positions and relations, however, one realizes, one is nothing. The basic feature of Understanding is said to be the recognition of one's nothingness in one's own death as the ultimate possibility. In Heidegger's view, to die is to be extinguished, which is true realization of nothingness. To recognize and accept one's nothingness through anxiety and understanding is to achieve authenticity (*Eigentlichkeit*), unique individuality. To flee from one's nothingness is to fall—the Fallenness of Dasein.

These specific features of Heidegger's existentialia can be valid only in highly individualistic societies. In traditional societies, where the ethos of communal togetherness reigns supreme, one is assumed to find one's true self in one's solidarity with the community. In these societies, the moments of breaking out of one's selfish shell, of feeling at one with the whole community, are considered moments of ecstasy, and are looked upon as the ultimate end of communal rituals and festivals. In these communal cultures, Heideggerian authentic existence would be the gravest sin.

To face one's own death as one's utter extinction is an inevitable syndrome of our atheistic, individualistic ethos. Obviously, such an attitude is incompatible with the theistic ethos, which is rooted in a firm belief in the immortality of the soul and the life after death. Even those who do not believe in life after death do not necessarily regard their death as the total extinction of their beings; they can believe that their true beings are perpetuated in the continuity of their families and tribes. The notion of familial perpetuity was the foundation for the Chinese ancestor worship; the notion of tribal continuity was the ancient Jewish conception of immortality. Only a highly individualistic self, living in a totally secular world and resolutely alienated from his community, can regard his death as the total extinction of his whole being.[18]

This is a sketchy summary of the first few strata of Heidegger's multilayered analysis, but even this summary shows the nature of the problem we have to face in determining the scope of Heidegger's existentialia. These structural universals can be taken in two ways: (1) in their bare generality, or (2) in their rich specificity. In their bare generality, they can be accepted as structural universals of human existence in all ages and in all cultures. However, as such they are not especially informative or significant because they embody no more than a definitional meaning of human existence. In their specificity, these existentialia are indeed informative and significant. But then they lose their universality, because they are valid only within Heidegger's own provincial world.

This categorial dilemma is especially acute because Heidegger never squarely faced the problem of determining the scope of his existentialia. There is only one passage in *Being and Time* in which he appears to be prescribing the limit of his structural universals. He mulls over the question whether or not the notion of worldhood analyzed in terms of Readiness-at-hand (*Zuhandenheit*) is applicable to primitive cultures. Readiness-at-hand is our existential attitude toward objects as objects of use, and as such is contrasted with Presence-at-hand (*Vorhandenheit*), which takes note of them as objects of mere presence. Heidegger concedes that the category of Readiness-at-hand may not be operative in primitive cultures.[19] This remark seems to imply that his existentialia are meant to be applicable at least to all advanced cultures.

Concerning the Dasein-structure he is about to analyze in *Being and Time*, Heidegger says, "In the interpretation of Dasein, this structure is something 'a priori'."[20] In philosophy, the expression "a priori" has generally meant the notion of necessity and universality since Kant's use of it in his transcendental philosophy (e.g., "the a priori conditions of human experience" means the necessary and universal conditions of human experience). If Heidegger follows this established usage, his existentialia must be construed as the a priori constituents of Dasein-structure in every culture. He also says that his Dasein-analysis is to exhibit "not just any accidental structures, but essential ones which, in every kind of Being that factical Dasein may possess, persists as determinative for the character of its Being."[21] Like the expression "the *a priori* structure," "the essential structure" usually means the invariant structure that can be found in every Dasein. Furthermore, Heidegger never thinks of discriminating the Daseins of different cultures, for example, the modern German Dasein from the ancient Greek Dasein. Throughout his Dasein-analysis, he refers to the object of his analysis with the general, abstract noun "Dasein" only. For these considerations, most readers of *Being and Time* have taken it for granted that his existentialia are meant to be applicable to all ages and cultures except perhaps for the primitive Daseins.

However, this presumed transcultural universality of Heidegger's existentialia has been a source of embarrassment because so many of them appear to be culture-bound.[22] To be sure, we can save Heidegger from this embarrassment by restricting the scope of his structural universals to his culture. Fortunately, Heidegger has never made any overt statements that can go against this restriction. Even his expressions "the

a priori structure of Dasein" or its "essential structure" can be
taken within this restriction, that is, his Dasein-structure is a
priori, essential only for the Dasein of European culture under
his analysis. This is the way Karsten Harries has proposed to
defend Heidegger's system of existentialia.[23]

Harries tries to buttress this defense of Heidegger's Dasein-
analysis by citing Heidegger's claim that Dasein is historically
determined and determines itself historically. Since Heidegger
emphatically stresses the historicity of Dasein, Harries argues,
he cannot be presumed to present his existentialia as the universal conditions of human existence in all ages and cultures.
This argument seems to miss the transcendental tone of *Being
and Time*; as David Hoy says, the aim of Heidegger's fundamental ontology is "to discover the apparently transcendental
conditions (the existentialia, which are not changeable or *ex-
istentiell*) that are to be the foundation of all other modes of
inquiry."[24]

Heidegger is indeed concerned with the historicity of Dasein, but the ultimate objective of his Dasein-analysis is to resolve even this concern in a transcendental mode, that is, by
spelling out the transcendental conditions for the possibility
of historicity itself. Those conditions cannot be historical any
more than the notion of historicity is historical. Heidegger's
claim that historicity is an essential feature of Dasein is meant
to be true in all ages and cultures. Likewise, the structure of
Dasein or existentialia that have been disclosed by his phenomenological analysis are meant to have transcendental validity, transcending all cultural and historical boundaries.

I have gone through this to show the difficulty of determining not only the scope of Heidegger's structural universals
but even his own intention. Of course, there is only one sensible
way of determining the scope of those universals, and that is
the empirical method. However, this method has been attempted neither by Heidegger himself nor by his followers.
Thus the scope of his existentialia remains unspecified. In sci-

entific investigations, a structural universal whose boundary remains unspecified is like a kingdom whose boundaries are unknown.

PARTICULARITY AND DISCONTINUITY

That the structural universals of formalist programs have not turned out to be transcultural is only one-half of their problem. Even when they are applied to the cultures where they originated, they are not powerful enough to capture all the particularities within those cultures. For example, Geoffrey Hartman has shown that the New Critical structural universal of paradox is too general to capture the important structural difference between the metaphysical poetry of the seventeenth century and the Romantic poetry of the nineteenth century.[25] Although the poetic structure of paradox is operative in both, it serves quite different functions. In the metaphysical poetry, this structural device expresses the poignancy of the arduous struggle to hold together the incomparable and the incommensurate. In the Romantic poetry, however, the same device is used to portray the fusion of the finite and the infinite, the natural and the supernatural, thereby achieving what M. H. Abrams has called natural supernaturalism.[26] In one case, poetic paradox is used to intensify and sustain a stringent dualism; in the other, it is used to transform a dualism into a pantheistic monism.

Such fine structural distinctions as the one between the metaphysical poetry of the seventeenth century and the Romantic poetry of the nineteenth century, or the one between modern European poetry and medieval European poetry, have been ignored and overlooked during the heyday of New Criticism. In chapter 3, we saw how Lévi-Strauss also quite unconsciously overlooked or even suppressed cultural differences in his eager attempt to prove the universal character of all myths and cultures. In most formalist programs, the unexamined confidence in the transcultural and transhistorical universality of formal structures has served as an intellectual blinder preventing the recognition and appreciation of cultural and historical diversity. As a natural reaction against this intellectual blinder, the formalist camps have generated a new concern for diversity and particularity.

This reaction has marked the emergence of post-formalism, or rather the transformation of formalism into post-formalism, e.g., the transformation of New Criticism into the new New Criticism, of structuralism into post-structuralism, of Freudianism into neo-Freudianism, the shift of attention from the analysis of Ideal language to that of natural languages in linguistic philosophy, and the corresponding shift in phenomenology from the analysis of the bracketed world of pure phenomena to that of the life-world (*Lebenswelt*).

This transition has involved a reversal in attitude toward universality and particularity. Whereas formalists in general were enamored of universality and uniformity, post-formalists have tended to disdain them because of their obsession with particularity and diversity. Roland Barthes expresses this reversal of attitude in the opening paragraph of his S/Z:

> There are said to be certain Buddhists whose ascetic practices enable them to see a whole landscape in a bean. Precisely what the first analysts of narrative were attempting: to see all the world's stories (and there have been ever so many) within a single structure: we shall, they thought, extract from each tale its model, then out of these models we shall make a great narrative structure, which we shall reapply (for verification) to any one narrative: a task as exhausting (ninety-nine percent perspiration, as the saying goes) as it is ultimately undesirable, for the text thereby loses its difference.[26]

What concerns Barthes most is difference rather than identity, diversity rather than uniformity, particularity rather than universality. It is this shift of concern to particularity that constitutes the heart and soul of Derrida's *differance*. This shift is, Derrida holds, inevitably dictated by the recognition of the primacy of temporality over structural universals.

Michel Foucault expresses the same concern for particularity and diversity by reversing almost every feature of Lévi-Strauss' structuralism.[28] Foucault accepts Lévi-Strauss' claim that there are unconscious forms or structures for thinking, perceiving, and representing the objects in the world, but rejects his claim that these structural universals are identical in every age and every culture. He calls these structural universals "epistemes" or "archives." He tries to disprove their transhistorical, transcultural universality by showing that there was a succession of three different sets of epistemes in European culture during the seventeenth, the eighteenth, and the nineteenth centuries. Not only does culture have its own unique set of structural universals, but there is no historical continuity or uniformity among those universals even in the career of one culture.

Although historical investigations have usually been concerned with historical continuities, Foucault holds, these continuities have only been surface appearances hiding deeply buried discontinuities and ruptures.[29] When they are excavated and exposed, he claims, they look like the ruptures between geological strata. For this reason, he regards his own historical inquiries as an archeology of human thought. He wants to show how one set of structural universals is abruptly replaced by another set. Since the investigation of historical continuities has been the central business of history, Foucault feels, his own inquiries should be called anti-history.

His emphatic stress on historical discontinuities is, of course, a violent reaction to the excessive concern on the part of Lévi-Strauss and his followers with the universality and continuity of structural universals. He is attempting to prove them wrong by demonstrating the discontinuities and diversities of those structural universals. For his concern with historical discontinuities, he has often been compared with Thomas Kuhn, who has emphasized the discontinuity in the succession of scientific paradigms.[30] As in the case of the Copernican revolution, Kuhn has argued, every scientific revolution introduces a radically new paradigm for scientific research and reasoning. The development of modern science has shown that the progress of science has been a series of abrupt revolutions rather than a continuous evolution.

Kuhn's theory of scientific paradigms came as a reaction against one of the central ideas which had long been firmly accepted in the philosophy of science, namely, the idea that there was only one valid model of scientific inquiry and discovery, and that this ideal model was operative in every phase of scientific development. This ideal may very well be called the structural universal of scientific inquiry. Kuhn's intent was to disprove the universality of the presumed model by demonstrating the historical diversity and discontinuity of past scientific paradigms.

Philosophers of science had developed the notion that a universal paradigm exists for every phase of scientific inquiry, such as the theories of observation and measurement, explanation and prediction, confirmation and falsification; they had done these things under the influence of Wittgenstein's *Tractatus*, in which the notion of ideal language was presented as the model for the study of all real languages. If there is one ideal model for all languages, then there must also be one ideal model for all scientific languages and inquiries. In his *Investigations*, Wittgenstein himself came to repudiate this dogma of one universal model, and advocated the importance of recognizing the diversity and variety of language games. Hence the focus of linguistic analysis must shift from the ideal language to natural languages, from the ideal paradigm to the real paradigms of scientific inquiry, from the philosophy of science to the history of science. The initial impact of this shift has been excitement over the newly discovered historical diversity in a vivid contrast to its hitherto presumed uniformity.

The awareness of historical diversity can take two different forms, the moderate and the radical. The radical form claims that the diversity in question is incommensurate; the moderate form claims that it is commensurate. Vico, Hegel, and Marx are well-known advocates of moderate historicism; all of them have conducted their formal-structural analyses within the framework of formal structures which are progressional. These historically oriented formal structures have given them their universal standards and transcendental perspectives.

As a general rule, the historicists who have grown up in formalist camps advocate the radical form of historicism by repudiating the very notion of universal standards and transcendental perspectives. These standards and perspectives were available not only in the progressional structural frameworks of moderate historicism, but also in the nonprogressional frameworks of ahistoricistic formal-structuralism such as New Criticism and Freudianism. The radical historicists reject the latter for their failure to recognize the importance of historical progression and for their commitment to their nonprogressional structures. They also reject the moderate historicists for their failure to appreciate the radical discontinuity of historical progression.

Whereas the structural frameworks of both moderate historicists and ahistoricistic formalists are closed-ended, those of radical historicists are emphatically open-ended. Of course, they are clearly progressional. The notion of an open-ended progression means that no stage of a historical progression, including its final result, can ever be determined by its previous stages. In that regard, every stage can be said to be radically discontinuous with its previous stages. There is neither causal nor teleological connection between any two stages of the progression. Their progression is a series of discontinuous events whose sequence is neither predictable in advance nor explainable in retrospect. It is a series of absolutely random motions, perhaps the type of motions that constitute Derrida's *differance*. Thomas Kuhn advocates this form of radical historicism in his theory of scientific revolutions. A scientific revolution takes place when an existing paradigm of scientific inquiry becomes ineffectual and is supplanted by a new one. Although natural science has developed as a series of revolutions, there are no transhistorical or transcultural criteria for explaining the succession of these revolutions. Scientists can have the benefit of using certain criteria or standards only insofar as they operate within an established paradigm, that is, only in the course of normal science. For standards and criteria are always instituted by the acceptance of certain paradigms, that is, they are intraparadigmatic and never transparadigmatic.[31] Since there are no transparadigmatic standards of validity or rationality, all scientific paradigms are incommensurate. Hence the problem of paradigm choice is like the problem of making a political choice or undergoing a religious conversion. In other words, paradigm choice and succession in the history of science are a matter of radical revolution rather than of rational reform.

Foucault's claims for his epistemes or archives can, almost point by point, be matched with Kuhn's claims for his paradigms. His emphatic stress on the discontinuity or rupture between different epistemes or archives is mainly to highlight their incommensurateness. To seek transcendental perspectives or transhistorical criteria is "transcendental narcissism," and his self-appointed task is to free the history of thought from this subjection to transcendence.[32] Through this freedom, Foucault maintains, we can accept the inevitable fact that we are always imprisoned in our historically or culturally conditioned subjectivity.

Thus the awareness of historical or cultural subjectivity has been an important gift of relativism, which has been developed in the post-formalist camps. Prior to this new awareness of subjectivity, formalists had taken for granted the objectivity of their structural universals and formal analyses. It had never occurred to them that the cognitive subject could be imprisoned in a structure, archive, or paradigm which was quite different from the structure, archive, or paradigm that constituted the nature of the object to be known. With the emergence of historical and cultural relativism, however, the focus of structural awareness has shifted from the ontic structure of the object to the cognitive structure of the subject. In this relativistic awareness, one instinctively senses the difficulty of breaking out of one's own subjective cognitive structure and comprehending the structure of the object without distortions. For these reasons, the awareness of subjectivity and the recognition of relativity have emerged as the hallmarks of post-formalism.

CHAPTER EIGHT

Relativity and Subjectivity

THE NEW VOGUE of relativism and subjectivism has produced a great deal of confusion, because the very logic of relativism inherently harbors many semantic paradoxes and ambiguities. To begin with, every relativistic or subjectivistic assertion has a built-in semantic ambiguity of reference. For example, Kuhn's claim that every inquiry is governed by its own paradigm may be construed as referring to itself or not to itself. If it refers to itself, Kuhn's own investigation of scientific paradigms has been governed by a paradigm, which has been conditioned by his historically situated circumstances. In that event, Kuhn's thesis cannot be objectively true; at best it can be claimed as a relative truth. On the other hand, it is more likely that Kuhn has presented his thesis as an objective truth which is not affected by any particular paradigm of inquiry. In that event, his thesis is not meant to refer to its own claim.

In order to clarify this ambiguity, we can divide all relativistic and subjectivistic assertions into two groups: reflexive and nonreflexive. The former refer to themselves; the latter do not. Whereas Thomas Kuhn has not told us whether his theory of scientific paradigms is meant to be reflexive or nonreflexive, Michel Foucault has declared that his theory of epistemes or archives is meant to be reflexive. That is, his theory that all knowledge is conditioned by some episteme or archive is itself conditioned by an episteme or archive, although "it is not possible for us to describe our own archive" as long as we are operating within it.[1]

In general, relativistic claims of the reflexive type emerge during the mature, self-conscious stage of relativism. In its initial, naïve stage, relativistic claims are usually presented as nonreflexive and hence as objective truths. For example, Foucault's thesis in his *Order of Things* has all the appearance of being an objective description of historical ruptures and discontinuities; he does not even consider the applicability of his own thesis to itself. Only in his *Archeology of Knowledge* is he forced by his critics to admit the applicability of his thesis to itself and thereby drops the objectivist posture with which he had initially announced his thesis.

As long as relativistic claims remain nonreflexive, they behave like any other objective statements. However, their objectivity can be retained only by making a special exception for their own truth. For example, let us take Karl Marx's well-known claim that all beliefs are ideological because they are determined by the economic conditions of their times. This claim is meant to be true of all beliefs, but not of itself; it is presented as a nonreflexive statement. This special exemption appears to be rather arbitrary and unreasonable. If it is the frailty of human reason that all its beliefs are shaped by economic conditions, it appears more sensible to assume that Marx's own beliefs should not be exempt from this frailty. The exemption seems to involve an unjustifiable inconsistency in Marx's position.

This awkward situation of inconsistency can be avoided by converting nonreflexive relativistic statements into reflexive ones. As we have seen with Foucault, relativistic claims are usually escalated from their nonreflexive to their reflexive stage for the sake of self-consistency. But this escalation creates further problems. Let us now assume that Marx's thesis about the ideological character of all beliefs is true of itself. In that event, it becomes a universal truth without any exception; however, Marx's own thesis becomes only an ideological product of a given age, devoid of universal validity. Thus we are driven to

the semantic paradox that inevitably haunts all reflexive relativistic positions. If Marx's thesis is a universal truth, it must
itself be an ideological product which can never be a universal
truth. That is, if it is a universal truth, then it is not a universal
truth.

We encounter the same semantic paradox in Foucault's
claim that there is no transcendental perspective. This claim
is itself a transcendental claim, which cannot be made without
adopting a transcendental perspective. If this claim is true, it
proves the existence of at least one transcendental claim and
perspective, thereby establishing its own falsity. For the sake
of self-consistency, Foucault is willing to make his relativistic
position reflexive, but he is forced to admit his embarrassment
with the logical consequence of this move.[2]

With this preliminary consideration on the logical complexity of relativism in general, we shall now turn to testing
the strength of some relativist programs of interpretation that
have recently become fashionable in our post-formalist era.

TEXTUAL SUBJECTIVISM

Norman Holland, Stanley Fish, and many other champions of
reader-oriented criticism have emphasized the subjectivity of
readers' responses in textual interpretation. Their concern with
the subjective dimension of textual interpretation has emerged
as a natural reaction to the naïve posture of textual objectivity
that the New Critics had assumed in their textual exegeses.
However, the new subjectivist theories of textual meaning and
interpretation are still saddled with many problems of ambiguity and uncertainty, because they inevitably involve the referential ambiguity of relativistic claims.

Let us first consider Stanley Fish's "affective stylistics."[3]
He says that our experience of textual meaning is temporal or

sequential rather than spatial. This claim appears to be indisputable. We cannot read a text and experience its meaning except in temporal sequence, any more than we can experience a musical performance except in temporal sequence. Kant has told us that all our experience is time-bound, even our experience of visual space. This is not yet a subjectivist theory of textual meaning. Stanley Fish is not yet saying that the meaning of a text is not in the text but in the reader; all he claims is that the experience of reading is in the reader. At this stage, Fish does not assert the identity of textual meaning and its experience. His theory of reading experience is subjectivist only in that it is meant to describe the subjective dimension of the reading experience. Furthermore, it is meant as an objective assertion, true of all reading subjects.

Stanley Fish gives many interesting examples to illustrate what difference the order of sequence makes to the affective tone of our reading experience. Let us consider one of his favorite examples: "That Judas perished by hanging himself, there is no certainty in Scripture: though in one place it seems to affirm it, and by a doubtful word hath given occasion to translate it; yet in another place, in a more punctual description, it maketh it improbable, and seems to overthrow it." This involved sentence is from Thomas Browne's *Religio Medici*. Let us rewrite this sentence by changing the order of its first two clauses: "There is no certainty in Scripture that Judas perished by hanging himself. . . ." Though these two sentences do not differ in syntax and semantics, Fish holds, they deliver two different reading experiences.[4]

In this statement, Fish makes a slight error. Although the two sentences have the same semantic content, they are not identical in syntax. The second sentence was written by changing the word order of the first sentence, and any change in word order is a change in syntax. What Fish really wants to say may be: Although the two sentences are semantically identical, they are syntactically different. Since syntax determines the sequence of our reading experience, two syntactically different sentences give us two different sequences of reading experience. When we read the original sentence, we begin with "That Judas perished by hanging himself," generally accepted as one of the emphatic certainties of Christendom, and then run into a denial of that certainty. This sequence of experiencing first an assured certainty and then its denial is reversed in the other sentence, in which the denial precedes the presumed certainty. The difference in sequence surely makes an important difference in our reading experience.

The effect of talking or writing can be distinguished from content. The former belongs to pragmatics; the latter, to semantics. If we make a distinction between what is to be said and how it is to be said, the former is a semantic question, while the latter is a pragmatic question. The same semantic content can be stated through different forms of expression. Insofar as they do not affect the semantic content, they do not belong to semantics. But they belong to pragmatics, because they carry different pragmatic efficacies. A poem and its paraphrase can be semantically identical but pragmatically different. Stylistics in general is concerned with the affective tone of our reading experience; it belongs to pragmatics.[5]

The pragmatic effect of talking or writing is often controlled by the order of sequence. For example, let us consider the terrible news of calamities that one day overtook Job: the first was that all his oxen and asses had been lost. The second was that all his sheep and servants had been destroyed. The third was that all his camels had been raided. And the final one was that all his sons and daughters had been killed. Now try to reverse the order of these messages of calamity, and you will find that they make a different impact on the receiver, although retaining the same semantic content. The change in the order of delivery does not change the semantic content of the news, but alters its pragmatic effect.

Another example can be given in the different ways of

telling the same story; it can be told to induce suspense in the listeners or to deliberately forestall it. These two ways require two different sequences of narration. What has been known as narrative structure or style is usually a matter of sequence. Through different narrative sequences, the same story can be given different pragmatic powers, although it retains its semantic identity. Any feature of a verbal act which does not affect the semantic identity of what is being said or written, and yet makes a difference in the world of *pragmata*, the world of action and emotion, belongs to pragmatics.

The intimate connection between style and emotion is one of the worthy points Stanley Fish has tried to propose. His so-called temporal theory of meaning-experience is a pragmatic theory which is meant to account for the emotive or rhetorical effect of temporal order in the experience of verbal meanings. There is nothing subjectivist about it except for the fact that the subject matter of his inquiry belongs to the experience of a reading subject.

Fish's program of affective stylistics presupposes the objectivity of textual meaning. For he says that two sentences can, though semantically identical, have different emotive effect. In this case, semantic identity means the identity of textual meaning, which cannot be affected by reading experience itself. Not only the semantic identity of the two sentences but also their stylistic difference has to be presupposed in Fish's program. Only by presupposing that the meaning of a text and its style belong in the objective domain can Fish meaningfully talk about the various ways in which reading experience is controlled by sequence.

As Norman Holland has pointed out, Fish's theory of reading experience is a theory of causal interaction between readers and texts—that is, readers do something to texts and texts do something to readers.[6] In this theory, texts are accepted as independent agents, which can act on readers by virtue of their independent meanings. Holland rejects this notion of independent textual meanings, for he believes that a literary text is just "a certain configuration of specks of carbon black on dried wood pulp" devoid of all meanings and significances.[7] In his view, a text can have meanings only insofar as those meanings are given to it by its readers. If a text is to act on a reader by virtue of its meaning, it can do so only to the extent that its meaning is constituted by the reader's interpretive synthesis. Holland's is clearly a subjectivist theory of textual meaning.

On his own, Stanley Fish has also embraced a subjectivist theory of textual meaning by proclaiming that even the formal units of a text are "always a function of the interpretive model one brings to bear; they are not in the text."[8] By "formal units" Fish seems to refer to linguistic units such as word, phrase, clause, sentence, etc. His claim that one has a totally free choice in adopting one's interpretive model means that one has complete freedom in deciding what is to be regarded as a word, a phrase, a clause, or a sentence. For example, I can regard every line of a text as a word, a phrase, a clause, or a sentence; I can treat every comma as an exclamation mark and every question mark as a comma; I can read every page from right to left and from bottom to top; I can read every other word and every third line instead of reading them all consecutively; I can give every word any meaning or no meaning at all; I can establish the connections between words in any manner I decide upon. There are infinite possibilities for interpretive models.

Since there is no limit to the possible number of interpretive strategies one can bring to any text, we are faced with two baffling consequences: (1) every text is a potential republic of an infinite number of equally valid readings and meanings; and (2) any number of different texts can be made to yield one and the same meaning. For example, Fish says, *Lycidas* and *The Waste Land* can produce exactly the same meaning, if they are read with suitable interpretive strategies.[9] The second baffling consequence follows, by logical necessity, from the first: if every text can be made to yield any meaning one may desire, it can deliver a meaning that can coincide with any of the meanings obtained from other texts.

This appears to be too wild a program of interpretation to be manageable. Even Fish does not illustrate its plausibility with some concrete examples—for instance, by producing the same reading from *Lycidas* and *The Waste Land*. The notion of producing the same meaning from these two poems is only a possibility entertained; likewise, Fish's program of subjectivist reading is no more than a proposal yet to be tested. All Fish can do to vindicate its viability is to cite the medieval allegorical practice: "Whatever one may think of this interpretive program, its success and ease of execution are attested to by centuries of Christian exegesis."[10] In Fish's view, the medieval tradition of allegorical exegesis vindicates his theory of interpretation, because medieval allegorists employed some incredible interpretive strategies. If they were successful, there can be no interpretive strategies that cannot be successfully executed.

The medieval program of allegorical exegesis originally had elaborate rules and constraints on its methods of interpretation and their legitimate scope; these rules were summed up in the doctrine of fourfold allegory.[11] The rules began to be relaxed in the twelfth century, and came to be completely ignored in the fourteenth century by those who tried to impute Christian messages allegorically to pagan classics. This complete freedom in allegorical exegesis produced an interpretive atmosphere much like the one that seems to lie dormant in Fish's program of interpretation.

Whereas Fish only talks of the possibility of producing the same meaning from *Lycidas* and *The Waste Land*, some medieval exegetes did produce the same Christian message from the book of Genesis and Ovid's *Metamorphoses*. This tendency eventually produced an information crisis and chaos: it became no longer possible to tell the difference between sacred and profane texts, or even to tell the different pagan texts from one another, because all of them were now claimed to embody the same sacred messages. This is why St. Thomas and other sober theologians emphatically repudiated the rampant allegorical fever and tried to institute more sensible ways of talking about God and his teachings. Saint Thomas' doctrine of analogy was one of these more sensible semantic devices designed to overcome the allegorical chaos in the theological world.[12]

However, the allegorical chaos of medieval exegetes was nowhere as critical as the chaos that can be produced by Fish's program of interpretation. Medieval exegetes never claimed interpretive freedom in construing the literal meanings of their texts; they exercised their fredom only in imposing allegorical meanings on them. In Fish's program, however, interpretive freedom is to be exercised from the ground level of formal units up; whether literal or allegorical, every type of textual meaning must be the function of an interpretive model or strategy. Whereas medieval allegorists had to cope with interpretive chaos only on the level of allegory, Fish cannot be spared it even on the level of literal sense.

If every text could be made to yield whatever meanings one might desire, the possession of one text should be sufficient for the needs of an entire library. The possession of any other text would be redundant in the technical sense (in information theory, "redundancy" means the transmission of gratuitous messages). Even if there is more than one text in any library, these texts cannot be distinguished from each other in terms of their meanings, because all can be made to yield whatever meanings one may desire. In information theory, this state of affairs is called maximum entropy; it spells the absolute end of all meanings, all information and all communication, and above all the end of the need for any interpretation.

Curiously enough, Fish's theory of textual meaning can lead to a consequence diametrically opposed to the one we have just drawn: there can never be two identical texts. Suppose there are two documents on our desk, and we try to determine whether they are two different texts or two copies of the same text. Within Fish's theory, the identity of texts is determined by the identity of their meanings; any two texts should be regarded as identical if they have the same meaning. Since the texts have no meaning whatsoever apart from their interpretations, they can be neither distinguished nor identified in and by themselves. Prior to an act of interpretation, every text is totally amorphous. Hence Fish concludes that the notions of the "same" or "different" texts are fictions.[13]

This is the sort of semantic or textual chaos that would result from a consistent execution of Fish's interpretive program. As Fish claims, the success and ease of its execution are beyond doubt; but the consequences of his program are impossible to cope with. Perhaps in order to avoid total chaos, Fish tries to establish some order with the notion of interpretive communities.[14] When different people share the same interpretive strategies, he says, they constitute one interpretive community. Even the notion of textual identity should be redefined in terms of the identity of interpretive communities: to say that there is one and the same text means that one and the same meaning can be produced by the members of an interpretive community who share the same interpretive strategies. Since their interpretation assigns meaning to an amorphous text, it might as well be regarded as an act of writing rather than reading. "And if a community believes in the existence of only one text, then the single strategy its members employ will be forever writing it."[15]

Within Fish's subjectivist program of interpretation, we can avoid semantic or textual chaos only by appealing to the identity of interpretive strategies shared by the different members of a community. But this identity can never be known through direct observation, but only through interpretation. Therefore, the problem of discovering and identifying interpretive strategies shared by different members of a community involves exactly the same difficulty as the problem of interpreting and identifying textual meanings. That is, the problem of discovering whether any two persons have the same or different interpretive strategies is no simpler than the problem of determining whether any two texts have the same or different meanings. As long as other people's interpretive strategies can be known only through interpretations, to determine the identity of textual meanings in terms of the identity of interpretive communities is as senseless as to determine the latter in terms of the former.

As a matter of fact, Fish seems to presuppose the identity of texts and their meanings in his very argument that it is determined by the identity of interpretive strategies. If two readers approach the same text with the same interpretive strategy, they are indeed likely to produce the same meaning. But if they use the same interpretive strategy in reading different texts, they are most likely to produce different meanings. That is, the identity of interpretive strategies alone can never assure the identity of interpreted meanings; it can do so only in conjunction with an identity of texts. The identity of texts and that of interpretive strategies are the codeterminants of the identity of interpreted meaning. Hence the identity of interpretive strategies or communities alone could not avoid Fish's semantic or textual chaos, even if it were available without the identity of texts and their meanings.

David Bleich has sought to vindicate the subjectivist programs of textual interpretation with his notion of "the subjective paradigm."[16] According to him, Thomas Kuhn has demonstrated the inevitable subjectivity and relativity of all scientific paradigms. If even natural science cannot avoid the subjectivity of its paradigms, there is no reason why humanistic inquiries and textual criticisms should try to do so. To be sure, this is the sort of conclusion that can be drawn from Kuhn's thesis on scientific paradigms, despite Kuhn's own protest against it.[17]

A consistent employment of a subjective paradigm, however, can only lead to the solipsist consequence of subjectivism.

Norman Holland quickly sees through this untenable consequence and says, "This lands [Bleich] in the thicket of extreme
Berkeleyan idealism."[18] So Holland attempts to avoid the new
paradigm of subjectivism as well as the old paradigm of objectivism, which he regards as no more than a security blanket of
illusion still clutched by many old-fashioned critics. He calls
his own a transactive paradigm: a transaction takes place between the reader and the text, just as it does between the subject
and the object of perception. "Perception is a function of *both*
its objective and subjective components."[19] Likewise, textual
meaning is a function of *both* the reader and the text. Since his
transactive paradigm involves both the subject and the object,
Holland seems to conclude, it is neither subjective nor objective.

If Holland means to establish his transactive model neither
in the subjective nor in the objective domain, he has yet to
demonstrate the existence of a cognitive domain which belongs
to neither. Let us now consider the plausibility of such a demonstration. In the transactive paradigm, every act of perception
(or interpretation) is given as a function with three variables;
the value of the variable P (perception) is determined by the
transaction or interaction between the values of two variables
S (the subject) and O (the object). Insofar as this transactive
function stands as a scientific model, the determination of all
these values must be given objectively. The fact that one of the
variables is called the subjective component or the perceiving
subject does not make the value of S subjective. The value of
S is as objective as that of O; the perceiving subject is now
functioning as an object of scientific investigation as much as
the perceived object.

If this model of perceptual transaction is applied to the
interpretive transaction, the interpretation of textual meaning
(M) can be reguarded as a joint function of the reader (R) and
the text (T). The value of M can be determined by the values
of R and T. This is the psychological model Norman Holland
has used in his effort to show how the readers' responses and

interpretations are determined by their psychological conditions, such as their memories and phobias, fantasies and aspirations, expectations and anxieties.[20] On the strength of his
experiments, he has formulated the general thesis that interpretive responses are functions of the psychological defense mechanism for coping with the problems of neuroses and ego-
identity.[21]

These experiments can be conducted only by a psychologist who can determine the objective values of his variables,
namely, the nature of the reader and that of the text. To know
the nature of the reader and the reader's response without
knowing the nature of the text is not enough for these experiments. For we cannot properly determine the nature of a response without knowing the nature of the object to which the
response is made. Suppose that one reader feels depressed from
reading Dante's *Inferno* and that another reader feels equally
depressed from reading his *Paradiso*. If these two texts are
totally amorphous and their meanings are absolutely indistinguishable, we cannot tell whether these two readers are making
the same response to the same or different texts. In that event,
we have no way of determining what psychological functions
are performed by their interpretive responses.

Moreover, to know the psychological conditions of a reader
is not any easier than to determine the meaning of a text. The
psychological state of an experimental subject is never open
for direct inspection and observation; it can be reached only
through the interpretation of words and behavior. To understand the nature of the reader's phobias and fixations will require the reconstruction of his emotional history, which cannot
dispense with the act of interpretation. If an experimental scientist has the capacity to determine the psychological conditions of a reader, he can also determine the meaning of a text.
If he cannot determine the objective values of his variables, he
cannot conduct his transactive experiment between texts and
readers. Thus the whole program of transactive interaction pre-

supposes not only the objective existence of textual meaning, but the scientist's access to it. Hence this program is as objectivist as Fish's program of affective stylistics; either of them can be called subjectivist programs only in the sense that it is concerned with the subjective dimension of reading experience.

To give the experimental scientist objective access to the meaning of a text or the psychological state of a reader is to allow an exception to the original premise of the transactive paradigm, namely, that every object of perception or interpretation is a function of transaction rather than an independent existence. This exception, which has given us an objectivist interpretation of Holland's transactive paradigm, destroys the consistency of his program. Its consistency can be restored only by denying the experimental scientist the privilege of objective access and by bringing him under the same constraints of the transactive model.

Within a consistent execution of Holland's transactive model, even the scientist can have access to texts and readers only through his subjective perception and interpretation. Since every perception (or interpretation) is a function of the perceiver (or interpreter) and the perceived (or interpreted) object, the scientist (S) cannot provide the objective or independent values of the variables T (the text) and R (the reader). He can provide the values of those variables only as they are perceived and interpreted by him. Let us designate them as T' and R'. Our experimental psychologist cannot investigate the transaction between T and R; he has no access to the values of these variables. But he can investigate the transaction between T' and R', and let us designate as M' the textual meaning that emerges as the result of this transaction.

Let us now introduce another experimental scientist, S'', to observe and interpret the same transaction between T and R. S'' cannot determine the objective values of these variables T and R any more than S' can. Let ùs designate as T'' and R'' the values of those variables as they are perceived and interpreted by S''. We can further designate as M'' the textual meaning that emerges through transaction between T'' and R''. Now the values of T' and R' are likely to be different from the values of T'' and R'', because they are functions of two different scientists, S' and S'', who have different aspirations and anxieties and who need different psychological defense mechanisms. If T' and R' are different from T'' and R'', then M' must be different from M''.

Norman Holland's transactive paradigm can produce as many different observations of the text, the reader, and the resultant textual meaning as the number of the scientists engaged in the experiment, although these scientists are presumably observing and interproting the same set of transactions. This makes it impossible to execute the transactive paradigm as an experimental model. No scientific experiment can be conducted without presupposing a unity of opinion or agreement among the participating scientists on their observational data.

In proposing the transactive paradigm as an experimental model, Norman Holland had surely anticipated the multiplicity of readers' responses to the same text, because this multiplicity was to be the object of the proposed experiment and explanation. On the other hand, it is unlikely that he had also anticipated the multiplicity of responses on the part of the experimental scientists. However, this second kind of multiplicity is dictated by the consistency of his transactive paradigm. If readers' textual perceptions and interpretations are determined by their psychological conditions, scientists' perceptions and interpretations of a reader must also be determined by their own psychological conditions.

In this consistent interpretation of Holland's transactive paradigm, his theory of textual meaning becomes as subjectivistic as Stanley Fish's theory of interpretive strategies. In fact, the latter can be transformed into the former by replacing the reader's interpretive strategies with his or her psychological conditions. In Fish's theory, textual meaning is a function of interpretive strategies; in Holland's theory, it is a function of psychological conditions.

Like Fish's subjectivist theory of textual meaning, the subjectivist version of Holland's transactive paradigm inevitably results in textual solipsism. Each reader has his or her own version of textual meaning shared by no other, because it is a unique function of that person's psychological conditions. Likewise, each scientist has his or her own version of experimental data shared by no other scientists. Of course, there can be no sharing between the observing scientist and the observed reader. Everyone is trapped in a private world of perception and interpretation.

Solipsism is perhaps the most embarrassing consequence of textual subjectivism. In the world of solipsism, one cannot even talk of the validity of subjectivism except for the world of one's own private experience. The very notion of discussion and validation becomes senseless in the world of solipsism; for the possibility of discussion and validation arises only in the world of intersubjective communication. The solipsistic success of textual subjectivism eradicates the intersubjective world, which was initially presupposed for the formulation of textual subjectivism itself. This is a pragmatic consequence difficult to accept under most circumstances.

CONTEXTUAL RELATIVISM

These tangled issues of textual subjectivism are inevitable as long as we confront the texts as independent objects by taking them out of their contexts. Elsewhere I have argued that a text can have meaning only in a given semantic or philological context.[22] Only within such a context does it become possible to establish the identity of a text and to have disputes about its interpretation. Taken out of all possible semantic contexts, a text becomes devoid of all possible meanings; it becomes a tabula rasa, as textual subjectivists have claimed. Even the talks about a reader's response to a text become meaningful only on the condition that responses are made to the text in a certain semantic context. If the reader cannot place a text in any semantic context, the text can have no meaning for him and he can make no responses to it as a text. Likewise, the responses of different readers to the same text can be meaningfully compared only when they respond to the same text in a shared semantic context.

The recognition of contextual importance in textual interpretation has been one of the salient features of the German hermeneutic tradition. Too often, the meaning of a text can be distorted by the unconscious misplacement of the text from the context of its composition to the context of its interpreter. In order to avoid this type of contextual distortion, Friedrich Schleiermacher formulated his first canon of interpretation:

> Everything in a given text which requires closer determination may be given such determination only from the linguistic context shared by the author and his original public.[23]

Schleiermacher's hermeneutic goal of interpreting every text in its own original context was reaffirmed in Wilhelm Dilthey's doctrine of transposition (Hineinversetzen), reconstruction (Nachbilden), and reexperience (Nacherleben): the interpreter should reconstruct the original context of the text, transpose himself to it, and therein reexperience or relive the original meaning of the text.[24]

The contextual approaches of Schleiermacher and Dilthey were animated with the confidence of historical objectivism, namely, the conviction that any historical contexts could be reconstructed and that the original meanings of any texts could be recovered. This confidence in the unlimited capacity for historical reconstruction and understanding has been undermined by Martin Heidegger's notion of the hermeneutic circle.[25]

The notion of the hermeneutic circle is not Heidegger's invention; it had originally been developed in the old German hermeneutic tradition, namely, the idea that the whole can be understood only in the context of its parts and that the parts can be understood only in the context of their whole. Heidegger adapts this well-known idea by shifting the focus of attention from the object of interpretation to its subject. He maintains that everything can be understood only in the context of the subject, whether it be a whole or parts, because no subject can jump out of his own historically given context. Just as the conditions of our existence are historically constituted, so are the conditions of our understanding and interpretation. The finitude of human understanding is irrevocably determined by historical contingencies; there is no way to transcend this circle of finitude and assume a transhistorical perspective. Heidegger's hermeneutic circle is this subjective circle of finitude and historicity.

One interesting feature of Heidegger's hermeneutic circle is that it was formulated in his criticism not of the German historical school and its historicism but of Edmund Husserl's phenomenology and his anti-historicism. In the early stages of his career, Husserl had been much disturbed with the dangerous consequences of historical relativism and tried to overcome it by taking his transcendental turn. This transcendental turn was most fully implemented in his program of transcendental phenomenology and his theory of transcendental subjectivity. His transcendental subject is never affected by historical contingencies; it is always assured of timeless truths.

Heidegger felt that Husserl's notion of transcendental subjectivity was too thin to do full justice to the temporal contingency of human existence. In his *Being and Time*, he tried to reformulate Husserl's phenomenology by highlighting the temporal and historical dimension of human existence, thereby giving a historicist turn to the phenomenological movement.

In taking this turn, he was not simply taking a lesson from German historicists, but was moving one step further than most of them had gone. Whereas they were mostly concerned with the historicity of the objects of knowledge, Heidegger wanted to emphasize the historicity of not only those objects but also the subjects of knowledge. With this subjectivist turn of Heidegger, not only did the phenomenological movement take a historicist turn, but also German historicism started to assume a truly radical form.

Hans-Georg Gadamer has inherited this radical form of historicism from his teacher Heidegger and tried to revamp the entire German hermeneutic tradition in accordance with it.[26] In his program of historicist hermeneutics, he puts his main emphasis on the context-boundness or context-dependence of a human subject and that subject's understanding. He claims that no one can transcend his own context or horizon (*Horizont*), which is determined by his tradition or history. Gadamer deliberately opposes his notion of a context-dependent subject to the notion of a context-independent subject, which had been operative in the old German hermeneutic tradition, namely, a subject who could freely transport himself to any historical contexts without any constraints of his own context. Gadamer attributes this old notion of context-free subject to "the questionableness of romantic hermeneutics."[27] He further claims that the context-free or context-independent subject is neither desirable nor possible.

It is simply impossible to shed one's own beliefs and values at will and assume the beliefs and values of other historical periods or cultures. There are certain beliefs which are given to us by our historical context and which we can never discard by an act of free will; for example, the belief in the roundness of the earth, in the mortality of human beings, or in the shortage of energy. If we had been born in a different age, we would have been bound by a different set of beliefs which were also determined by their historical context. If we had been born during the Middle Ages, we could not have viewed the world in terms of modern science. Many features of our thought and knowledge appear to be clearly determined by our historical context; Karl Mannheim also had these features in mind in formulating his notion of *Seinsverbundenheit des Wissens.*[28] The bondage of historical context appears to be as impossible to break as it is impossible for us to be born at some other historical period. All these inescapable constraints belong to what Heidegger has called the situatedness or thrownness of our human existence.

Let us now consider what would happen if we were to shed all the beliefs and values given by our historical context. Culturally, we would become a tabula rasa, which could neither understand nor interpret anything. Gadamer holds that we can understand the beliefs and values of other ages only through our own beliefs and values. For example, we can understand the works of Dante or Chaucer to the extent that we still share their beliefs and values. If we had no beliefs or values, we would never know what it means to have beliefs or values, and consequently would never understand any works that portray beliefs or values. We understand the beliefs and values of other historical periods not by shedding all our own but by using them. Hence Gadamer holds that our beliefs and values are the necessary preconditions for our understanding.

Gadamer calls these preconditions "prejudgments" (*prea-judicium* or *Vorurteil*).[29] He says that prejudgment was given a wrong characterization during the Enlightenment; it was assumed to distort or hinder understanding. Hence the Enlightenment produced the idea of the context-free or context-independent subject, who could discard all his prejudgments and understand another age or culture without any distortions. In his view, this was clearly a mistaken understanding of prejudgments. No doubt, improper prejudgments can distort our understanding. But there are prejudgments that can be not only right but also necessary, because every understanding can operate only within a set of prejudgments.

Once we recognize the indispensability of prejudgments, the only question we can ask ourselves is whether we have the right or the wrong kind of prejudgments. According to Gadamer, the right kinds of prejudgments are provided by the continuity of tradition. We can have the right kind of prejudgments for reading Dante or Chaucer, because we are still living in the same European tradition that had reared Dante and Chaucer. That is, we share the same prejudgments with those authors through the continuity of tradition. Without this continuity, we would not be able to understand even their languages. On the other hand, we do not have the right kind of prejudgments for reading the classics of some non-European cultures, because we do not live in the same tradition as their authors had and do not share the same prejudgments with them. Thus tradition plays the central role in Gadamer's program of historicist hermeneutics, namely, the role of securing the right kind of preconditions for understanding.[30]

To be sure, Gadamer never disputes the old view that the meaning of a text is dependent on the context of its composition. But he insists that the understanding of that meaning inevitably involves the context of the interpreter. Hence every act of interpretation involves the operation of two contexts or horizons, that is, the context of the subject as well as the context of the object. The latter can be understood only within the former. This is Gadamer's theory of horizon-fusion (Horizontverschmelzung).[31] The theory is not meant to be an ethical recommendation; Gadamer is not advising us to interpret all our texts from the perspectives of our horizons. Rather it is meant to be an "ontological structural" description; he is simply describing the nature and process of understanding and interpretation, which is always there, whether we commend or condemn it.[32]

The claim that every interpretation is dependent on the context of the interpreter can be called contextual relativism. The truth of this relativism appears to have been borne out by the history of interpretation. It has often been said that every age gives its own interpretation of great classics and that the changes in the interpretation of those classics have reflected the changes in the interests and concerns of the different ages. The same thing can also be said about changing interpretations of historical events and personages. In short, it seems plausible to give an objective confirmation to Gadamer's thesis.

However, the notion of objective basis goes against the very idea of contextual relativism. Suppose that five different historical contexts have produced five different interpretations of the *Divina Commedia*. Before one can say that all those interpretations are determined by the historical contexts in which they were produced, one must know that they have been presented as interpretations of one and the same poem, that they differ from one another, that they have been produced from different contexts, that different contexts cannot produce the same interpretation of the same poem, and many other things. Most important of all, one's knowledge of these things is presumed to be objective or context-independent. But this presumed context-independent knowledge is possible for Gadamer only if he alone has the privilege of being exempt from the constraints of his own contextual relativism.

This exemption cannot, however, be granted without rendering Gadamer's position inconsistent. If everybody is trapped within his or her own historical horizon, so must be Gadamer and his theory of interpretation. In that event, there is every reason to believe that his theory is determined by the unique character of his own historical context; his historical relativism may simply reflect the gradual loss of confidence in European rationalism, or our increasing awareness of cultural and ethnographic diversity. In due course, the loss of confidence in rationalism may be replaced by a boredom with irrationalism, and our awareness of cultural diversity may be replaced by an awareness of a fundamental unity among different cultures. Under those historical circumstances, Gadamer's historical relativism would surely go out of fashion. This is meant to be not a historical diagnosis and prognosis, but an application of Gadamer's theory to its own genesis and destiny. In short, if Gadamer's theory is true, its own truth is only a historical episode.

Gadamer is prepared to admit that the emergence of historical relativism and its acceptance are no more than historical products.[33] But this admission is quite different from the assertion that the truth of historical relativism is a historical product. Every theory, relativistic or nonrelativistic, emerges as a historical product, and its acceptance or rejection also takes place as a historical event. But to say that the truth of any theory is a historical episode is an entirely different matter, and this claim can be maintained only by identifying the notion of being true with the notion of being taken as true. Gadamer's theory is true only so long as it is taken as true; it will become false as soon as it is no longer held to be true.[34] Even now it is true only for those who accept its truth and false for those who reject it. This goes against Gadamer's claim that his contextual theory is meant to be an ontological truth about the structure of human understanding, that is, it is meant to be true of all human beings, whether they are or are not aware of the historicity of their understanding. This sort of ontological assertion can neither allow the identity of being true and being accepted as true, nor be made without presupposing a transcendental perspective which cannot be bound by any historical contexts.

Let us now consider the historicity and contingency of human nature and reason. According to Gadamer, the nature of interpretive subjects has no transhistorical universality; it is constituted differently in different historical contexts, largely due to the existential or cultural contingency of those contexts. In that case, it is quite likely that some historical contexts may produce context-free interpretive subjects, while other historical contexts may produce context-bound interpretive subjects. The nature of interpretive subjects must change from age to age, context to context, and makes it impossible for Gadamer or anyone else to disclose the ontological structure of all interpretations, which is true of all historical contexts. The very idea of an ontological structure presupposes an invariant feature of human nature.

Gadamer's theory cannot be formulated without assuming a transcendental perspective because it is meant to be true of all ages and contexts. However, the same theory denies the very possibility of a transcendental perspective, because such a perspective becomes possible only with the admission of context-free subjects and because Gadamer's theory of the context-boundness of human understanding rules out the possibility of context-free subjects. Paradoxically, however, even the denial of the possibility of transcendental perspectives can be made only from a transcendental perspective. For the claim that there can be no transcendental perspective refers to all historical contexts and subjects. This appears to be the semantic paradox inherent in any form of contextual relativism. Gadamer can avoid this paradox only by exempting himself and his perspective from the constraints of his own theory. But this exemption produces an awkward inconsistency; Gadamer alone is context-free while everybody else is context-bound.[35]

Apart from this logical problem of consistency, Gadamer's theory of horizon-bound understanding harbors some practical problems. We run into these problems when we try to extend his theory to the province of cross-cultural understanding. Let us assume that there are two quite different cultures; their identities and their integrity have been established by their respective traditions. Let us further assume that someone who has grown up in one of these two cultures tries to understand the other culture. According to Gadamer's theory, he can understand the other culture only from the context of his own culture. Since the two cultures do not share a common tradition, he cannot share the same fundamental prejudgments with the people of the other culture. Hence he cannot understand the other culture. Thus Gadamer's theory of horizon-bound understanding makes it impossible for us to have cross-cultural understanding, when the cultures to be understood do not share the same tradition.

This conclusion that inevitably follows from Gadamer's theory of horizon-bound understanding goes directly against the empirical fact that many American and European anthropologists and missionaries have adequately understood other cultures which have developed in radically different traditions from their own. I am not sure what Gadamer would have to say about this. He might say that those anthropologists and missionaries have adopted the contexts of other cultures by physically transporting themselves into those contexts and acquiring the prejudgments operating in them. He might further claim that this way of understanding another culture is quite different from understanding another culture from the perspective of one's own. When one moves over to another culture and understands it by living in it, one understands it not from the context of one's previous culture but from that of one's adopted culture. This type of understanding, Gadamer might say, involves only one cultural context rather than two.

In order to avoid confusion, we had better give different labels to these two different ways of understanding other cultures. We may call them intellectual understanding and existential understanding. In an existential understanding, one understands another culture by living in it and adopting its perspective in place of one's own; in an intellectual understanding, one understands another culture from the perspective of one's own culture. An existential understanding of a culture involves only one context or horizon, whereas an intellectual understanding of it involves two. Gadamer's theory of horizon-fusion applies to the latter, but not to the former.

In response to these distinctions, Gadamer might say that

we can never gain an existential understanding of past cultures, because we can never find ways to transport ourselves into them and live in them. Since only an intellectual understanding of past cultures is available to us, our understanding of past cultures inevitably involves two contexts. Hence our understanding of historical past is always governed by his theory of horizon-fusion or context-bound understanding. Thus the ultimate thrust of Gadamer's theory of understanding is the claim that we can never suspend the constraints of our own cultural or historical context as long as we live in it.

This claim goes against one of the premises which had been firmly accepted in the German hermeneutic tradition from Schleiermacher to Dilthey. There it had been assumed that one could suspend the constraints of one's own living context, transport oneself into a past historical context, and live in it at least in imagination. We may call this way of understanding past cultures the imaginative existential mode in distinction from the factual existential mode in which one moves into another culture not merely in imagination but in fact. We seem to employ an imaginative existential mode when we read ancient classics and relive or reexperience their world. The same imaginative mode has been reaffirmed as a legitimate method of historical and anthropological understanding by R. G. Collingwood, Peter Winch, and a few others.[36]

To be sure, the imaginative existential mode is more difficult to achieve than the factual existential mode, but its difficulty need not be mistaken for impossibility. Gadamer's theory of context-bound understanding seems to dictate its impossibility rather than merely its difficulty. According to his theory, the only possible existential mode is the factual one, because one can never leap out of one's own historical or cultural context through the act of imagination alone. In his view, to presuppose the possibility of such an imaginative act was "the questionableness of romantic hermeneutics." Thus, his theory of context-bound understanding is implicitly grounded on his theory of human imagination; it stands on the presumed limits to what we can imagine and understand.

What really is the limit of human imagination? This appears to be an empirical question which requires empirical investigations. The empirical contingency of this question becomes even more stringent if we accept Gadamer's historicism. If the nature of human subjectivity or simply human nature is historically constituted, it may change from one historical period to another. In that event, the nature of human imagination cannot remain fixed, whatever limits it may have. Although its limits can be established by empirical investigations for any given age, those limits will change from age to age. Consequently, if Gadamer lives up to his historicism, he can never assume that there are permanently fixed limits to human imagination. Without making this assumption, of course, he cannot formulate his theory of horizon-fusion or context-bound understanding. Thus we come to the same conclusion through a different route, namely, that Gadamer's contextual relativism is inconsistent with his theory of understanding and interpretation.

This problem of consistency which has repeatedly cropped up in our discussion of relativism may be avoided by amending one common flaw in the very conception of relativism. As we have seen at the beginning of this chapter, the initial impetus for the conception of relativism has come from our awareness of difference and diversity. Our awareness of historical diversity has nurtured our historical relativism; our awareness of cultural diversity has yielded our cultural relativism. However, the category of difference or diversity is not enough for the formation of relativism; the category of sameness or identity is equally indispensable to it.

Let us consider Benjamin Whorf's investigation on the difference between the Hopi culture and the SAE (Standard Average European) culture. He has shown how the Hopi conception of time is different from SAE conception of it.[37] However, this conceptual difference cannot be identified and recognized until and unless both the Hopi and the SAE concept are seen as different concepts of the *same* time. Identity of reference is the fundamental condition presupposed for the recognition of the conceptual difference in question. If we did not know that the Hopi concept of time has anything to do with time, we could not even understand the meaning of that concept. That is, difference without identity should be totally incomprehensible.

As Martin Hollis and Donald Davidson have argued, we can understand another culture or conceptual system only by presupposing a framework of massive identity or similarity for it and our own.[38] We have to assume that the natives of another culture have to cope with the same kinds of problems in human life as ours, for example, the problem of coping with birth and death, growth and decay, hardship and comfort, etc. Their conventions of marriage and education may be different from ours, but we can recognize the difference between theirs and ours only after identifying their conventions of marriage and education as such. This identification can be made only by presupposing a fundamental identity between their conventions and ours. This requirement for understanding their conventions also holds for understanding their beliefs and values. This principle of shared experience and problems is also operative in our understanding of animal behavior; we try to understand the behavior of a dog or a snake by attributing to them desires and feelings of the same sort as ours.

We may have to use the distinction between total and partial diversity or difference. The difference or diversity that is recognized within a framework of identity or similarity is partial difference or diversity. The difference or diversity that is claimed without presupposing such a framework is total difference or diversity. The latter kind has also been called radical difference or diversity. However, the radical or total difference in concepts and beliefs can neither be discovered nor be understood. Total difference is totally unintelligible. Hence the notion of total relativism is equally unintelligible, because total relativism is the relativism of total difference. The only form of relativism that we can meaningfully talk about is partial relativism, the relativism of partial difference.[39]

As a matter of fact, this notion of fundamental identity and partial difference is operative in Gadamer's theory of horizon-fusion:

> Every encounter with tradition that takes place within historical consciousness involves the experience of the tension between the text and the present. The hermeneutic task consists in not covering up this tension by attempting a naïve assimilation but consciously bringing it out. This is why it is part of the hermeneutic approach to project an historical horizon that is different from its own. On the other hand, it is itself, as we are trying to show, only something laid over a continuing tradition, and hence it immediately recombines what it has distinguished in order, in the unity of the historical horizon that it thus acquires, to become again one with itself.[40]

The tension between the text and the present, or rather between the two contexts concerned, is no doubt generated by the difference between them. However, this difference can become intelligible and recognizable only when the two contexts share a fundamental identity. Thus the difference in question turns out to be a partial difference. Gadamer refers to this interplay of identity and difference as "the polarity of familiarity and strangeness."[41]

Unfortunately, Gadamer's account of this polarity is incomplete and inadequate. As we have seen, he has tried to provide this account by using the notion of tradition. The continuity of tradition, however, can account for only the identity of different historical contexts, not their difference. As long as understanding and interpretation take place within one cultural tradition, they cannot involve two different horizons. If tradition always secures the identity and continuity of prejudgments, the two horizons are so identical that they cannot be distinguished. There is no need to fuse them; there is no room for the interplay of familiarity and strangeness.

As long as Gadamer regards tradition as the only ground for contextual identity or similarity, he has no way of explaining the possibility of cross-cultural understanding. As Barry Stroud says, we can understand another culture or conceptual system only by using our own conceptual system.[42] This insight is quite similar to Gadamer's claim that we can understand other historical periods or cultures only through our context. But there is no reason to maintain that tradition is the sole determinant of conceptual or contextual identity. Tradition is only one of its determinants along with many others; furthermore, it is a breeding ground for discontinuity as well, because every tradition undergoes perpetual transformation.

Gadamer must presuppose a fundamental identity of all cultures and historical periods as a necessary framework for his historicism and his theory of horizon-fusion. Only this identity can give him a transcendental perspective, from which he can formulate his transcendental thesis. No doubt, his notion of the finitude of human understanding and its historical situatedness is a valuable insight, but this insight can remain intelligible only within the framework of fundamental identity and similarity between different cultures and historical periods. This fundamental identity can be secured only by establishing a set of transcultural or transhistorical universals. Without presupposing such universals, the assertion of relativism and historicism can never avoid semantic paradoxes and logical inconsistencies. Thus we come back to the problem of universals.

CHAPTER NINE

Objectivity and Transcendence

WE HAVE COME around almost full circle. We began this volume with an inquiry into the nature of formal-structural analysis. We have seen how uncritically the pioneers of formalist programs had presumed the transcultural and transhistorical validity of their formal-structural universals. We have also seen that the critical awareness of this presumption has led to the rise of relativism and historicism within formalist circles and dictated the emergence of post-formalism. We have finally seen that historical relativity and cultural diversity are, however, incomprehensible without presupposing a framework of fundamental identity or generality for all cultures and historical periods.

But such a framework does not prove the transcultural, transhistorical validity of any particular structural universals. All cultures may have certain structures, but their structures need not be that of binary opposition. Their structures are products of historical contingency; they can vary from one culture to another, and from one historical period to another even within the same culture. This is also true of poetic forms. All poems may have some forms, but they need not have the same form of paradox and irony. The unique structure of any poem or culture can be regarded as a specification of the general notion of structure. This general notion provides the framework of generic identity for recognizing the structural differences as specific differences. This is another way of saying that structural differences are only partial rather than total.

The generic identity of different poems or cultures is not limited to their structure, although it is one of the salient features that constitute their overall generic identity. Beside structure, all cultures have beliefs and values, practices and customs, and many other things, by virtue of which they are regarded as cultures, or rather as members of a generic class called culture. Their generic identity is the identity of their class, which consists in the defining characteristics of that class. This is also true of poems. There are certain features of poetry which constitute the generic identity of all poems as a class, whether this class is conceived as an essentialistic or a nominalistic entity. However, the discovery of generic identity has never been regarded as an objective of formal-structural analysis.

Formal-structural analysis has been regarded as exciting and revelatory only insofar as it has been assumed to disclose some formal structures which lie hidden beneath the commonplace surface of generic identity. Furthermore, formal-structural universals appeared to have special magic, because they were believed to account not only for universal properties but also the nature of any particular entity. For example, the New Critical universals of paradox and irony were not only accepted as universal properties of all poems, but also used in explicating the nature of any particular poem. This may be called the dual function of formal-structural universals, the function of designating universal properties and at the same time that of disclosing the specific nature of a particular entity.

In this dual function, many formalists assumed, their formal universals could perform exactly the same task as the universals of natural science. In their view, the magic of natural science seemed to be its power to account for a vast range of difference and diversity within the framework of a single universal law or a set of universals. For example, Charles Darwin's theory of evolution is not only applicable to all the different species of plants and animals, but also appears to explain how their differences have come about. Niels Bohr's theory of atomic structure seems to explain not only the atomic properties common to all elements, but also those which differentiate these elements from one another. The universals of natural science appear to be truly *comprehensive*; they seem to account for both universal and particular properties and relations of natural objects.

The comprehensive power of scientific universals seems to become even greater when the scope of those universals becomes broader, and when the number of those universals decreases. For example, Newton's theory of gravitation seemed to have a greater power of comprehension and explanation than the theories of Galileo, Copernicus, and Kepler, because the universals used in the former were fewer in number and yet had a broader scope of coverage than the universals used in the latter. The scope of generality appeared to be in proportion to the degree of simplicity; the simpler a scientific theory was, the greater generality it appeared to gain. In short, simplicity and generality appeared to be the twin hallmarks of truly scientific universals.

Formalists had these hallmarks in mind when they devised their structural universals. These universals were meant to be as simple as possible, and their simplicity was intended to be the epistemic basis for their comprehensive generality. In fact, the structural universals of most formalist programs appear to have attained these twin hallmarks of true science. It was indeed difficult to think of simpler and more comprehensive universals than the structural universals of New Criticism, structuralism, phenomenology, etc.

The notion that the universals of natural science are comprehensive, that is, that they can account not only for the common properties of their objects but also for their differences, is quite mistaken. Universals can account for only common properties and relations, whether they are used in natural science or in the humanities. For example, Niels Bohr's theory of atomic structure covers only those properties which are common to all atoms, and leaves out those properties which differentiate one type of atom from another. Bohr's theory by itself cannot explain why heavy atoms are unstable, whereas light atoms are stable; it cannot explain the difference between the unique nature of a hydrogen atom and that of a helium atom. We can say exactly the same thing about Darwin's theory of evolution. Although it can specify those features common to the evolution of all species of plants and animals, it cannot, by itself, explain the difference between the evolution of mammals and that of reptiles. The claim of scientific generality (e.g., that Darwin's theory is applicable to all species of plants and animals) is one thing; the claim of scientific comprehensiveness (e.g., that Darwin's theory can explain even the differences as well as the common properties of their evolution) is an altogether different issue. The former has often been mistaken for the latter.

To be sure, Bohr's theory is useful in understanding the unique nature of the atom of any particular element, e.g., platinum; however, his theory has to be supplemented by a set of universals which describe the unique properties of platinum atoms. The same general theory can also be used in specifying the difference between a platinum atom and a zinc atom; in this case, it has to be supplemented by two sets of universals, one of which characterizes the properties of platinum atoms, while the other characterizes the properties of zinc atoms. That is, the differences and particularities of scientific objects can be known only through the use of additional universals.

The distinction between universality and particularity can be drawn on many different levels. To be alive is a common property of all living things; it also constitutes the difference between living and nonliving things. The capacity to move around is the particular property that differentiates most animals from other living beings; it is at the same time the property that establishes the generic identity of animals. Any property can be used to establish the identity of a class, and its difference from other classes. Any class can be divided into subclasses, or be grouped together with other classes into a larger one. A hierarchy of classes (genera and species) embodies a hierarchy of universalities and particularities.

A similar hierarchy of genera and species (or universality and particularity) also obtains in the world of culture. For example, that all poems have certain structural properties is a generic feature of poetry. This generic feature can be manifested in many specific typos of structures, and the New Critical forms of ambiguity and irony can be regarded as two of these specific types. According to William Empson, the form of ambiguity itself can be manifested in seven different types.[1] No doubt, each of these seven subtypes can be manifested in many different ways, and so forth.

Just as the distinction between generic identity and specific difference can be drawn on many different levels, so the identity and difference of various cultures and cultural objects can be established on many different levels. This notion of various levels of identity and difference is the central point in Wilhelm Dilthey's conception of objective mind (*objektive Geist*) as the ontological locus of cultural objects.[2] Dilthey defines the objective mind of a community as the objectification of the patterns of thinking and feeling shared by the members of that community; as such the objective mind expresses whatever generality obtains in that community and also establishes its differentia from other communities. However, this implies neither that a community has nothing in common with other communities nor that it allows no room for diversity within itself.

Every community can be divided into smaller and smaller communities, each of which has its own objective mind. Conversely, every community can be regarded as a unit in any number of larger communities, each of which also has its own objective mind. In Dilthey's view, there is a vast pyramid of objective minds, whose smallest unit is the objective mind of an individual and whose largest unit is the objective mind of all mankind. Dilthey says, "And indeed the objective mind comprises within itself an order of differentiation (or articulation), which ranges from mankind down to the most narrowly circumscribed types."[3] He admits that this was Hegel's idea; however, Hegel's mistake lay in his attempt to construct the entire system of objective minds by logical deduction.

Dilthey's notion that there is a vast pyramid of objective minds is another way of stating that there are many different levels of sharing conventions. Some conventions such as eating and mating are shared by all mankind; there are no cultures without them. But these universal conventions are given different forms in different cultures; to that extent, they are particular. Of course, the degree of particularity can vary from convention to convention, and the most "particular" convention is the one that can characterize the uniqueness of an individual. For example, the style of a writer is a convention shared by nobody else except those who imitate him. Since the style of an author can change from period to period or from work to work, there is no reason to assume that the objective mind of an individual must remain identical at all times. Even at any given period, an individual may operate with more than one objective mind. Kierkegaard wrote and published his *Either/Or* almost simultaneously with the first two of his *Edifying Discourses*, using quite different styles and conventions in each of them.

Probably the most serious misunderstanding about Dilthey's theory of objective mind has been the assumption that the objective mind of a culture or community has a monolithic unity. For example, the notion of the medieval mind is sometimes erroneously assumed to imply that there was a monolithic unity in the medieval culture of Christendom. To be sure, this fallacy of cultural homogeneity has been committed by some historians engaged in the reconstruction of the spiritual milieus of past ages, and by some anthropologists intent on portraying the cultural patterns of primitive communities. Some of those who are disappointed in finding no such monolithic unity have gone to the other extreme of denying the existence of any unity whatsoever in any culture or historical epoch. These radicals have overlooked Dilthey's unassailable claim that it is impossible for the members of a community to interact with one another without the benefit of shared conventions, because their shared conventions constitute the context of their interactions. This sharing is what is meant by the unity of a culture or community, or its objective mind.

Perhaps we do not have to accept Dilthey's notion of objective mind, but we cannot dispense with his notion that there is a hierarchy of generic identities and specific differences. This hierarchy provides the conceptual framework in which we can compare different poems and different cultures and in which we can specify their similarities and differences. Since these similarities and differences can be found on many different levels of this conceptual hierarchy, there can be many grades of difference and identity between various cultures and historical periods. Consequently, there can be many grades of relativism and historicism.

This conceptual framework of generic identities and specific differences is a metaframework; it is the framework through which we observe and compare different cultures. This metaframework should be distinguished from the conceptual frameworks which are constitutive of those cultures, and which may be called the object framework. The former stands to the latter in the same relation as a metalanguage does to its object language.

The distinction between object language and metalanguage has been made to clarify the dual character of language in linguistics. In most sciences, language is used only as an instrument of inquiry; most scientists must use language in observing and describing the objects of their investigation. In linguistics, however, language also functions as the object of inquiry. The language that serves as the object of inquiry is called the object language; the language that is used as its instrument is called the metalanguage. The object language can also be described as the language being talked about, and the metalanguage as the language used in talking about the object language. If Chinese is used in talking about the nature of Korean as a language, Korean is an object language and Chinese its metalanguage. Their roles can be reversed; Korean can be used as a metalanguage of Chinese. We can also use a third language, Japanese, as the metalanguage of both Korean and Chinese. We can also use the same language as a metalanguage and an object language; we can use Korean in talking about Korean.

A language becomes a metalanguage as an instrument of our reflexive awareness. As long as we simply use our language and do not talk about it, it is neither an object language nor a metalanguage. Only when we become aware of language and talk about it do we begin to use language in two different ways, as an object of discourse and as its medium. In this metaconsciousness, we can become aware of the similarities and differences between various languages. Likewise, our awareness of cultural and historical similarities and differences is a product of our metaconsciousness on cultural and historical levels, which may be called our metacultural or metahistorical consciousness. Since relativism and historicism are the manifestations of this metaconsciousness, we can reexamine their nature by explicating the logic of the metaconsciousness and its relation to the object consciousness.

THE LOGIC OF METACONSCIOUSNESS

The conceptual framework of generic identities and specific differences that is used in the formation of a metacultural or metahistorical consciousness can be called a metaconceptual framework, as distinct from an object-conceptual framework operative in any given culture or historical period. The meta-conceptual framework can be value-neutral. For example, we can compare and describe different cultures or historical periods without evaluating them. We can take this impartial, non-evaluative approach in understanding their beliefs and values, their customs and conventions, etc. We are most likely to take this nonevaluative approach when we find it difficult to discover objective standards for their evaluation. Even if standards of evaluation are readily available, we can still take a non-evaluative approach by simply leaving them aside for a while.

In contrast to this nonevaluative approach, we can imagine an evaluative one. We do not stop at merely comparing and describing different cultures or historical periods, but appraise their differences, whether they be matters of values or beliefs. This appraisal, of course, requires a set of standards, which can be derived from one of the cultures being appraised or be constituted anew in the metaconsciousness. In either event, the standards of appraisal do function as components of the metaconsciousness. That is, the evaluative metaconsciousness employs a metaconceptual framework which has an evaluative mechanism, while the descriptive or cognitive metaconsciousness employs a metaconceptual framework free from any evaluative mechanism.[4]

These two types of metaconsciousness can produce two different kinds of emotional effect. If we are exposed to more and more different cultures or historical periods, and get to know their beliefs and values without being able to appraise the validity of these, we are bound to experience some chaos or even paralysis in matters of beliefs and values. Toward the end of a long career devoted to the investigation of historicism, Wilhelm Dilthey expressed this feeling of a helpless chaos: "But where are the means for overcoming the anarchy of convictions which threaten to break out upon us?"[5] On the other hand, the evaluative metaconsciousness can give the feeling of progress and development, because it can provide a unified view of all known cultures and historical periods through its appraisals. This feeling is expressed by Karl Mannheim:

> The most promising aspect of the present situation, however, is that we can never be satisfied with narrow perspectives, but will constantly seek to understand and interpret particular insights from an ever more inclusive context.
>
> . . . An unquestioning espousal of any point of view that is at hand is one of the most certain ways of preventing the attainment of the ever broadening and more comprehensive understanding which is possible today.
>
> . . . A total view implies both the assimilation and transcendence of the limitations of particular points of view. It represents the continuous process of the expansion of knowledge, and has as its goal not achievement of a super-temporally valid conclusion but the broadest possible extension of our horizon of vision.[6]

These two types of metacultural or metahistorical consciousness can be either reflexive or nonreflexive. If they are nonreflexive, they are assumed to be exempt from the constraints of their own relativistic views. Since they are not self-critical enough to realize that they must be also the products of historical contingencies and cultural relativities, they produce what may be called the naïve forms of historicism and relativism. In these naïve forms, historicism and relativism are formulated from presumably objective (nonrelativistic) positions. That is, the metaconceptual frameworks are presumed to be objective, whether they are merely descriptive or evaluative frameworks.

The naïve forms of relativism can be divided into two different types: the relativism of noncognitive norms and values, and the relativism of cognitive norms and knowledge. By "cognitive norms" I mean the standards for determining the truth value of our beliefs and knowledge, and the acceptability of the premises and conclusions in our inference. By "noncognitive norms and values" I mean those norms and values which operate in such noncognitive domains as ethics, aesthetics, religion, etc. Cognitive relativism in its naïve form claims the relativity of cognitive norms and knowledge in the object consciousness; noncognitive relativism in its naïve form claims the relativity of noncognitive norms and values in the object consciousness. In these naïve forms of relativism, both the cognitive and the noncognitive dimensions of the metaconsciousness are supposed to be still immune from the claims of relativity. Both forms of naïve relativism are expressions of a naïve metaconsciousness, unaware of its own relativity.

It is certainly possible that these two types of relativism on the naïve level can be combined into one, that is, the relativity of both the cognitive and the noncognitive dimensions at once. But I have distinguished them because many have claimed the relativity of noncognitive norms without claiming the relativity of cognitive norms and knowledge, and because some have claimed the exact opposite. What is even more important for us is the interesting fact that these two types of relativism present different problems for the self-consistency of naïve relativism.

It seems to be inconsistent for the naïve metaconsciousness to claim the relativity of cognitive norms and knowledge in the object consciousness without acknowledging the relativity of that claim itself. If the object consciousness is infected by cognitive relativity, it is most likely for the metaconsciousness to be infected by the same relativity, because both the object consciousness and the metaconsciousness belong to the same human mind. The problem of self-consistency alone seems to force the naïve cognitive relativism to shed its original naïveté and accept the reflexivity of its own relativity claim. But this does not mean that there are no self-inconsistent metaconsciousnesses; in fact, many have asserted cognitive relativism in its naïve form without recognizing their reflexivity. In claiming that every culture or historical period has its own cognitive norms and truths, they have uncritically assumed that their own knowledge of those relative norms and truths is objective.

The problem of reflexivity in the case of naïve noncognitive relativism is quite different. It is clearly inconsistent for the naïve metaconsciousness to claim the relativity of noncognitive norms and values in the object-consciousness without acknowledging the relativity of its own noncognitive norms and values. But it is quite consistent for the same metaconsciousness to assert the relativity of noncognitive norms and values in the object consciousness without acknowledging the relativity of its own cognitive norms and knowledge. As a matter of fact, most assertions of naïve noncognitive relativism presuppose cognitive objectivism on the part of the metaconsciousness. For example, the assertion that each culture or historical period has its own noncognitive norms and values presupposes that the noncognitive norms and values of each culture or historical period are objectively known or knowable.

Since noncognitive relativism in its naïve form confines its relativity claim to the domain of noncognitive norms and values, it cannot affect its own validity as a cognitive claim. The fundamental point is that every relativity claim of the naïve metaconsciousness is presented as a cognitive claim, although it may concern either the cognitive dimension of the object consciousness or its noncognitive dimension, or both of them. As long as the relativity claim is confined to the noncognitive dimension, it cannot affect its own validity as a cognitive claim. On the other hand, as soon as it is extended to the cognitive dimension, it can affect its own validity. Whereas the problem of consistency alone can force the naïve cognitive relativism to become reflexive, it cannot force the naïve noncognitive relativism to accept the reflexivity of its own relativity claim. Hence it is much easier for the metaconsciousness to recognize and acknowledge the historical and cultural relativity of its evaluative framework than that of its descriptive or cognitive framework.

For these reasons, we can distinguish two distinct levels in the naïve metaconsciousness: (1) the metaconsciousness that presumes the objectivity of not only its cognitive but also its evaluative framework, and (2) the metaconsciousness that presumes the objectivity of only its cognitive framework and recognizes the relativity of its evaluative framework. The former may be regarded as totally naïve; the latter, as partially naïve. The naïve claims of relativity are more likely to be presented as expressions of the partially naïve metaconsciousness than the totally naïve one, because it is not easy to accept the relativity of one's own cognitive framework even in the discussion of relativistic claims. For example, it is not easy for many to concede that their own relativistic claims are only relatively true.

Moreover, the simply descriptive, cognitive metaconceptual framework of generic identities and specific differences does not seem to be bound to any particular culture or historical period, because such a conceptual hierarchy appears to be a universal logical framework operative in every age or culture. However, this hierarchy of generic identities and specific differences can be considered in two different ways: in its formal mode and in its material mode. In its formal mode, this hierarchy does not specify any material properties as generic traits or specific differences. In its material mode, it does specify those generic traits and specific differences. When we compare two cultures, we have to specify their generic traits and specific differences. Until this specification is made, the hierarchy of generic identities and specific differences in our metaconsciousness is only formal. With the specification, it becomes material.

The specification of generic identities and specific differences is mainly the matter of specifying the points of similarity and difference, which can be done in any number of different ways. For example, let us consider the similarity and difference of an eagle and a lion. These two animals are similar in that they have legs; they are different in that one has two legs while the other has four legs. They are similar in that they are predators; they are different in that one hunts by flying while the other hunts by running. They are similar in that they have bodies; they are different in that the body of one is covered by fur while the body of the other is covered by feathers. The comparison of these two animals can go on indefinitely, and the point of every comparison is determined by our perspectives or selected by our interests. Since our interests and perspectives are shaped by our own cultural or historical contexts, the specification of generic traits and specific differences is context-bound.

The comparison of two cultures is not essentially different from the comparison of two animals. Both of them have to use the conceptual hierarchy of generic identities and specific differences in its material modes. Now there is an interesting difference between its formal and material modes. Whereas there is only one formal mode, there can be any number of material modes. The former is clearly context independent; the latter appear to be context dependent. Since the descriptive metacultural or metahistorical consciousness is dependent on the conceptual hierarchy not only in its formal mode but in one of its material modes, it appears to be as firmly context dependent as the evaluative metaconsciousness.

With the recognition that even cognitive framework is also context dependent or relative, the metaconsciousness completely sheds its original naïveté and fully achieves self-critical maturity. Until the metaconsciousness reaches this stage of reflexivity, all its claims of relativity are presented as objective claims. For example, the assertion that every culture has its own cognitive or noncognitive norms is meant to be objectively true. In general, the claims of relativity in their naïve forms are grounded on the presumed objectivity of the metaconsciousness.

The objectively grounded claims of relativity can be produced by not only a naïve metaconsciousness, but also a self-critical one. By using Bertrand Russell's theory of types, a self-critical metaconsciousness can deliberately exempt itself from the relativity of an object consciousness. Russell's theory of types can be expressed in many different ways. For our purpose, however, it can be stated as the stipulation that no statement can say anything about itself.[7] For example, the assertion that all truths are relative cannot be construed to mean that the truth of that assertion itself is also relative. Under this stipulation, no assertion can be allowed to be reflexive; it cannot say anything about itself. Consequently, a metaconsciousness can make assertions about an object consciousness, but not about itself. Statements about a metaconsciousness can be made by another metaconsciousness for which the first metaconsciousness becomes an object consciousness. Thus Russell's theory of types enables a metaconsciousness to maintain its objectivity by exempting itself from the reflexivity of the relativity claims it makes about an object consciousness.

The relativity claims which are grounded on the objectivity of either the naïve or the self-critical metaconsciousness present no serious epistemological problems, because they can be accommodated within the framework of objective knowledge or values. What cannot be so accommodated are the claims of relativity made by a metaconsciousness which denies its own objectivity and affirms its own relativity. Those claims of relativity are not meant to be objectively true; they are meant to be true only within the relativistic framework of the metaconsciousness. Even at this height of relativity, however, the metaconsciousness cannot dispense with one requirement of objectivity. That is the requirement for objective reference in presenting relativity claims.

By extending Frege's distinction between the sense of a name and its reference, Israel Scheffler distinguishes between the objective reference of a statement and its descriptive content.[8] Let us compare the two statements, "The moon is devoid of air," and "The moon is made of green cheese." The descrip-

tive contents of these statements are different; their truth values
are also different. Nonetheless, they have the same objective
reference, namely, the moon. The same distinction can obtain
in an evaluative statement. For example, "The moon is beau-
tiful," and "The moon is depressing," have different evaluative
contents but the same reference.

When we say that a descriptive or an evaluative statement
is subjective, we may mean two different things. In one case,
we may mean that the descriptive or evaluative content of the
statement is subjective or not objective, although its reference
is objective. In the other case, we may mean that not only the
descriptive or evaluative content of the statement but also its
reference is subjective. These two cases display two different
senses of the words "subjectivism" and "relativism," namely,
strong and weak senses. When we use these words in their
strong sense, we call our descriptions or evaluations subjective
not only because their contents are believed to be subjective,
but because they lack objective references. Employed in their
weak sense, "subjectivism" and "relativism" concern only the
content of descriptions and evaluations, while the references
are assumed to be objective.

The weak sense of "subjectivism" and "relativism" is the
normal one; it is used in the normal discussions of subjectivism
and relativism. If we say that our view of the Hopi culture is
subjective or relative to our perspective, we do not normally
mean that our view has no objective reference. If it had no
objective reference, we would rather call it hallucination. Our
subjective views are admittedly distorted by our prejudiced
perspectives, but they are not usually even branded as subjective unless they have objective references. Thus the objectivity
of reference appears to be a necessary condition for the constitution of normal metaconsciousness. Without the objectivity
of reference, our metaconsciousness would become solipsistic.

The inevitability of objective reference is more or less obvious in the case of nonreflexive (or naïve) historical or cultural
relativism. I shall now show that the objectivity of reference

cannot be avoided even by the most sophisticated form of self-reflexive relativism. For this illustration, let us use Jack Meiland's meticulous examination of Charles A. Beard's historical relativism.[9] Meiland tries to determine whether Beard's historical relativism is consistent or inconsistent. For the sake of consistency, Beard has to acknowledge the relativity of relativism itself. Since all historical conceptions are dependent on their times, and historical relativism is one of those historical conceptions, Beard believed, historical relativism will be discarded at a certain point of history. However, this statement cannot be made without presupposing one "absolute"—namely, what Beard calls "the totality of history as actuality which embraces all times and circumstances and all relativities."[10] This "absolute" can be briefly described as those objects and events which must be presupposed for the objective reference of that statement. Even a relativistic view of relativism cannot be expressed without presupposing its objective reference.

The objectivity of reference is the objective pole for the constitution of subjective views and positions. The conceptual framework which is used for the constitution of those views and positions is the subjective pole, whether the conceptual framework is descriptive or evaluative. The subjective pole can be subjectivistic, but the objective pole cannot be. These two poles are the necessary conditions for the constitution of any normal metaconsciousness, regardless of its level of reflexivity. Hence no espousal of subjectivism and relativism can make much sense without acknowledging at least one objective element, the objectivity of reference.

INTERSUBJECTIVE TRANSCENDENCE

Recent years have witnessed quite a few attempts to revive the pragmatic notion of truth as a way of coping with the problems of subjectivism and relativism. Especially Peirce's idea of a community of inquirers and their intersubjective communication has gained some popularity. If the domain of objectivity is difficult or even impossible to reach, it can be replaced with the domain of intersubjectivity. Whatever can be agreed upon by members of a community can be accepted as objective or even as true at least within that community. This device may enable us to avoid the logical embarrassments of subjectivism and free us from the impossible dream of objectivism.[11]

A German Peirce scholar, Karl-Otto Apel, has reaffirmed the importance of intersubjective communication as the foundation of all inquires, especially in the humanities.[12] He regards the recognition of intersubjective community as the most essential feature of the later Wittgenstein's conception of language games:

> Indeed, the later Wittgenstein even explained his conventionalism by pointing out that one person alone cannot be said to follow a rule. Thus he has shown that conventions presuppose language games. However, language games cannot be founded by conventions in the same way that artificial semantic frameworks can. Instead, they must on their own provide the foundations for rule conventions in a communication community.[13]

In Apel's view, the early Wittgenstein had made the mistake of not seeing the importance of intersubjective community in the use of language. Since logical positivism developed under this faulty view of language, he holds, it was forced to adopt methodological solipsism as its metaphysical presupposition. This presupposition led to the common bias of logical positivism "that *objective* knowledge should be possible without *intersubjective* understanding by communication being presupposed."[14] Apel says that this tendency toward methodological solipsism is especially pronounced in the use of formalized languages, because "the very point of constructing formalized languages for scientific use is to get rid of the *hermeneutic* problems of communication." "In short," he explains, "the logically reconstructed language of science is destined for describing and explaining a world of pure objects; it is not suited to express communication which is the intersubjective dimension of language."[15] Convinced that methodological solipsism can never secure the path to objective knowledge, Apel tries to reinstate intersubjective communication as its only legitimate foundation in the name of "transcendental hermeneutics," or "transcendental pragmatics."

Jürgen Habermas has tried to substantiate Apel's idea in his program of universal pragmatics.[16] In this program, Habermas distinguishes the constitution of objects from the certification of truths. The former is prescientific or prediscursive; the latter belongs to the province of discourse or intersubjective communication. The latter requires arguments, disputes, and reasoning, while the former precedes arguments, disputes, and reasoning.[17] The domain of objects guarantees the objective reference of our statements; the domain of discourse determines their truth values. Both domains are intersubjective. One is determined by intersubjective perception; the other, by intersubjective communication.

The domain of discourse belongs to pragmatics. If the truth values of statements are to be determined in the domain of discourse, the question of truth will be treated as a question of pragmatics. However, Habermas says, not every discourse can correctly determine the truth value of a statement. As Marx and Freud have pointed out, some discourses are hopelessly distorted by repressions and constraints, whether they be conscious or unconscious, psychological or social.[18] In order to avoid distorted communications, Habermas postulates what he calls "the ideal speech situation (die ideale Sprechsituation)," in which all participants are totally free of repressions and constraints, have equal opportunities for expression and communication, and sincerely cooperate with one another.[19] Such an ideal situation may never obtain in fact, Habermas admits; it is a counterfactual idea. Nevertheless, truth can be defined as the consensus reached in such an ideal situation. This is his consensus theory of truth.

Habermas' consensus theory of truth has provoked many

kinds of criticism. As a matter of fact, it cannot avoid most of the objections which have been raised against Peirce's notion of truth formulated in terms of the community of inquirers. The most obvious and the most formidable objection is that the notion of truth for a solitary individual becomes meaningless under this definition of truth. This objection may be countered by saying that consensus is not the nature of truth but only its criterion. Even under this modification, truth becomes unreachable for solitary individuals, because the criterion is not available to them. Then, there is the problem of communal ability. John E. Smith explains it in the following way:

> We do not escape the liability of error which the isolated individual brings with him, merely by multiplying the number of such individuals and setting them all to work. Their effort must be unified in some determinate way, and the principle of that unity is our only guide against subjectivism. But that principle is something more than the fact that they work together or co-operate. This is the mistake of those who appeal to a "social" principle in an uncritical way. That principle avails nothing in the pursuit of truth unless we know how the individuals engaged in a co-operative effort actually qualify for their task. We need, in short, to know the basis upon which the operation takes place, the ideal to which it is dedicated, and the standards governing the activity of those who participate.[20]

Habermas appears to be fully aware of this problem; he tries to resolve it by specifying the normative conditions for the constitution of communicative acts. These conditions are called universal validity claims:

    a. *Uttering* something understandably;
    b. Giving [the hearer] *something* to understand;
    c. Making *himself* thereby understandable; and
    d. Coming to an understanding *with another person.*

The speaker must choose a comprehensible [*verständlich*] expression so that speaker and hearer can understand one another. The speaker must have the intention of communicating a true [*wahr*] proposition (or a propositional content, the existential presuppositions of which are satisfied) so that the hearer can share the knowledge of the speaker. The speaker must want to express his intentions truthfully [wahrhaftig] so that the hearer can believe the utterance of the speaker (can trust him). Finally, the speaker must choose an utterance that is right [richtig] so that the hearer can accept the utterance and the speaker and hearer can agree with one another in the utterance with respect to a recognized normative background.[21]

The enumeration and explication of these four conditions are Habermas' way of saying that two persons can communicate fully with each other by truthfully expressing and understanding something mutually understandable under appropriate circumstances.

To be sure, all these four conditions are important, but Habermas seems to have left out one condition that is even more important than these four. That is the capacity of interlocutors to attribute expressions and utterances, thoughts and feelings, to one another. For example, if you tell me that you are depressed, I can understand your statement by recognizing it as yours and attributing to you the emotional state of being depressed. In making this attribution, I must presuppose a domain of objective entities, namely, you, your utterance, your feeling, etc. If I cannot make this attribution in objective terms, I cannot be said to understand or communicate with you. Intersubjective understanding or communication is essentially a matter of intersubjective attribution of statements and expressions, thoughts and feelings. Without presupposing the competence for such attribution, Habermas' four speech conditions would have no efficacy at all. Hence the competence for interpersonal attribution should be considered the foundation for every type of communication, whether the communication be distorted or undistorted, factual or ideal.

The attribution of thoughts and feelings, statements and expressions, to persons can be described through the use of statements. For example, we can attribute a feeling to Henry by saying, "Henry is depressed," and a statement to him by saying, "Henry says that he is depressed." Since every statement has two components, its reference and its content, every intersubjective attribution can also have the same two components. Because of these two components, the mistakes we can make in intersubjective attributions can concern only the content, only the reference, or both the content and the reference of attributions. In what Habermas calls a well-functioning language game, I suppose, both the error of reference and that of content are to be avoided. That simply means that the participants can understand one another objectively or without any subjective constraints. It is this objective intersubjective communicative competence that is presupposed as the foundation for his consensus theory of truth. Thus his pragmatic theory of truth is now shown to be ultimately based on one special type of objective knowledge.

This objective foundation of Habermas' universal pragmatics can be avoided by reformulating it in subjectivist terms. This requires a subjectivist reformulation of intersubjective attributions. Since every intersubjective attribution has two components, its reference and its content, subjectivist reformulation of it can involve either one of the two components or both. However, there is an important difference between a subjectivist reformulation of its content and that of its reference. The former appears to be quite plausible. Suppose that I attribute a feeling of disappointment to someone by understanding it only in terms of my own experience and cultural background, which are radically different from his. This can be regarded as a case of making an intersubjective attribution in subjectivist terms as far as its content is concerned. Such a case is quite conceivable and acceptable in intersubjective communication.

Let us now try to extend this subjectivist reformulation of intersubjective attribution to its reference. To say that its reference is subjective can mean either that the person referred to does not exist or that he is described in the subjective language of the speaker. In the former case, the speaker cannot be said to be engaged in intersubjective communication because he is talking about nobody. In the latter case, he is clearly engaged in a communicative action. Even his reference to the person he is talking about should be regarded as objective insofar as that person is an objective entity. The fact that this reference is formulated in his subjective language does not make the object of that reference a subjective entity, which does not exist objectively. All this shows the indispensability of objective reference in intersubjective attribution; its indispensability is as indisputable as the necessity of objective reference for any communicable statements.

The objectivity of reference enters intersubjective communications in two regards. First, the interlocutors must have the common objective reference of what they are talking about; second, they must establish objective reference in attributing thoughts and feelings to one another. George Herbert Mead seems to sum up these two requirements of objectivity by saying, "We are unconsciously putting ourselves in the place of others and acting as others act."²² He goes on so far as to say that we understand ourselves from the perspective of others: "We are more or less unconsciously seeing ourselves as others see us. We are unconsciously addressing ourselves as others address us."²³ Intersubjective communication is intersubjective understanding, which is impossible without the reciprocal objectification of interlocutors.

Although subjectivists and relativists have no sense of objectivity, it has often been claimed, they can at least communicate with one another and form an intersubjective community as long as they have the same subjective or relative beliefs and values. In making this assumption, people have often overlooked an important difference between having the same beliefs and sharing them. Two persons can have the same views without knowing that they do. For example, two psychotics can entertain the same megalomaniac views of themselves without knowing that they do. In this, they need no sense of objectivity;

they do not have to attribute any thoughts and feelings to each other. They can be said to *have* the same views, but they cannot be said to *share* them. They can share them only by communicating with each other, and their communication cannot be established without the requirements of objectivity we have just examined. The minimal feature of these requirements is objectivity of reference.

Thus we come back to the overriding importance of reference and its presumed objectivity. We cannot avoid the problem of reference, even after consensus is freely reached and fully accepted as the criterion of truth. For every consensus must be about something, and this *aboutness* is a matter of reference. In fact, reference is indispensable not only for agreement but also for disagreement, because two persons cannot disagree with each other without presupposing the object of their disagreement. Thus the problem of reference is unavoidable at every stage of Habermas' universal pragmatics or transcendental hermeneutic, that is, from the initiation of a discussion through the exchange of opinions to its conclusion with a well-founded consensus.

TRANSCENDENCE AND REFERENCE

The problem of reference is inevitable in our thought, because our thought is always about something. This *aboutness* of our thought is due to what Edmund Husserl has called its *intentionality*. The range of our intentionality can be divided into two areas: the area of immediate intentionality and the area of remote intentionality. For example, the objects of direct perception belong to the former area, while the thoughts of things lying beyond the range of direct perception belong to the latter area. These two areas can also be called the areas of immanent and transcendent intentionality.

These two areas of intentionality produce two different types of reference: immediate or immanent reference and remote or transcendent reference. We can establish the objects of immediate or immanent reference by directly pointing at them and by using demonstratives such as "this" or "that," because they lie within the field of our immediate awareness. The objects of remote or transcendent reference cannot be established in the same direct manner, because they lie beyond the field of our immediate awareness and because they cannot be designated by our demonstratives. They can be established only indirectly through the use of descriptive phrases such as "the man who killed Caesar" or "the event called World War II."

These two types of referential intentionality present two different problems of referential certitude. Although the objects of immediate or immanent reference are given in immediate certainty, the objects of remote or transcendent reference cannot be so given. Hence we can never be sure of the efficacy of our intentionality, when we try to refer to their objects through descriptions. For example, when we use the phrase "the founder of Rome," we may fail to capture accurately the object of our transcendent reference for any one of the following reasons: (1) there was no founder of Rome, (2) there were more than one founder of Rome, (3) there was no Rome, etc. The objects of transcendent reference are always located in the vast area of uncertainty, while the objects of immanent reference are confined to the small area of immediate certainty.

Husserl tried to overcome the uncertainty of historicism, psychologism, and relativism by establishing the privileged domain of transcendental subjectivity. He tried to situate this privileged domain within the narrow area of immanent referential intentionality by bracketing or leaving out of account the vast area of transcendent referential intentionality. His doctrine of bracketing or phenomenological reduction is to dispense with the domain of transcendent reference, at least for his project of securing transcendental subjectivity.[24] To be sure, the area of immanent reference can give us certitude of reference; we can be clear and distinct about the objects of our thinking. But this assurance is procured at the high cost of renouncing the possibility of transcending the small area of immediate experience.

As long as we bracket the area of transcendent reference, our thoughts are doomed to be imprisoned within the narrow scope of immediate awareness. By such a phenomenological reduction, we are cutting off our only means of reaching out for the objects lying beyond the narrow scope of immediate subjective experience. For transcendent reference is the only conceptual avenue of transcendence for our thought. To cut this off is especially devastating to those engaged in cultural or humanistic studies, because no cultural or historical object can ever be understood in the immediate awareness of natural perception. Even the mere recognition of a cultural object, whether it be a poem or a political system, requires an intricate network of interpretation which can never be available in the narrow zone of immediate phenomenological intuition.

Without relying on transcendent reference, neither can we establish intersubjective communications. I can point at the objects of my immediate perception and treat them as objects of immanent reference, but I cannot do the same with the objects of my neighbor's perception because I cannot directly inspect his perceptual field. It is ultimately a matter of judgment or inference for me to determine which of the perceptual objects or their features my neighbor is pointing at. For that reason, every object of his immanent reference can be understood by me or any other person as an object of transcendent reference, that is, through their descriptions rather than their ostensive designations. The act of ostensive denotation is a disguised form of descriptive reference when it is used in intersubjective communications.

When we talk about the transcendence of our thought, we

can generally conceive of it in two dimensions: the objective and the intersubjective. In either dimension, we cannot get out of the narrow zone of subjective awareness without relying on transcendent reference. Every act of transcendent reference involves description of the objects or subjects we try to reach, and the formulation of those descriptions requires the use of language or conceptual framework. Whatever language or conceptual framework we may use, it is given to us as a historical or cultural product. There is no point in denying the historicity and contingency of our language and conceptual system, but we should not make the mistake of assuming that their historicity and contingency automatically nullify their power of objective reference. Without such power, it would be impossible for us even to formulate the idea of historical contingency and cultural relativity.

If we have the power to establish the objectivity of transcendent references, we should also have the power to gain some objective knowledge of the objects of those references. Both the knowledge of those objects and their reference involve their descriptions. For example, the referring expression "the man who killed Caesar" and the knowledge that Brutus was the man who killed Caesar involve the use of the same description. In the former, it is used for reference; in the latter, it is used for ascription. If we know how to handle its referential use, we can also handle its ascriptive use. There can be no fundamental difference between the capacity for referring to something and the capacity for knowing it.

In fact, there is an isomorphism between knowledge and reference. As the domain of reference can be divided into the area of immanent reference and the area of transcendent reference, so can the domain of knowledge be divided in two. The area of immanent reference coincides with the area of evident knowledge; the area of transcendent reference, with the area of inferential knowledge. The latter is the area of uncertainty; the former is the area of certainty. Accordingly, the transcendence of our thought can be characterized as our cognitive exodus from the area of evident knowledge into that of inferential knowledge as much as it can be conceived as the expansion of our referential intentionality from the area of direct to that of indirect awareness.

Moreover, there may be no sharp line of demarcation between the area of immanent reference and evident knowledge on one hand, and the area of transcendent reference and inferential knowledge on the other. These two areas are what Jacques Derrida might call the domain of presence and the domain of absence. As many have argued, one area may gradually shade off into the other; their difference may be a matter of degree rather than of kind.[25] As Derrida seems to say, the opposition of presence and absence may be no more than a conceptual abstraction of one continuum, which can allow no neat binary division.

Given such a continuum, the problem of transcendence is not how to leap out of one area into the other, but how to expand and articulate the domain of reference and knowledge. This enterprise of expansion and articulation can indeed be conducted only in terms of our own conceptual and linguistic frameworks, because they are the only cognitive resources at our command. Since they are our own resources, they may be called subjective. But they are objective in one emphatic sense; that is, they are irrevocably linked to our sense of objectivity, which is inseparable from our apparatus of reference.

No doubt, linguistic and conceptual frameworks are historical products, and our cognitive enterprise may have been shaped and determined by historical contingencies. But there is no reason to believe that its historicity places any inexorable constraints on its further progress and eventual outcome. On the contrary, our recognition of its historicity can, all by itself, stand as tangible evidence that our cognitive enterprise for transcendence has been given a solid justification.

CHAPTER TEN

Language and Reference

BY THE END of the last chapter, reference was shown to be the most fundamental function in signification and communication. Through this function, we can establish our relation to the objects of our discourse, and our relation with each other as members of a speaking or writing community. But this function of language has been condemned as a disreputable legacy of an outmoded tradition by some radicals. For example, Roland Barthes has proclaimed that the so-called classical language, the language of reference, is the language of bad faith, and that the new language of good faith should be free of referential constraints.[1]

This new language is claimed to magnify immensely our pleasure in reading and writing by delivering the art of reading and writing from the burden and constraint of reference and representation. To write in freedom from reference and representation is "to write intransitively" or "writing degree zero."[2] This new style of writing, Barthes maintains, is one of the most sophisticated accomplishments in human history, because it has finally established the sovereignty of human language. Up to this point of linguistic revolution, human language has presumably been yoked to the servile function of reference and representation. Now the language of good faith has resolutely discarded this servile function and adopted the lordly function of referring to nothing but itself.

Before we can properly celebrate this epochal liberation of language, we had better know what it really is to have a language free from reference and representation. The expression "a nonreferential language" or "a nonrepresentational language" is not easy to understand; it seems to contain a self-contradictory notion. How can anything be called language, if it neither represents nor refers to anything? It appears to be impossible even to conceive of such a strange entity.

The language of fiction is sometimes called a language of nonrepresentation or nonreference, because it neither represents real people and events, nor refers to them. But there is no reason to restrict the domain of reference and representation to the actual world. It is quite proper to hold that the language of fiction represents or refers to fictive or possible persons and events. On purely semantic grounds, the function of representing or referring to fictive entities is not fundamentally different from the function of representing or referring to actual entities. Hence the language of fiction cannot be properly called nonrepresentational or nonreferential language.

It has been said that our emotive outbursts such as "Ouch" or "Hurray" express only our emotions. This expressive function has been specifically distinguished from the descriptive function of language. If the representational or referential function is identified with the descriptive function, emotive language can be said to be nonrepresentational or nonreferential. But emotive language does not seem to enjoy the sort of sovereignty that is attributed to the language of good faith. For its expressive function is not truly autonomous; it is still dependent on the world of inner states. Michel Foucault has this point in mind:

> the writing of our day has freed itself from the necessity of "expression"; it only refers to itself, yet it is not restricted to the confines of interiority. On the contrary, we recognize it in its exterior deployment. This reversal transforms writing into an

interplay of signs, regulated less by the content it signifies than by the very nature of the signifier.[3]

If this new language is released from the traditional function of representation and reference, it cannot refer to itself either. The linguistic function of referring to oneself is fundamentally the same as the function of referring to others. Hence it is a mistake to say that a truly sovereign language refers only to itself. Such a language is good only for play, the free play of words and signs, as can be found in Samuel Beckett's "stories and texts for nothing." Of course, there is no reason for leaving this new play as the prerogative of only creative writers, for this play obliterates the traditional distinction between creative and interpretive writings by releasing all our words and signs from their chain of reference. In this spirit of total release, Jacques Derrida plays with the words of Hegel and Genet in his *Glas*.[4]

If it is possible to play with mud or feces, it should be equally possible to play with words and signs. The pleasure of playing with one may be as good as the pleasure of playing with the other. Neither can the danger and effect of playing with one be greater than the danger and effect of playing with the other. Nevertheless some champions of this new language have voiced their concern with its nihilistic consequence. If the new language and its new art of play make no sense through either representation or reference, they may create only semantic void. So Paul Bové says,

> How do then these texts escape nihilism? Not only by generating an image of the struggling creator who, somewhat heroically, keeps on going, but also by sketching this creator as a writer intentionally, purposively frustrating his audience. That is, we can watch the drama of this creator as he undermines the expectations of an audience which has learned to read according to formal conventions which originated with the novel itself in the seventeenth century. The texts enact with an almost parodic

purity the Modern drama of a reader-writer alienated from the models of understanding which no longer work as expected. But the discomfort which results from this alienation is not merely impatience or even a neurotic response to an unknown context. Rather Beckett's creator intentionally sets about arousing the "ontological insecurity" which we know as "angst," i.e., dread or anxiety. This is part of the fundamental ontology of Modern man. It is felt both by the writer who finds he cannot control a non-representational language and by a critical reader who experiences his Modern tools of understanding sliding into ineffectiveness. It is worth pointing out that in the story and character of Moran, Beckett represents both sides of this experience of failure. Yet, this failure of the tools of reading and writing is a victory over nihilism because Beckett generates and dramatizes anxiety to recall to mind man's fundamentally active and temporal being.[5]

This anti-nihilistic verdict on the character of Beckett's writings is a surprising reversal in Paul Bové's exposition. At the outset of his essay, Bové takes it for granted that Beckett's writings are eminent examples of the new language, which neither represents nor refers to anything. Now he is arguing that this new style of writing *represents* the angst of modern man as a writer and as a reader, and that it even *dramatizes* the fundamentally active and temporal character of his existence. He calls these functions of representation and dramatization a victory over nihilism.

This victory over nihilism is doubly suspect if it is to be claimed for the glory and power of the new language free of reference and representation. First, it is a victory for representation; the victory is achieved by representing the ontological insecurity of modern man. Second, it is achieved by using the old-fashioned linguistic expectations, those expectations that have been nurtured in the matrix of representational languages. It stands on a borrowed ground. It can last only so long as the slow-witted audience cannot divest themselves of their old linguistic habits, that is, the habits of expecting to find some reference and representation in linguistic expressions. As soon as they master the *modus operandi* of the new language, they will experience neither anxiety nor insecurity, but only the nothingness of Beckett's writings.

The idea of achieving a victory over nihilism clearly reflects our old notion of language, which is surely incompatible with the notion of nihilism. The old-fashioned victims of representational language have every reason to be terrified at even the notion of linguistic nihilism. But the champions of the new revolutionary, nonrepresentational languages should be free of this anxiety over linguistic nihilism. A truly revolutionary language is meant to be absolutely free of all references and representations; it cannot even be allowed to represent the nothingness of our existence. By this new standard of linguistic reference and representation, Beckott's language is still old-fashioned. What is achieved by a truly nonrepresentational language is verbal nirvana, which should be distinguished from linguistic nihilism, the chaos produced by the total failure of a representational language. Whereas linguistic nihilism might be an object of anxiety, verbal nirvana should be an object of rejoicing.

In the domain of language and signification, the function of reference and representation performs the role of *karma*. As the chain of karma places constraints on the freedom of an individual, the chain of reference provides semantic constraints on the freedom of a signifier. Released from this chain, every signifier becomes a meaningless cipher, whose function can never be distinguished from that of any other. Only through the chain of verbal karma can signifiers retain their semantic identity and individuality. The chain of reference is the chain of semantic individuation. To be released from this chain of verbal karma is to enter the mysterious realm of verbal nirvana.

Language without reference is the language of nirvana. To institute such a language is indeed a linguistic revolution. Although this great revolution has been promised by many manifestoes and praised in many eulogies, its theoretical justification has yet to be given. Such a justification cannot be given by the traditional theories of language and signification, because they are theories of reference-bound languages and signs. It can be given only by an equally revolutionary theory of language and signification—as revolutionary as the new language. Some have hailed Saussure's theory of language and Derrida's theory of signification as such revolutionary theories.

REFERENCE AND DISTINCTION

As we saw in chapter 6, Saussure rejects the traditional view of linguistic function as naming. If language derives its meaning through its naming function, its signification function can never be separated from its referential function. If the word "red" names red objects or the ideal object of redness, it cannot avoid referring to those objects or object. Hence the naming function entails what Derrida calls the metaphysics of presence; the objects referred to by their names must be present before they can be named or referred to. Since Saussure's linguistic conceptualism rejects the naming function of language, it may be regarded as a way of conceiving of language and its meaning function without presupposing its referential function and without the stigma of the metaphysics of presence.

If the meaning function is derived from referential function, linguistic distinctions are governed by the extralinguistic distinctions. For example, the distinction between the words "red" and "blue" must reflect an extralinguistic distinction between what is red and what is blue. If the meaning function is not derived from referential function, linguistic distinctions can have no reference to any extralinguistic distinctions. This referential freedom in linguistic distinctions gives language its total autonomy, but this autonomy also means the totally arbitrary character of its distinctions. Hence Derrida correctly observes that the arbitrariness of signs and their differential character are inseparable in Saussure's theory.[6] In Saussurian linguistics, language can be defined as a totally arbitrary system of distinctions.

This notion of arbitrary linguistic distinction is the fountainhead of linguistic relativism, namely, the claim that our experience is language-dependent and that every language is a different way of organizing experience. As Benjamin Whorf says, the Hopi Indians have a different experience of time from ours because their language carves up time in a different way from ours.[7] If one grows up in a culture that has seven color words, a linguistic relativist holds, he can experience only seven colors. On the other hand, someone who has grown up with three color words can recognize only three colors. That is, color distinctions are dependent on linguistic or conceptual distinctions. This is the hallmark of conceptualism.

Conceptualism advocates the underivativeness of conceptual and linguistic distinctions in opposition to the traditional view that they are derived from the ontological distinctions that obtain in the extralinguistic domain. If language does not derive its distinctions from reality, it must create them. The autonomy of language means its creativity. How can our language create its system of distinctions without relying on extralinguistic reality, for example, the distinction of colors, without appealing to colors? This is the enigma of distinction that is contained in conceptualism. Saussure tries to resolve this enigma with his thesis that linguistic differences are "differences without positive terms," that is, linguistic distinctions are established through the mutual negation and opposition of linguistic signs.[8]

The validity of Saussure's thesis depends on the viability of negative definitions. Let us assume that our language contains three color words "med," "ned," and "ped." According to Saussure's thesis of negative definition, these three words can be defined in their mutual negation or opposition. "Med" can be defined as neither "ned" nor "ped"; "ned" as neither "med" nor "ped"; "ped" as neither "med" nor "ned." But this operation of mutual opposition and exclusion cannot, in itself, give these color words any determinate meaning. Notwithstanding Spinoza's famous dictum that all determination is negation, negation alone can never make anything determinate. This is the stumbling block for the notion of absolutely negative definition.

Let us now take Saussure's notion of negative definition only as one of the two elements for establishing color distinctions. The other element is the color spectrum or sensation, which will function as the positive element in our determination of color words, while their mutual negation will function as the negative element. Now suppose that the meaning of "ned" is determined by fixing it on the color spectrum, and then defining the meaning of "ped" as not "ned." This definition of "ped" gains certain determinateness to the extent that the meaning of "ned" is determinate. Even then, this negative definition of "ped" cannot, by itself, tell us exactly what color the word stands for. There is no way to give it a determinate meaning without locating it on the color spectrum along with the other color words.

By locating all our three color words on the spectrum, we can divide the whole spectrum into three zones of mutual opposition and exclusion. This operation of mutual opposition and exclusion requires the use of negative definition, but this negative procedure is inseparable from the positive content of the color spectrum. Negative definition and positive content are like two hands for clapping. Even Spinoza's dictum should be understood as a description of only one of these two hands for our linguistic performance. One-handed clapping may produce clappings without sound. Without presupposing a semantic matrix of positive content, the negative definition of linguistic terms can produce only linguistic distinctions without difference.

This linguistic operation of using the three color words for carving up the entire color spectrum into three sectors may appear to restore the old linguistic function of naming. But the function of these three words is the function of not naming but ordering. The color spectrum contains a potentially infinite number of different colors and shades of colors, and an infinite number of entities can never be named. The naming function is really impossible to perform, and this is the main objection to the traditional view of linguistic function. Since the domain of reality or its perception is the domain of infinite multiplicities, it is a domain of potential chaos. The function of linguistic distinction is to overcome this potential chaos by imposing its own order upon it.

The potentially infinite number of different colors and shades in the color spectrum can be divided and ordered in any number of different ways. It is possible to use any number of color words for this ordering function. To that extent, any system of linguistic distinctions is autonomous, but this autonomy is partial because it depends on the positive content of the extralinguistic world. Just imagine that our color spectrum consists of only one uniform color. There is no way of establishing a system of color distinctions for that spectrum simply by using the mutual negation of color words. If the operation of linguistic distinction were totally autonomous, even the blind could have their own color words and give them their determinate meanings solely through the linguistic operation of defining color words.

We have given two different accounts of linguistic autonomy that underlie Saussure's notion of linguistic distinction, that is, the total autonomy and the partial autonomy of language. Before Saussure, these two notions had already been tried out by Kant and Hegel. Kant had advocated partial autonomy; his famous dictum "Percepts without concepts are blind; concepts without percepts are empty" described the mutual dependence of concepts and percepts. Without the content of perception, conceptual distinctions are empty because they are distinctions without differences. Without conceptual distinction and ordering, perceptual contents are blind because they cannot escape the chaotic state of potentially infinite multiplicity.[9]

Hegel was gravely dissatisfied with Kant's notion of partial autonomy, because he was driven by a relentless craving for the absolute. He was determined to secure the total autonomy of conceptual distinctions. He was convinced that the use of any positive terms in establishing a system of conceptual distinctions always undermines its total autonomy. Since positive terms are concepts of determinate beings, Hegel refuses to admit any determinate concepts as the basis for establishing his absolute system of conceptual distinctions. The only concept he can use is the concept of pure being, absolutely indeterminate being. From this single concept, he tries to derive all other concepts through the dialectical operation of deduction. This is his program of logical dialectic. Since the concept of pure being and the dialectical operation of deduction are not dependent on the positive content of reality, the resulting system of concepts or conceptual distinctions can have total autonomy.

Let us now see how well Hegel has carried out this program of logical dialectic. Since the concept of pure being is totally devoid of determinateness, Hegel says, it is the same as the concept of pure nothing, the second concept in his conceptual system. Through this identity, the first concept leads to the second concept. Since the second concept also leads back to the first, Hegel says, there is a constant oscillation between the two. This oscillation produces the third concept, the concept of becoming. These three concepts constitute the first triad in Hegel's logical dialectic. The concept of becoming then produces the concept of determinate being, which sets the stage for generating all other determinate concepts. Thus Hegel's logical dialectic gives the impression that his entire system of concepts is generated from the concept of pure being or absolute nothingness.[10]

Unfortunately, Hegel's logical dialectic is full of dubious claims and tricky maneuvers. If the concept of pure being is truly indistinguishable from the concept of pure nothing, they cannot be regarded as two concepts. When two concepts are indistinguishable, they are one and the same concept, although they may have two names. Since there is only one concept and not two, there can be no oscillation between the two. Even if there were such an oscillation, it could not produce the concept of becoming in its ordinary sense, that is, the concept of becoming determinate, which presupposes the concept of determinate being instead of producing it. The only concept of becoming that can be produced by the oscillation between two concepts of absolute indeterminateness is the concept of remaining totally indeterminate. This strange concept of becoming may be called the concept of totally indeterminate becoming. But this concept is neither distinguishable from the first two concepts of absolute indeterminateness nor capable of producing the concept of determinate being.

It is not easy to decide whether Saussure's notion of linguistic distinction and its autonomy should be understood as the Kantian partial autonomy or the Hegelian total autonomy. Saussure appears to be operating in a Kantian framework when he talks of sound-images as the constituents of linguistic signs. They are said to be the imprints of physical sounds, and that seems to presuppose the perceptual framework for the constitution of linguistic distinctions. On the other hand, when he gives his formal account of linguistic distinctions, he appears to accept the Hegelian framework. He stresses the totally negative character of linguistic distinctions by claiming that they are "differences without positive terms" or that "concepts are purely differential and defined not by their positive content but negatively by their relations with the other terms of the system."[11]

So long as Saussure's operation of linguistic distinction relies solely on the notion of negation and negative relation, it is fundamentally the same as Hegel's logical dialectic. To be sure, there are some surface differences between the two. Whereas Hegel begins his logical dialectic with only one negative concept, Saussure seems to set up his linguistic distinctions with a plurality of negative terms. In the domain of purely negative concepts, however, there can be no real difference between one and many, unity and plurality, because all purely negative terms are truly identical. Saussure's operation of negative definition and opposition can be different from Hegel's operation of dialectical negation and opposition, if the terms of definition and opposition are positive. But if those terms are totally negative, the two operations are indistinguishable.

If the autonomy of language can be total, its distinctions can also be totally free of the referential matrix. If it is only partially free, it is only partially free of that matrix. As we said in the last chapter, the linguistic function of reference is inseparable from the issue of relativism. If the doctrine of total autonomy is valid, it can provide a solid linguistic foundation for total relativism. In that event, all our perceptions and cognitions must be totally relative to our system of linguistic distinctions, which depends on nothing but itself and refers to nothing outside itself. Every linguistic system must be absolutely incommensurate with every other, because they share no common referential base.

Jacques Derrida fervently embraces Saussure's notion that linguistic distinctions are not derivative but original.[12] But he cannot accept Saussure's thesis that the values of linguistic signs are established through their mutual negation and opposition. Saussure's thesis presents the genesis of linguistic distinctions as a synchronic operation, because the mutual negation of linguistic signs is a synchronic operation. Every synchronic operation is liable to capitulate to logocentrism and the metaphysics of presence. If all the values of linguistic signs are generated in a synchronic operation, they must be simultaneously present to one another. Derrida tries to avoid this trap of presence and logocentrism by constructing his diachronic account of the genesis of linguistic differences. As we saw in chapter 6, he has constructed this diachronic account by transforming Saussure's notion of linguistic difference into his doctrine of differance and by asserting the primacy of genesis over structure.

Saussure's account of linguistic distinctions is structural; it is given in terms of the structure of the mutual opposition of linguistic signs, which are simultaneously present to each other. Derrida's account is genetic; it is given in terms of the temporal relation between a trace and its origin, which can never be present to each other. The meaning of a trace as a signifier is determined by its retentional relation to its origin; hence the distinction of all signs is grounded on their retentional relations. This retentional account renders all signs reference dependent. If a signifier is a trace of something, the former must refer to the latter. This referential relation is unavoidable whether the sign is conceived as a trace, a remainder, or a supplement; it is a trace of something, a remainder of something, or a supplement to something. Hence Derrida says, "The instituted trace cannot be thought without thinking the retention of difference within a structure of reference."[13] This inescapable referential relation makes Derrida's theory of sign too conservative. It cannot account for signs which are not traces of what has already been in the past.

How can Derrida explain the existence and operation of the signs whose constitution appears to be protential rather than retentional? If all signification relations are retentional, how is it possible for us to have the signs representing tomorrow's weather, next week's appointments, next year's vacation, and the future itself. These entities projected into the future and the future itself cannot leave traces because they have never been in the past.[14] Even more difficult to explain, within Derrida's retentional theory, than the protentional signs are the signs and ideas produced by creative imagination. They can never come into existence as traces of anything past or present, precisely because they transcend the domain of what is and what has been.[15]

Some of Derrida's followers have touted his theory of signs for having transformed the function of textual interpretation into a creative one. Because of Derrida's differance, no two readings of any text can ever be the same. Hence it is impossible to implement the traditional notion of textual interpretation as the uncreative role of merely reconstructing and recovering the original textual meaning. Derrida's differance makes every reading of a text a creative act of producing a new meaning. No doubt, differance is the play of becoming different, but to become different is not the same as being creative. Every rock becomes different at every moment, but it is never being creative at any moment. The play of difference can never be any more creative than rocks, so long as it is contained within the framework of retention.

Derrida has praised Nietzsche for his attempt to liberate signs from their dependence on the domain of presence, and his theory of differance is meant to restate and amplify Nietzsche's fight against logocentrism and the metaphysics of presence.[16] But he does not seem to realize that Nietzsche's theory of sign is fundamentally protentional. That is, signs or ideas are expressions of the will-to-power, which is always future-oriented rather than past-oriented. In this protentional account of ideas and signs, whatever is retained from the past is not for its own sake but for the sake of future use. Hence Nietzsche's account of signs is meant to liberate them from the yoke of not only the present but also the past. In that regard, Derrida's retentional theory of signification bluntly goes against the Nietzschean spirit of free play.

DIFFERANCE AND POLYSEMY

The conservativism in Derrida's theory of signs is the unavoidable consequence of divorcing the genesis and function of signs from the notion of subjectivity. This is the same problem that is encountered in the behaviorist account of language. In spite of its conservatism, Derrida's theory has been presented as a radical position, which has some revolutionary consequences. One of these consequences is said to be the inevitable polysemy of all signs. Since every sign is a product of differance, Derrida has maintained, it differs and defers its meaning perpetually. Although iterability constitutes the nature of every sign, every iteration involves its alteration. The perpetual alteration of a sign means that every sign is polysemous. This universal polysemy is the dictate of differance, the play of becoming different.

Here are some salient examples of the Derridian polysemy. In Plato's dialogues, the word *pharmakon* moans both remedy and poison. In Mallarmé's *Mimique*, the word *hymen* stands for both virginity and marriage. Again in the *Mimique*, the word *blanc* perpetually changes its meaning. As we shall see, these examples represent three different problems of polysemy, although Derrida regards all of them as exemplifications of the same problem. Let us first take the last example. In the *Mimique*, the word *blanc* appears in many different contexts: white cloud, white snow, white swans, white veils, etc. In all of these occasions, Derrida holds, the word *blanc* has different meanings, whether they be literal or symbolic, metaphoric or metonymic.[17] The meaning of *blanc* is dispersed in a potentially infinite number of loci, and the totality of its meaning can never be given. The Derridian differance is said to be this infinite movement of dispersion and dissemination.

In this description of polysemy, the identity of a sign is implicitly equated with the totality of its meanings. This implicit equation is consonant with Derrida's definition of ideal content or the ideality of a sign in terms of its repetition:

> But this ideality, which is but another name for the permanence of the same and the possibility of its repetition, *does not exist* in the world, and it does not come from another world; it depends entirely on the possibility of acts of repetition. It is con-

stituted by this possibility. Its "being" is proportionate to the power of repetition; absolute ideality is the correlate of a possibility of infinite repetition.[18]

Derrida's claim that the ideal content of a sign is constituted by the possibility of its repetition is meant to invert Husserl's idealist account of ideal content. Idealists in general hold that the repetition of a sign depends on its ideal content. For example, the repetition of the word "horse" in many different places can be recognized because of the self-identity of its ideal content. Empiricists in general maintain the opposite view, that is, the ideality of a general term like "horse" is established by the association of particular impressions, that is, its repetitions. Hence, Derrida's view of ideal content is hardly distinguishable from the empiricist account of general ideas.

Derrida fully recognizes the affinity of his position with empiricism and materialism.[19] If the empiricist account of general ideas is correct, the meaning or ideal content of every general term is dispersed in an endless number of occasions. On the other hand, if the idealist account of ideal content is correct, ideal content can always maintain its unscattered self-identity. Its self-identity can never be affected by its repetitions; it is a perfect example of self-presence. Hence Derrida regards idealism as the most uncompromising expression of logocentrism. But his espousal of empiricism seriously endangers his doctrine of semiotic independence. As we saw in chapter 6, Derrida maintains that every sign can discharge its function of signification in total independence of any human subjects. This notion of semiotic independence ultimately hinges on the independence of ideal content, that is, its self-identity cannot be affected by any contextual changes. So Derrida asserts ideal content as the requisite condition for repeatability:

> Iterability supposes a minimal remainder (as well as a minimum of idealization) in order that the identity of the *selfsame* be repeatable and identifiable *in*, *through*, and even *in view of* its alteration. For the structure of iteration—and this is another of its decisive traits—implies *both* identity and difference.[20]

This is the central contradiction in Derrida's theory of signs. When he advocates his notion of dissemination, he maintains that the ideal content of a sign is derived from its repetition and dispersal. When he argues for his notion of semiotic independence, he admits that the repeatability of a sign presupposes the self-identity of its ideal content. The former is the empiricist position; the latter is the idealist position. The contradiction in Derrida's theory of signs reflects the conflation of these two incompatible positions. These two positions have been combined in his theory because Derrida has constructed his theory by combining Husserl's notions of expressive and indicative signs.

Husserl's notion of indicative signs is an empiricist view of signs; his notion of expressive signs is an idealist view. The indicative relation is the relation of one particular to another. This is an empirical relation which involves no ideal content. The expressive relation is the relation of one idea to its many instances. That is not an empirical relation and is impossible without the function of an ideal entity. Derrida's notion of trace retains Husserl's notion of indicative signs; the relation of a trace to its origin is an indicative relation. But it also contains Husserl's notion of expressive signs; it has ideal content. This Derridian trace which is at once indicative and expressive is called the instituted trace.[21] The contradiction in Derrida's theory of signs is the incompatibility of the two constituents for the constitution of this instituted trace.

This contradiction can be resolved by recognizing the primacy of one over the other, for example, by saying that the indicative function of a sign is dependent on its ideal content, or that its ideal content is derived from its repeated and repeatable indicative function. The trouble with Derrida is that he admits both of these claims. When he wants to discredit idealism, he maintains that the ideal content is not primordial but derivative from its repeatability, that is, its indicative relations. But this empiricist notion of ideal content makes the meaning of a sign totally context-dependent; its ideal content is totally dispersed. For example, the meaning of the word *blanc* perpetually changes with the context of its use. But this notion of context-dependence is incompatible with Derrida's notion of semiotic independence, which presupposes the invariance of ideal content. So for the sake of semiotic independence, he espouses the idealist notion of context-independence, and admits the dependence of indicative relations on ideal content, that is, the ideal content of a sign is presupposed for its repeatability.[22] Derrida asserts both the derivative and the underivative character of ideal content.

Whether the ideal content of an instituted trace is derivative or underivative, its ideal content can be regarded as its semantic focus or nucleus. A sign may have one or more than one semantic focus. The polysemy of *blanc* is the polysemy of a word with one semantic focus; it is the dispersion of meaning around its single semantic focus. But the polysemy of *pharmakon* is more complicated, because it has two semantic foci, which can be designated with the words "remedy" and "poison." It is truly a word of what Derrida calls a *double séance* or double register. Let us introduce a distinction between two types of polysemy: monofocal and multifocal. The monofocal polysemy is the polysemy of a word with one semantic focus; it is dictated by dispersion and dissemination. The multifocal polysemy is the polysemy of a word with more than one semantic focus; it is dictated not only by dispersion and dissemination but by the plurality of semantic foci.

Derrida has shown why his notion of differance and dispersion dictates the monofocal polysemy, but not the multifocal polysemy, as the norm of any language. To have more than one semantic focus is a much more complex phenomenon than to have the meaning of one semantic focus dispersed to different semantic loci. The formation of more than one semantic focus requires a different retentional account from the one for the formation of only one semantic focus. The latter requires a theory of simple retention, and the former that of composite retention. Imagine the track of a snake on the sand; it is a simple retention. Now suppose that a dog steps on this track; it becomes a composite retention. One is a simple trace, the other composite. The composite trace and retention produce the multifocal polysemy, while the simple trace and retention produce the monofocal polysemy. In the physical world, the production of simple traces is the norm, while that of composite ones is an accident, the accident of compounding simple traces. Without showing the universality of this accident, Derrida cannot claim that the multifocal polysemy is a universal norm dictated by his theory of differance and retention.

Our distinction between monofocal and multifocal polysemy has introduced some complexity into our vocabulary. Perhaps we should eliminate this complexity for the following considerations. The monofocal polysemy is really indistinguishable from the traditional notion of univocity, while the multifocal polysemy coincides with the traditional notion of polysemy. Hence we may, from now on, use the word "polysemy" to designate only multifocal polysemy, and the word "univocity" to designate monofocal polysemy.

In natural languages, polysemy is accepted as a matter of abnormality. If it were a universal norm of any language, that is, if every word in any given language had more than one semantic focus, a serious semantic problem would be created. Let us assume that we are using such an unusual language and try to explain the polysemy of *pharmakon* by designating its semantic foci as "remedy" and "poison." But each of these two words must have more than one semantic focus, whose designation can be made only by using some other words, each of which has more than one semantic focus, and so forth ad infinitum. Neither can the assertion that every word has more than one semantic focus have a univocal meaning, nor can its polysemy be described in univocal terms because they are not available. The acceptance of polysemy as a universal norm inevitably creates a semantic chaos. This chaos can be avoided only by containing polysemy within the framework of univocity. So long as it is so contained, it can be translated into the language of univocity; it is reducible to univocity.

This is the traditional notion of polysemy, which has always accepted the semantic matrix of univocity. Derrida's doctrine of polysemy is not a restatement of this moderate notion. If it were, it would not be Derridian. Since the Derridian polysemy is dictated by his differance as the universal generator of signs, it is the universal norm rather than an abnormal occurrence within the framework of a univocal language. Hence it is irreducible. This irreducible polysemy is called the undecidable polysemy. He explains it with the polysemy of *hymen.* He says that this word means neither virginity nor marriage. The undecidable polysemy is governed by the logic of neither/nor, which is also the logic of between (*entre*).[23]

Derrida has given many different accounts of the undecidable polysemy, and they can be divided into two groups: the semantic and the syntactic accounts. Let us first consider his semantic accounts, which generally involve the notion of semantic oscillation, for example, the meaning of *hymen* oscillates between the two semantic foci of virginity and marriage. This oscillation can take place between any number of semantic foci. A multifocal semantic oscillation is exemplified in Derrida's involved explication of Nietzsche's remark, "Perhaps truth is a woman."[24] The word "truth" can have many different meanings or semantic foci: the dogmatic notion of truth, the critical notion of truth, the skeptical notion of truth, the Christian notion of truth, the pagan notion of truth, etc. Likewise, the word "woman" can be given various semantic foci: the woman as castrating, as castrated, as deceiving, as simulating, as evading, as affirming, as denying, etc. As the two words "truth" and "woman" oscillate between these various semantic foci, the meaning of Nietzsche's statement perpetually changes.

Derrida says that the perpetually oscillating meaning of

Nietzsche's statement can express three fundamentally different propositions or positions. The first of them depicts the
woman as a figure or potentate of falsehood; as such she is
censured, debased, and despised. Derrida calls it a phallogo-
centric deposition of classical metaphysics which equates truth
with the phallus. The second position presents the woman as
the figure or potentate of truth. This is the Christian notion of
truth, the truth that cannot be pierced through by the phallo-
gocentric metaphysics. In this role, Derrida says, she is again
censured, debased, and despised. The second position is another expression of phallogocentrism. The third position is the
double negation of the first two; it negates phallogocentrism
which negates the woman once as truth and once as nontruth.
Through this double negation, "woman is recognized and affirmed as an affirmative power, a dissimulatress, an artist, a
dionysiac."[25] Although these three positions are decidable and
specifiable, Derrida holds, the semantic oscillation of Nietzsche's
statement between these three is undecidable, because it is an
infinite operation whose determination requires an infinite calculus. An infinite calculus is unmanageable and undecidable
for the finite human intellect.[26]

The undecidability of semantic oscillation is no more than
its interminability. As far as semantic operation itself is concerned, it is described in univocal terms. The three positions
are stated in the language of univocity, and this semantic space
of univocal language is the basis for the interminable operation
of semantic oscillation. To that extent, the Derridian polysemy
is dependent on univocity. Semantic oscillation is very much
like the mathematical operation of generating an infinite series
from finite numbers, which is reducible to the mathematics of
finite numbers. Likewise, the polysemy of semantic oscillation
is no more than an extension of univocity; it is reducible to the
operation of a univocal language. Inevitably, a semantic account of Derridian polysemy creates a semantic trap, the trap

of a univocal space as the matrix of its operation. The recognition of this inevitability appears to have induced Derrida to construct a syntactic account.

Derrida's syntactic account is constructed by exploiting Gödel's proof of undecidability. This proof concerns the completeness of formal systems. A proposition (or formula) is said to be decidable if it can be proven or disproven within a formal system; it is said to be undecidable if it can be neither so proven nor so disproven. Gödel has demonstrated that given any formal (or axiomatic) system, there is always an undecidable proposition (or formula) for that system. A formal system is said to be incomplete if it cannot provide a decision procedure for every proposition or its negation. Hence Gödel's proof is the demonstration of the inevitable incompleteness of formal systems, at least, those formal systems rich enough to cover arithmetic or a second-order predicate calculus.

Derrida's use of Gödel's proof is ingenious. The ingenuity lies in his claim that Gödel's is the proof of not semantic but syntactic undecidability. What counts in this proof, Derrida argues, is not the semantic richness, equivocity, or ambiguity of a word, but "the formal or syntactic convention."[27] He goes on to say that this syntactic notion of undecidability governs the undecidability of *hymen* in the *Mimique*. With this he is prepared to give a syntactic account of *hymen*'s undecidability: "Its effect is first of all produced by the syntax which positions the *between* (*entre*) in such a way that the suspense is created only by the place and not by the content of the words."[28] Since the suspension or undecidability of *hymen* depends on not its semantic content but its syntactic position, Derrida concludes, *hymen* can be replaced with any other word without affecting the syntactic suspension or undecidability in question. From this premise of universal syntactic suspension or undecidability, he finally draws the following unfathomable conclusion: "Those words admit in their play contradiction and noncon-

tradiction (and the contradiction and noncontradiction between contradiction and noncontradiction)."[29]

The syntactic position of a word means its position in a
sentence. The word "syntax" generally means the relation of
words in a sentence. In this sense of "syntax," the semantic
content of a word can be contrasted with its syntactic position.
But this notion of syntax has nothing to do with Gödel's proof.
His proof is called a syntactic proof because it concerns the
completeness of uninterpreted formal systems. The interpretation of a formal system is to give its primitive signs some
semantic content. Prior to its semantic interpretations, a formal
system can be called a syntactic system, because it is composed
of uninterpreted primitive signs and the syntactic rules for their
combination and transformation. To prove a formula is to derive it from the primitive signs by using these rules for their
combination and transformation. The undecidable formula is
the one that cannot be so derived; its undecidability is its un-
derivability from a formal system. This relation of an undecidable formula to a formal system can be called a syntactic relation
only because neither the formula nor the formal system is given
semantic interpretations. Hence the syntactic character of
Gödel's proof has nothing to do with ordinary notion of syntax.
Furthermore, his proof cannot open up the magic land of free
play which violates the laws of contradiction and noncontradiction because his proof cannot take a single step without presupposing those laws.

Derrida's syntactic account of his polysemy thus turns out
to be too ingenious to make any sense, or it is too ingenious
because it makes too many senses. It makes too many senses
because it trades on the *double séance* of the word "syntactic."
Hence his syntactic account is no more than an equivocation.
This sort of equivocation may be an inevitable outcome of any
argument given in a language of polysemy. The notion of argument or account usually presupposes univocity; words must

retain the same meanings throughout any argument or account. This identity of meaning cannot be guaranteed by a language of polysemy. The meaning of a polysemous term can change from premise to premise, from premise to conclusion. Such an argument necessarily degenerates into an equivocation. Hence even the equivocation in Derrida's syntactic account is apparently unintentional; it is only a reflection of Derrida's confusion about the notion of syntax.

Paul de Man has made a sustained attempt to salvage Derrida's syntactic account. This is his singular contribution to the Derridian movement. De Man's account is based on the fact that every linguistic expression contains incompatible meanings. He illustrates this point with an example from the TV show "All in the Family." In one of the scenes, Archie Bunker asks his wife Edith to lace his bowling shoes, and she asks him whether he wants them laced over or laced under. Archie replies to her, "What's the difference?" Taking this question literally, Edith patiently explains the difference between the two ways of lacing bowling shoes. But this explanation immensely irritates Archie, because his question was meant not to ask for the explanation, but to express his indifference to the difference. From this example, de Man draws the following moral:

> But suppose that it is a de-bunker rather than a "Bunker," and a de-bunker of the arche (or origin), an archie De-bunker such as Nietzsche or Jacques Derrida for instance, who asks the question "What is the Difference"—and we cannot even tell from his grammar whether he "really" wants to know "what" difference is or just telling us that we shouldn't even try to find out.[30]

De Man explains this indeterminacy of meaning by using J. L. Austin's theory of illocutionary forces. With the same sentence (the constative), Austin has shown, many different speech acts (the performatives) can be performed. Exploiting this idea, de Man says, "A perfectly clear syntactical paradigm (the question) engenders a sentence that has at least two meanings, of which one asserts and the other denies its own illocutionary mode."[31] This account of polysemy may be regarded as syntactic because it is based on the notion of syntactic paradigms. It does not depend on the multiplicity of semantic foci in any given word. It can also be regarded as a rhetorical account because it depends on what de Man calls the rhetorization of grammar:

> The grammatical model of the question becomes rhetorical . . . when it is impossible to decide by grammatical or other linguistic devices which of the two meanings (that can be entirely incompatible) prevails. Rhetoric radically suspends logic and opens up vertiginous possibilities of referential aberration.[32]

Thus de Man introduces the notion of rhetorical suspension: every linguistic expression is suspended between its own conflicting rhetorical or illocutionary forces. He tries to establish the rhetorical space for this suspension by exploiting Derrida's magic word entre. This space is said to lie in "the aporia between performative and constative language" which is "merely a version of the aporia between trope and persuasion." Sometimes he tries to locate this space between the cognitive and the performative functions of language, or between the constative and the performative.[33] There is just one trouble with these magic spaces. Their location is a big mystery; only Paul de Man seems to know their whereabouts.

At any rate, de Man regards this power of generating rhetorical spaces and forces as the essence of literature.[34] But his notion of rhetoric is quite confusing (or polysemous). He regards rhetoric as the province of performatives, because they involve rhetorical questions. He also accepts the traditional notion of rhetoric as the art of persuasion. This second meaning of "rhetoric" may be compatible with its first meaning, because the speech act of persuasion is only a special type of performatives. He also regards the use of figures and tropes as rhetoric on the ground that the art of persuasion depends on their use.

This is done on Nietzsche's authority: "There is no difference between the correct rules of eloquence [*Rede*] and the so-called rhetorical figures."[35]

De Man now maintains that the rhetorical figures or tropes have their own grammar, and that the operation of their grammar also creates the multiplicity of meanings for every figure of speech. He illustrates this point with a passage in which Proust describes a summer reading scene. This description asserts the mastery of metaphor over metonymy, but its persuasive force is derived from the use of metonyms. Hence Proust's metonymic description of metaphor's superiority to metonymy discredits its own assertion. This reflexive operation of rhetorical figures is called the grammar of rhetoric. By generalizing from this example, de Man claims that the grammar of rhetorical figures is a linguistic device for generating conflicting meanings for the same figure or troupe. Hence the grammatization of rhetoric produces the same linguistic effect of polysemy as the rhetorization of grammar.[36] Of course, this final symmetry stands on the dubious *double séance* of the two words "rhetoric" and "grammar."

It is hard to tell whether or not Derrida would regard de Man's account of polysemy as a correct interpretation of his own syntactic account. As we have seen, Derrida's motive for attempting a syntactic account was to avoid the semantic trap of univocity. At least, this motive cannot be fulfilled by de Man's account. The various rhetorical or tropological meanings of a linguistic expression and their relations cannot be mapped out without using the semantic space of a univocal language. For that reason, de Man's rhetorical account falls into the same semantic trap of univocity as Derrida's semantic account. Derrida eventually takes the bold step of getting out of this trap by employing the logic of neither/nor in its most radical form. This is the logic of semantic diffusion and elimination; it eliminates or diffuses a binary distinction. For example, the statement that hymen means neither virginity nor marriage asserts neither that the meaning of the word lies somewhere between virginity and marriage, nor that it oscillates between them. The statement obliterates the distinction between the two semantic foci of virginity and marriage.

Although Derrida has not openly advocated the logic of semantic elimination and diffusion, it appears to be what he has in mind in his invocation of Gödel's proof. He calls it a proof of "*tertium datur*, sans synthèse."[37] In another occasion, he describes his notion of undecidable polysemy as an escape from the philosophical binary opposition without ever constituting a third term, for example:

> The pharmakon is neither the cure nor the poison, neither good nor evil, neither the inside nor the outside, neither speech nor writing; the *supplement* is neither a plus nor a minus, neither an outside nor the complement of an inside, neither an accident nor an essence, etc.; the *hymen* is neither confusion nor distinction, neither identity nor difference, neither consummation nor virginity, neither the veil nor the unveiling, neither the inside nor the outside, etc. . .[38]

The escape from these distinctions can be achieved only by eliminating them, but their elimination turns out to be an ironic terminus for Saussure's notion of linguistic distinction.[39] For it is dictated by Derrida's differance, which has been produced by transforming Saussure's synchronic operation of linguistic distinction into a diachronic operation of perpetual alteration and deferment. In Derrida's hands, the Saussurian operation of producing distinctions has been turned into the operation of eliminating them. This peculiar turn of events may also characterize the fortune of structuralism as a movement. It has thrived by exploiting the notion of binary opposition and distinction; it may shrivel by diffusing all binary distinctions and oppositions.

POLYSEMY AND DECONSTRUCTION

The notion of deconstruction has been regarded as the most serious practical consequence that Derrida's theory of signs and their polysemy has for textual interpretation. Since Derrida had never given a formal exposition of this notion, the program of textual deconstruction has been variously interpreted. It has been compared to Husserl's notion of *Abbau*, Heidegger's notion of *Destruktion*, Lyotard's notion of figural operation, and Merleau-Ponty's notion of hyper-reflexion.[40] Perhaps we can clarify the diffuse notion of deconstruction by treating it as a corollary of Derridian polysemy. That is, the various senses of Derridian polysemy may dictate different programs of textual deconstruction.

Derrida's interpretation of Nietzsche's statement "Perhaps truth is a woman" illustrates the nature of textual deconstruction that is based on the semantic operation of perpetual oscillation. This semantic operation deconstructs the illusory notion of a fixed textual meaning. Every presumed meaning or position is shown to be no more than a simulation and dissimulation. To mistake any meaning or position as the privileged or ultimate one is the hermeneutic somnambulism. Deconstruction destroys this hermeneutic illusion by demonstrating the true nature of every text as a simulacrum which has no determinate essence. In this regard, Derrida compares the nature of text to that of woman:

> There is no such thing as the essence of woman because woman averts, she is averted of herself. Out of the depths, endless and unfathomable, she engulfs and distorts all vestige of essentiality, of identity, of property.[41]

Since she is free of any fixed essence, Derrida says, she is an expert mountebank and an acrobatic artist. Textual deconstruction is her acrobatic art of constantly shifting semantic positions and of never being caught in any fixed position. She is the hymen that can never be pierced by a stylus, because it is only a simulacrum in perpetual motion. This art of perpetual oscillation involves what Derrida calls the dialectical operation of inversion or reversal. Every one of the three positions, which Nietzsche's statement "Perhaps truth is a woman" can take, involves "a violent hierarchy" of values or rather a hierarchical opposition of values, for example, phallogocentrism vs. antiphallogocentrism. Hence to shift one position to another is to invert or reverse a hierarchy of values.[42] But the inversion or reversal can never produce a new fixed hierarchy, because the operation of inversion and reversal is as ceaseless as the operation of textual deconstruction itself.

This perpetual motion of reversal and inversion can also be regarded as an attitude of ambivalence. "Perhaps truth is a woman," Derrida says, reflects, simultaneously or successively, Nietzsche's ambivalent attitude toward woman: (1) he dreaded this castrated woman, (2) he dreaded this castrating woman, and (3) he loved this affirming woman.[43] Derrida compares this ambivalent position of Nietzsche to a spider lost in his own web. The web of ambivalence that is constructed by the program of textual deconstruction is very much like the textual ambivalence and ambiguity that have been the central concern for the New Critics.

Paul de Man's notion of deconstruction is twofold, because it is derived from his two notions of textual polysemy: the rhetorization of grammar and the grammatization of rhetoric. We have seen how the rhetorization of grammar produces two incompatible meanings for Archie Bunker's question "What's the difference?" De Man applies the same rhetorical operation to Yeats's poem "Among School Children," which ends with the question "How can we know the dancer from the dance?" Depending on whether this question is taken literally or rhetorically, he says, the poem can deliver two incompatible meanings, and those two meanings undermine and deconstruct each other.[44] This is the program of textual deconstruction dictated by the rhetorization of grammar.

The deconstruction through the grammatization of rhetoric is illustrated by Proust's metonymic description of the supremacy of metaphor over metonymy, that is, it discredits its own assertion. Another example is Nietzsche's thesis that language is fundamentally rhetoric, that is, it consists of purely rhetorical tricks and devices.[45] At first this philosophical statement appears to expose and demystify the deceptive character of literary language, but this procedure of exposure and demystification applies to Nietzsche's own statement, thereby exposing its own deceptive character. In this case, textual deconstruction means the deconstruction of textual pretense, which is called the rhetorical reversal. This reversal or deconstruction is based on the reflexivity of a statement or a text.

The difference between these two deconstructive procedures is described as follows: the rhetorization of grammar produces indeterminacy or "a suspended uncertainty," whereas the grammatization of rhetoric "seems to reach a truth, albeit by the negative road of exposing an error, a false pretense."[46] The uncertainty or indeterminacy produced by the former can be described as ambiguity or ambivalence. The negative truth realized by the latter is called rhetorical irony or the irony of allegory. This irony is produced by the reflexive character of rhetorical figures, which exposes their own blindness.[47] Evidently, the indeterminacy or ambiguity produced by the rhetorization of grammar is incapable of reflexion and irony.

The most baffling feature of de Man's deconstructive program is the limitation of reflexion to figurative language. Whether figurative or literal, any assertion can be made to refer to itself. However, it is not the assertion or sentence that does or does not have the power of self-reference, but the human subjects that do or do not give that power to it. Hence the notion of textual self-reference implicitly reflects the old-fashioned notion of subjectivity, which can never be found in Derrida's own writings. Even de Man cannot invoke the authority of Derrida in his discussion of the reflexivity of tropes and figures. As to his notion of irony, he has to trace it back all the way to Friedrich Schlegel and other Romantics, the last custodians of old-fashioned ideas in good faith, although it may be more familiar to us through the old fashioned New Critic Cleanth Brooks's notion of poetic irony.

At any rate, the two deconstructive procedures—the rhetorization of grammar and the grammatization of rhetoric—deliver ambiguity and irony, the two standard products of New Criticism. As interpretive procedures, they are indistinguishable from the familiar procedures of New Criticism. De Man's technical terms appear to be no more than new labels for renaming old brands. These technical labels seem to have two different effects. Sometimes they give an appearance of strangeness to old familiar procedures and guard against our natural response of contempt. But most of the time they shroud de Man's deconstructive exegeses in the opaqueness of technical jargon. Most often, these two effects intermingle with each other and generate the profound aura of strange opaqueness and opaque strangeness. And it is hard to tell whether they are due to the rhetorization of grammar or the grammatization of rhetoric.

Paul de Man's program of deconstruction is a rhetorical program, whereas Jacques Derrida's is a semantic one. The former trades on rhetorical polysemy; the latter treads on semantic polysemy. In spite of this difference, they involve the same idea of generating conflicting meanings from the same text, and playing those meanings against each other. It is this play of meaning against meaning, or reading against reading that securely establishes their affinity with New Criticism. But this play of ambiguity and irony cannot be found in the deconstructive program dictated by the logic of eliminatory diffusion. For instance, let us take Derrida's eliminatory interpretation of the word *hymen* in Mallarmé's *Mimique*. His demonstration that this word means neither virginity nor marriage is meant to eliminate the distinction between virginity and marriage, which is generally presupposed as the semantic fundamentum for the play of ambiguity, ambivalence, or irony. In this regard, the eliminatory deconstruction is not only radically novel, but also unequivocally destructive. It destroys the very conceptual or linguistic foundation of a theoretical structure.

This mode of deconstruction can be called positional deconstruction in distinction from textual deconstruction, which produces the play of ambiguity, ambivalence, and irony. The program of positional deconstruction is exemplified by Derrida's deconstruction of Husserl's theory of signs; it is meant to destroy Husserl's position by demonstrating its internal inconsistency. Of this internal operation, Derrida says, "The movements of deconstruction do not destroy structures from the outside."[48] This internal operation can be performed only in the context of univocity, because the notion of internal consistency and inconsistency makes no sense without presupposing univocity. If theoretical terms are not used univocally, any theory can be shown to be consistent and inconsistent with itself at the same time. This presupposition of univocity is the fundamental difference of positional deconstruction from textual deconstruction, which can be performed only in the context of textual polysemy.

Let us now see how internal Derrida's deconstruction of Husserl's theory of signs is. As we saw in chapter 6, Derrida's internal criticism of Husserl is to demonstrate that his notions of expressive and indicative signs are inconsistent. He says that Husserl's notion of expressions as an internal soliloquy is inconsistent with his own admission that all expressions in the context of intersubjective communication function as indications. But this is not a theoretical inconsistency, because my expressive signs can be expressive to me and indicative to you at the same time. Husserl's notion of expression as an instantaneous act is said to be inconsistent with Husserl's later phenomenological view of temporality, which entails the impossibility of an instantaneous act. Again this is not an internal criticism. Husserl's phenomenological view of temporality is no part of his theory of signs, which belongs to his prephenomenological period. As a matter of fact, his phenomenological position is meant to be the rejection of his prephenomenological position. As to Husserl's notion of indicative signs, Derrida says, it is faulty because it fails to recognize their ideal content. This failure can be recognized only by appealing to the nature of indicative signs, which is an outright external appeal.

None of Derrida's criticisms turn out to be truly internal. Whether his criticisms are internal or external is perhaps not essential for the ultimate objective of his positional deconstruction, which is to destroy Husserl's distinction between expressive and indicative signs and all other binary distinctions related to this distinction, such as the sensible vs. the intelligible, existence vs. essence, interiority vs. exteriority, presence vs. absence.[49] As long as Derrida can achieve this deconstructive objective, he does not seem to care whether his methods and arguments are even legitimate or illegitimate. This Machiavellian approach may very well be the essence of the Nietzschean play that is supposedly dictated by his program of deconstruction.

The same Machiavellian maneuvers underlie his deconstruction of the metaphysics of presence. He tries to demonstrate the untenability of logocentrism and its metaphysics of presence on the ground that the notion of full presence is illegitimate. He argues for the illegitimacy of this notion on the ground that it is based on the illegitimate distinction between present and past. Finally he claims the illegitimacy of this distinction by invoking Husserl's phenomenological theory of temporality, which asserts the inseparable connection between present and past. But this theory of temporality clearly recognizes the legitimacy of the notion of full presence. Consequently Derrida's critique of logocentrism turns out to be a series of specious arguments, and the only thing it really accomplishes is the willful elimination of the distinction between present and past.

The elimination of conceptual (or linguistic) distinction produces conceptual (or linguistic) unity. Derrida's rejection of Husserl's distinction between expressive and indicative signs entails a unified theory of signs. As a matter of fact, the absence of this unified theory in Husserl is one of the sources for Derrida's dissatisfaction, and to establish "the essential unity" of all signs is one of his objectives in his critique of Husserl's theory.[50] But Derrida's way of establishing the essential unity of two classes produces logical contradictions.

In his view, Husserl has failed to capture the "essential" unity of all signs, because he has been unable to define their common essence. He has indeed defined the essential unity of indicative signs and that of expressive signs. But to regard these two classes of signs as subclasses of the unified class of signs without defining the latter's essential attribute is to give only a nominal unity of all signs. Derrida claims to provide the "essential" unity of all signs by designating indication and expression as the common attributes of every sign, the two attributes used by Husserl as the defining attributes of indicative and expressive signs respectively. But these two attributes arc incompatible, as we have seen; they cannot be predicated of the same entity without contradiction any more than the attributes of male and female can be.

Derrida seems to handle this problem of logical conflict in two different ways: (1) by eliminating the properties that produce conflict, and (2) by recognizing the inevitability of their conflict. The first of these two methods is used in his handling of the distinction between speaking and writing, which he regards as based on the distinction between presence and absence. His rejection of the primacy of speaking appears to invert the traditional hierarchy of spoken and written words. But this apparent inversion is only his rhetorical maneuver for establishing the essential unity of speaking and writing. Both spoken and written words are equally writing; they perform their signification function through the same property of semiotic independence, which is incompatible with the property of being present or absent. Hence the distinction between these two properties is eliminated.

This maneuver of eliminating the conflicting properties from the notion of a unified class is not acceptable when those properties cannot easily be dispensed with. If they are indispensable, they must be retained in spite of their logical conflict. This is the second of Derrida's two methods for dealing with the conflict of properties in a unified class; it is illustrated in his handling of the distinction between expressive and indicative signs. Husserl proposed this distinction to separate two meanings (*Doppelsinn*) contained in the word "sign."[51] He believed that the dual sense of this word reflects the two different functions, namely, expression (of ideal content) and indication (of an object). Since they are incompatible functions, Husserl assigned them to two different classes. Derrida's rejection of Husserl's distinction between expression and indication brings together those two functions as the common properties of all signs. This creates the *double séance* for Derrida's unified notion of signs.

This *double séance*, as we have seen, contains a logical conflict, namely, the conflict between the primacy of ideal content over indicative function and the primacy of indicative function (repetition) over ideal content. This conflict also appears in Derrida's definition of differance as the conjunction of identity and difference. Although he presents these two properties as independent features of differance, he cannot avoid the problem of their ontological relation in the course of his exposition. When he stresses the identity of a sign as the necessary condition for its iteration and alteration, he asserts the irreducibility of its identity to its difference, which entails the reducibility of its difference to its identity. On the other hand, when he stresses the perpetual deferment of its meaning, he asserts the irreducibility of its difference to its identity, which entails the reducibility of its identity to its difference. As Derrida has said, his notion of differance can really be said to differ from itself, that is, it contradicts itself.

It is hard to tell whether or not Derrida is aware of this logical conflict in his unified theory of signs. But he recognizes the "conflictual character" of his differance as its essential difference from Hegel's *Aufhebung* (synthesis).[52] In Hegel's synthesis, the conflict of properties is resolved by finding a third term. Against this Hegelian maneuver, Derrida holds that such a third term cannot be found, or that the only third term available is *sans synthèse*. This conflictual synthesis defies the law of noncontradiction. Probably for this reason, Richard Rorty has said that Derrida's theory of signification should be regarded not as an attempt to construct a philosophy of language but to demonstrate the impossibility of constructing such a philosophy.[53] Derrida's synthesis without resolution may also underlie what Newton Garver calls "Derrida's unrestrained literary extravagance": "Their possibility [of Husserl's essential distinctions] is their impossibility," "The *infinite* differance is *finite*," or "*A voice without differance, a voice without writing, is at once absolutely dead.*"[54] These overtly contradictory statements are no more than a few surface symptoms of the systematic contradiction that permeates the language produced by Derrida's synthesis without resolution.

This systematic conflict does not arise in Derrida's other method of positional deconstruction, because it rejects the conflicting properties along with the binary distinction itself. This elimination of distinguishing properties generates a different problem, that is, language without distinction. This language obliterates the distinction between speaking and writing, signs and objects, supplements and origins. If everything is a sign, nothing is gained by calling something a sign. If everything is a text, there is nothing startling to hear it said that there is nothing outside the text. Language without discriminations is like Schelling's Absolute, which Hegel compares to the dark night in which all cows are black. In effect, however, this language is not much different from the language saddled with inner contradictions, because contradictions dissolve all distinctions. Either way, the final outcome of Derrida's positional deconstruction is to produce a language or a unity devoid of all distinctions.

Derrida has often derided the notion of unity as a hopelessly outmoded nostalgia of logocentrism. All along, however, he has been hiding his own notion of unity, the unity devoid of distinctions, or saddled with contradictions. Whereas the Derridian unity is negative, the logocentric unity is positive. The former dissolves all distinctions; the latter preserves them all. The distinctions can be preserved by virtue of their positivity, their possibility of being presented. The elimination of this possibility generates the language of absolute negativity, the mechanism for Derrida's negative dialectic and negative specularity. This new language of negative unity is supposed to deliver us from the snares of the metaphysics of presence and from all the evils of her offspring, the positive sciences.

Derrida has inherited this fight against positivity and his longing for the language of total negativity from Heidegger. Heidegger was deeply distressed over the fact that positive sciences investigate the nature of only determinate beings (*Seiende*) and completely overlook the question of their true being (*Sein*). Since *Sein* is totally devoid of any determination, Heidegger calls it nothing (*Nichts*). This ontological notion of *Nichts* should not be confused with the ordinary notion of nothing. The latter is derived by the negation of determinate beings; it is ontologically posterior to the notion of determinate beings. On the other hand, the former is ontologically prior to the notion of determinate beings. Even the notion of negation and denial, which is used in deriving the ordinary notion of nothing from determinate beings, stems from the ontological notion of *Nichts*: "'Nothing' is more original than the Not and negation."[55]

The total indeterminacy of *Sein* presents a serious problem of language for Heidegger's ontological project of posing and responding to the *Seinsfrage*. None of our existing languages can be used for this enterprise. All our languages are languages of determinate beings; they conceal the nature of *Sein* instead of revealing it. As a matter of fact, Heidegger holds, our language of determinate beings has imprisoned us in the domain of *Seiende*, and made us forgetful of *Sein*. The language of *Seiende* can be discarded, if it is possible to design a language of *Sein*. But that is impossible. So Heidegger is forced to use the language of determinate *Seiende* for the disclosure of the indeterminate *Sein*. But his use of this language cannot be a normal one; it has to be stretched and twisted to overcome the difference between *Sein* and *Seiende*. This tortuous linguistic operation has produced what has been known as the Heideggerian word mysticism.

The Heideggerian word mysticism abounds in opaque phrases, oracular expressions, paradoxical statements. They are all about Nothing; they can be said to constitute a metaphysics of absence. They can also be regarded as assertions in a metaphysics of presence, if they are taken as descriptions of *Sein*. The interchangeability of *Sein* and *Nichts*, thus, creates a metaphysical ambiguity, which prompts Derrida to say that Heidegger's enterprise is at once contained within the metaphysics of presence and transgresses it.[56] Derrida has resolved this ambiguity by resolutely dismissing the notion of *Sein* as the lingering nostalgia of logocentric tradition and converted Heidegger's language of *Sein* into his language of total negativity.

The language of total negativity is the language of nirvana. The Derridian maneuver in this language may very well be the ultimate Nietzschean play, but this play is quite different from the plays of semantic oscillation and rhetorical suspension, which are better known as Nietzschean plays. The two are as different as *Sein* and *Seiende*. One is the play of *Sein*; the other is the play of *Seiende*. The latter is the play of perpetual motion and countermotion, which presupposes distinctions and discriminations. The former is the play of nirvana. In the unity of nirvana, there is no longer any distinction between Nietzschean and non-Nietzschean, play and nonplay, motion and nonmotion, is and is not. Neither can there be any more pleasure or displeasure of writing and reading, nor any more anxiety over truth and untruth, sense and nonsense, and contradiction and noncontradiction.

This blissful state of hermeneutic nirvana can no longer admit the distinction between polysemy and monosemy, nor recognize the difference between differance and difference. In this end-state, Derrida's celebrated program of deconstruction cannot avoid the ultimate fate of dissolving its own existence and operation. The same fate of self-dissolution is reserved for all post-structuralist programs of reading and writing. This common fate is dictated by their mysterious semiotic mechanism, language finally released from the verbal karma of reference and representation.

NOTES

ONE: PROGRAMS FOR THE HUMAN SCIENCES

1. Wilhelm Dilthey, *Gesammelte Schriften* (Göttingen: Vandenhoeck, 1924), 5:144, 242–58. Edited by Georg Misch. (Second edition in 1957).

2. W. Windelband, *Geschichte und Naturwissenschaft* (Strassburger Rektoratsrede, 1894), in *Präludien: Aufsätze und Reden zur Philosophie und ihrer Geschichte* (Tübingen: J. C. B. Mohr, 1907), pp. 142–45.

3. F. de Saussure, *Course in General Linguistics* (New York: Philosophical Library, 1959), pp. 6–20. Trans. by Wade Baskin.

4. Roman Jakobson and Morris Halle, *Fundamentals of Language* (The Hague: Mouton, 1956), pp. 37–51. Roman Jakobson et al., *Preliminaries to Speech Analysis*, 2d ed. (Cambridge, Mass.: MIT Press, 1952).

5. Martin Heidegger, *Being and Time* (New York: Harper, 1962), pp. 201–4. Trans. by John Macquarrie and Edward Robinson. My references are to this translation.

6. Claude Lévi-Strauss, *Structural Anthropology* (New York: Basic Books, 1963), pp. 33–34. Trans. by Claire Jacobson and Brooke Grundfest Schoepf.

7. Lévi-Strauss, *Structural Anthropology*, p. 33.

8. Jakobson and Halle, *Fundamentals of Language*, pp. 37–51.

9. A. J. Greimas, *Sémantique structurale* (Paris: Larousse, 1966).

10. Roman Jakobson, "Concluding Statement: Linguistics and Poetics," in *Style in Language* (Cambridge, Mass.: MIT Press, 1960), p. 353. Ed. by Thomas A. Sebeok.

11. There are many other obvious examples which cannot fit into the schema of binary opposition: the three tenses of verbs, three or four genders of nouns in some languages, three grammatical persons (the first, the second, and the third person). Some languages have three voices for their verbs, the active, the passive, and the middle voice.

12. Many champions of structuralism have thought that their structural prin-

ciple of binary opposition has been emphatically vindicated by the ascendancy of the binary computer, a prominent child of mathematical logic, which has supposedly replaced the outmoded Aristotelian logic. This view is erroneous on two counts. First, binary opposition cannot be programmed into a binary computer; the former takes three values, while the latter takes only two. Second, most of Aristotle's logical insights still remain unsurpassed even by mathematical logic, and his distinction between contrariety and contradiction is one of those insights.

13. Immanuel Kant, *The Critique of Pure Reason*, A264–65 = B320–21, A282 = B338; "Attempt at Introducing Negative Qualities into Philosophy," in Gabriele Rabel, *Kant* (Oxford: Clarendon Press, 1963), pp. 46–50.

14. This fundamental logical error in Hegel's system is the central theme of Benedetto Croce's *What Is Living and What is Dead in the Philosophy of Hegel* (London: Macmillan, 1915), trans. by Douglas Ainslie. For a good discussion of logical problems in Hegel's dialectical method, see J. N. Findlay, *Hegel: Re-Examination* (London: Allen and Unwin, 1958), pp. 58–82.

15. Even such a sympathetic champion of Lévi-Strauss as Edmund Leach says that the linguistic model Lévi-Strauss has borrowed from Roman Jakobson's structural linguistics is now largely outmoded. This criticism is made on the ground that the structure of language now accepted in today's structural linguistics is too complex to be analyzed by Jakobson's simple schema of binary oppositions. Leach does not yet recognize the logical confusion between binary opposition and binary distinction, which has contaminated Jakobson's allegedly universal schema. See, for details, Leach, *Claude Lévi-Strauss* (New York: Viking, 1970), p. 122.

16. Lévi-Strauss, *Structural Anthropology*, pp. 47–48.

17. Ibid., pp. 60–61.

18. Claude Lévi-Strauss, *The Savage Mind* (Chicago: University of Chicago Press, 1966). Trans. from the French.

19. Lévi-Strauss, *Structural Anthropology*, pp. 62–63.

20. Paul Ricoeur has labeled Lévi-Strauss' structuralism a Kantianism without a transcendental subject; *The Conflict of Interpretations* (Evanston: Northwestern University Press, 1974), p. 52, ed. by Don Ihde. This label indeed applies to his psychological structuralism, but not to his linguistic structuralism. Kant's transcendental philosophy is a version of psychological structuralism; he appeals to the structure of the human mind in explaining the structure of our experience.

21. It may be said that the principle of homology or equivalence can be found in its embryonic form in *Structural Anthropology*. There Lévi-Strauss often talks of the four-term relation which is constituted by the conjunction of two bipolar relations (e.g., p. 49). This four-term relation is the fundamental matrix even for his analysis of the so-called Oedipus myth, although it may appear to involve a little more complex structure than a four-term relation (pp. 213–16). This structural device of conjoining two polarities into a four-term relation may appear to play the same structural role that is played by the

principle of homology in *The Savage Mind*. But the principle of conjunction can be accounted for without introducing the notion of homology. It can be regarded as another case of binary opposition, that is, the binary opposition between two polarities or its operation on the second level.

22. Lévi-Strauss, *The Savage Mind*, p. 93.

23. In structural linguistics, the interrelation between binary oppositions is established not by the principle of homologies or equivalences but by scientific mapping and charting. The latter is a univocal maneuver; the former is not. The principle of homologies is unacceptable in any scientific discourse, because it is not univocal.

24. Lévi-Strauss, *Structural Anthropology*, pp. 213–29.

25. Roman Jakobson and Claude Lévi-Strauss, "Les Chats de Charles Baudelaire," *L'Homme* (1962), 2:5–21.

26. Lévi-Strauss, *The Savage Mind*, pp. 232–34.

27. Noam Chomsky, *Cartesian Linguistics* (New York: Harper, 1966).

TWO: TYPES OF PSYCHOLOGICAL STRUCTURE

1. Claude Lévi-Strauss, *The Savage Mind* (Chicago: University of Chicago Press, 1966). Trans. from the French.

2. Ibid., pp. 35–74.

3. Ibid., p. 233.

4. G. E. R. Lloyd, *Polarity and Analogy: Two Types of Argumentation in Early Greek Thought* (Cambridge: Cambridge University Press, 1966).

5. Lloyd, *Polarity and Analogy*, p. 95.

6. Ibid., p. 35.

7. Lévi-Strauss, *The Savage Mind*, p. 93.

8. Ibid., p. 94.

9. Lloyd, *Polarity and Analogy*, p. 103.

10. Ibid., p. 100.

11. The Neo-Confucianists Chou Tun-i (1017–1073) and Chu Hsi (1130–1200) tried to reduce the dualism of yin and yang to a monism by claiming that yin and yang had been generated from the Great Ultimate. This Neo-Confucian monism was later elaborated into a systematic metaphysical doctrine of universal genesis: In the beginning, there is Nonultimate, which generates the Great Ultimate, which generates yin and yang, which generate four figures (old yin and young yin, and old yang and young yang), which generate the eight trigrams. The sixty-four symbols of *I Ching* are then produced by the permutation and combination of these eight trigrams.

12. Socrates has no technical term for definition. He pursues definitions by asking what-questions: "What is justice?" "What is courage?" "What is virtue?" etc.

13. W. K. C. Guthrie points out the similarity between Socrates' search for definitions and Confucius' campaign for the rectification of names; A History of Greek Philosophy (Cambridge: Cambridge University Press, 1969), 3:488n. Confucius' rectification of names indeed played a similar role to Socrates' definition. The former was instrumental in transforming pre-Confucian Chinese thought, which was dominated by yin-yang, into a complex system, just as the latter was instrumental in transforming polarity-ridden pre-Socratic thought into an architectonic system.

14. Socrates has no technical term for a universal or essence. His expression kata olou was contracted into Aristotle's katholou, which is translated as "universal."

15. Lévi-Strauss, The Savage Mind, pp. 1–33. Lévi-Strauss expresses the same point in saying, "The elements of mythical thought similarly lie half-way between percepts and concepts."

16. Ibid., p. 106.

17. J. D. Denniston, Greek Prose Style (Oxford: Clarendon Press, 1952), p. 60.

18. These general traits of pre-Socratic thinkers often cannot be found in one exceptional group, the Eleatics. Their style of expression and discourse was more like that of the Sophists than that of other pre-Socratics. Among the pre-Socratics, they alone abhorred the use of polarities and analogies in their discourses; for example, Parmenides maintained that Being is One which cannot permit any contraries. To the best of my knowledge, the Eleatics were the first to distinguish thought and being. This surely indicates a close affinity between them and the Sophists. W. K. C. Guthrie mentions "a profound influence" the Eleatics had on the development of Sophistic tradition (History of Greek Philosophy, 3:47), but no one has yet explored the exact nature of this influence.

19. On these technical matters, I am relying on the expert judgment of my friend David Francis.

20. In Structural Anthropology (New York: Basic Books, 1963), p. 312, Lévi-Strauss talks of the "order of orders," that is, the overall social order which embraces the different types of social order, such as the kinship system, the economic system, the political system, etc. But he does not clarify whether this order of orders is meant to be a system of coordination or of subordination. In one important respect, the structure of primitive cultures appears to be a system of subordination: in many instances, a primitive society is divided into two moieties, each of which is then further divided into three or four tribes. Hence the social order seems to employ two levels of organization.

21. Lévi-Strauss, The Raw and the Cooked: Introduction to a Science of Mythology (New York: Harper, 1969), 1:33–78. Trans. by John and Doreen Weightman.

22. Lévi-Strauss, Structural Anthropology, pp. 232–34; G. Charbonnier, ed., Conversations with Claude Lévi-Strauss (London: Jonathan Cape, 1969), pp. 35–47.

23. On this point, Lévi-Strauss has often been mistaken to mean that prim-

itive societies have no history and that history is a prerogative of advanced societies. This misunderstanding has been partly due to his own careless language such as "people without history." To correct this sort of misrepresentation and misunderstanding, he says, "We should not, then, draw a distinction between 'societies with no history' and 'societies which have history'. In fact, every human society has a history. . . ." Charbonnier, Conversations with Lévi-Strauss, p. 39.

24. As we shall see in the next chapter, this is one of the main criticisms Terence Turner makes against Lévi-Strauss' structural analysis of the Oedipus myth; see Turner, "Narrative Structure and Mythopoesis: A Critique and Reformulation of Structuralist Concepts of Myth, Narrative and Poetics," Arethusa (1977), 10:140. Lévi-Strauss' transformational account of myths has been given in many different places, but his Mythologiques, 3 vols. (Paris: Librairie Plan 1964, 1966, 1968), is the most extensive one.

25. Edmund Leach, ed., The Structural Study of Myth and Totemism (London: Tavistock, 1967), p. 23.

26. For example, Auguste Comte in Cours de philosophie positive, vol. 4; Wilhelm Dilthey in Einleitung in die Geisteswissenschaften; and lately Paul Ricouer in The Conflict of Interpretations (Evanston: Northwestern University Press, 1974), pp. 40–41.

27. By Rupert of Deutz in De sancta trinitate et operibus eius and Joachim of Floris in Concordia vetris et novi testamenti.

28. Stephen Usher, The Historians of Greece and Rome (New York: Taplinger, 1970), p. 108.

29. F. W. Walbank, "Polybius," in T. A. Dorey, ed., Latin Historians (London: Routledge, 1966), pp. 57–58.

30. Ludwig Edelstein, The Idea of Progress in Classical Antiquity (Baltimore: Johns Hopkins University Press, 1967).

31. E. R. Dodds, The Ancient Concept of Progress and Other Essays on Greek Literature and Belief (Oxford: Clarendon Press, 1973), pp. 1–25.

32. Perhaps this sense of value-neutral movement can be better expressed by the word "directional" rather than "progressional," but "directional" can be too inclusive, since the range of its application can be coextensive with that of the word "irreversible." That is, any irreversible sequence of events can be regarded as a directional one, including a nonprogressional sequence.

33. Dodds, Ancient Concept of Progress, p. 20.

34. Edelstein, Idea of Progress in Classical Antiquity, p. 3.

35. There can be one more distinction in the notion of historical progression: it can be either open-ended or closed-ended. But this distinction has no immediate relevance to our discussion of Lévi-Strauss' structuralism.

THREE: STRUCTURE OF A GREEK MYTH

1. Lévi-Strauss, Structural Anthropology (New York: Basic Books, 1963), p. 214. Trans. by Claire Jacobson and Brooke Grundfest Schoepf.

2. *The Savage Mind* (Chicago: University of Chicago Press, 1966), p. 69. Trans. from the French.

3. Terence Turner, "Narrative Structure and Mythopoesis: A Critique and Reformulation of Structuralist Concepts of Myth, Narrative and Poetics," *Arethusa* (1977), 10:103–63.

4. Ibid., p. 109.

5. In most religions, the doctrine of gods and goddesses is meant to answer two related questions: What is the ultimate nature of the world, and what is the ultimate origin and destiny of man? The myths of creation (of man and the world) are meant to give specific answers to these questions, which are ultimately the questions of birth and origin. For example, the doctrine that man shall return to dust because he has come from it, or that he shall return to nirvana because he has come from it, is an attempt to answer the question of man's destiny in terms of his origin and birth.

Even Plato follows this line of thinking, although he repudiates ancient Greek religion and its myths. He says that our noble self is more akin to the gods than to beasts and should feel more at home in the eternal world of Forms than in the temporal world. With his doctrine of the recollection of Forms, he thinks, he can prove the divine origin of our souls. Since our souls came from the divine world, he argues, they are destined to return to it.

6. Lévi-Strauss, *Structural Anthropology*, p. 216.

7. Turner, "Narrative Structure and Mythopoesis," p. 111.

8. Ibid., p. 140.

9. Lévi-Strauss, *Structural Anthropology*, p. 217.

10. Lévi-Strauss' *Mythologiques* can be considered as his most extensive attempt to prove the uniformity of human nature through a structural analysis of myths. As Edmund Leach points out, the massive volumes of *Mythologiques* are designed to prove the thesis "that when we really get down to the roots of the matter the interdependence of logical structure and emotional response is much the same everywhere—for the nature of man is everywhere the same." *Claude Lévi-Strauss* (New York: Viking, 1970), p. 126.

11. Lévi-Strauss, *Tristes Tropiques* (New York, Atheneum, 1975), p. 57. Trans. by John and Doreen Weightman.

12. Lévi-Strauss, *The Savage Mind*, p. 12.

13. Ibid.

14. Sigmund Freud, *Civilization and its Discontents* (New York: Norton, 1961), pp. 14, 24, 30, 70. Trans. and ed. by James Strachey.

15. Karl Marx and Frederick Engels, *The German Ideology*, Part One (New York: International Publishers, 1978), pp. 42, 88–89. Ed. with Introduction by C. J. Arthur.

16. There can be a collision between two physical objects or forces, for example, two cars. But it is absurd to call it a conflict, or say that there is a conflict between two cars. The notion of conflict presupposes a teleological or intentional world for its semantic context; the notion of collision presupposes a nonteleological or nonintentional world for its semantic context. The word

"equilibrium" can be used in both types of semantic context, that is, an equilibrium can be said to obtain between two physical objects or forces as well as two social agencies or forces. Nevertheless, the former equilibrium cannot be regarded as the resolution of a conflict, while the latter can be so regarded.
17. Lévi-Strauss, The Savage Mind, p. 69. Taking seriously the ultimacy of structure in Lévi-Strauss' analysis of myths, K. O. L. Burridge says: "Really what a myth 'is about' or is 'telling' us or its bearers is, for Lévi-Strauss, a secondary consideration, a by-product of the main point at issue: the structure of articulate thought"; see his "Lévi-Strauss and Myth," in Edmund Leach, ed., The Structural Study of Myth and Totemism (London:Tavistock, 1967), p. 100.

FOUR: STRUCTURE OF A FRENCH SONNET

1. Roman Jakobson and Claude Lévi-Strauss, "'Les Chats' de Charles Baudelaire," L'Homme (1962), 2:5–21. An English translation of this essay by Katie Furness-Lane can be found in Michael Lane, ed., Introduction to Structuralism (New York: Basic Books, 1970), pp. 202–21. From the many critical discussions of this essay, I will cite two representative examples: one largely in favor of Jakobson's and Lévi-Strauss' structural approach, and the other against it. The former is James A. Boon, From Symbolism to Structuralism (New York: Harper and Row, 1972), pp. 38–61; the latter is Michael Riffaterre, "Describing Poetic Structures: Two Approaches to Baudelaire's Les Chats," in Jacques Ehrmann, ed. Structuralism (Garden City: Doubleday, 1970), pp. 188–230, originally issued as Yale French Studies 36 and 37 (1966).
2. The "demonstration proper" ends on p. 17 of the essay, and the "recapitulation" begins on the same page after a line of blank space, and ends on p. 20.
3. Jakobson and Lévi-Strauss, "'Les Chats' de Charles Baudelaire," p. 7.
4. The complete independence of the rhyme and punctuation schemes can be illustrated by the following hypothetical considerations. Let us assume that each of the two quatrains were composed of two or three sentences rather than one. This change in the punctuation scheme could not affect the rhyme scheme. In the 1847 La Corsaire text, as our authors point out, the sestet was divided into two sentences, whereas it constitutes one sentence in the present test (ibid., p. 8). But the rhyme scheme of the La Corsaire text was the same as it is in the present text.
5. Jakobson and Lévi-Strauss, "'Les Chats' de Charles Baudelaire," p. 17.
6. Ibid., pp. 7–8.
7. Ibid., p. 8.
8. It was clearly an oversight on the part of our authors to include the noun reins in this group. Although it is a subject term, it is not related to an object term because its verb is intransitive. Hence it cannot have the subject-object relation.

9. Jakobson and Lévi-Strauss, "'Les Chats' de Charles Baudelaire," p. 18.

10. Our authors' characterization of the second quatrain incorrectly presupposes that in the second quatrain the cats are placed in darkness. The second quatrain says that the cats are searching for the silence and the horror of darkness. Therefore, it is more accurate to say that the second quatrain defines the cats in terms of the darkness they are seeking.

11. In Jakobson's structural linguistics, the distinction of metaphor and metonym plays a far more significant role than a rhetorical distinction. These two rhetorical figures represent two most fundamental linguistic functions, selection and combination. Jakobson holds that every utterance or sentence involves two acts of *selecting* words and *combining* them into a meaningful assertion.

The act of combination establishes the contiguity of words in a sentence. Hence the act of combination can be said to be governed by the principle of contiguity. The act of selection involves a class or group of words from which the selection is made. Since this group is established by the resemblance relation of those words to each other, the act of selection can be said to be governed by the principle of resemblance. For these reasons, the principles of resemblance and contiguity are not only principles of rhetorical figures but the most pervasive linguistic principles governing all linguistic events. For details, see Roman Jakobson and Morris Halle, *Fundamentals of Language* (The Hague: Mouton, 1956), pp. 58–82.

12. It is not altogether accurate to admit this rhetorical progression or transition. It is more accurate to say that the third stanza asserts the resemblance of the cats to the sphinxes, and that the contiguity of the cats to *solitudes* is contained in this resemblance. The third stanza asserts the resemblance of the cats not to the sphinxes pure and simple, but to those sphinxes *allongés au fond des solitudes*. The contiguity of the sphinxes to *solitudes* is presented as an essential step in asserting their resemblance to the cats. Hence this contiguity is already contained in the metaphorical relation depicted by the third stanza.

13. Jakobson and Lévi-Strauss, "'Les Chats' de Charles Baudelaire," p. 9. The binary principle is involved even in the ternary thematic analysis of the sonnet. This principle is first used in setting up the thematic opposition, and then in relating the opposition to its resolution. This double use of the binary principle produces a complex binary system rather than a simple one. Such a complex binary system involves a more complex imbalance than any simple binary system can ever create.

14. Claude Lévi-Strauss, *The Savage Mind* (Chicago: University of Chicago Press, 1966), p. 69. Trans. from the French.

15. Jakobson and Lévi-Strauss, "'Les Chats' de Charles Baudelaire," p. 9.

16. Ibid., p. 10.

17. Ibid., p. 11.

18. Ibid., pp. 11–12.

19. Ibid., p. 14.

20. Ibid., p. 12.

21. Ibid., p. 13.
22. Ibid., p. 14.
23. Ibid., p. 17.
24. Ibid., pp. 18–19.
25. Ibid., p. 19. "Le but de cette modulation est de résoudre l'opposition implicite ou explicite depuis de début du poème, entre démarche métaphorique et démarche métonymique. La solution apportée par le sizain final consiste à transférer cette opposition au sein même de la métonymie, tout en l'exprimant par des moyens métaphoriques."
26. Ibid.
27. Ibid., p. 20.
28. Ibid.
29. Ibid., p. 21.
30. Ibid., p. 19.
31. Ibid., p. 15.
32. Ibid., p. 17.
33. When we compare the purely structural versions with the thematic ones, we find one striking coincidence. With one intriguing exception, all the purely structural versions belong to the demonstration proper, while all the thematic versions belong to the recapitulation. The single exception is the thematic version of the isometric analysis, which appears at the end of the demonstration proper. This textual evidence may support the following conjecture. In the demonstration proper, our authors relied on the purely structural approach and tried out their thematic approach only at the end of it. Probably better satisfied with this approach, they stayed with it exclusively in the recapitulation and abandoned the purely structural approach. It is equally plausible that they decided to write the recapitulation mainly as a way of doing over the analysis of the sonnet with the thematic approach which they had tried out only at the end of the demonstration proper.
34. Jakobson and Lévi-Strauss, "'Les Chats' de Charles Baudelaire," pp. 11–12.
35. Our authors claim an ambiguity in the expression *orgueil de la maison*: it can mean either "that the cats, proud of their home, are the incarnation of that pride, or that the house, proud of its feline inhabitants, tries, like Erebus, to domesticate them" (p. 15). Their claim of ambiguity can be better expressed by saying that *les chats* can be regarded either as the semantic subject of *orgueil de la maison* or as its semantic object. But this ambiguity does not seem to be in the text; the first stanza clearly presents *les chats* as the semantic object of *orgueil de la maison*.

The semantic subject and object should be distinguished from the syntactic subject and object, which are sometimes known as the grammatical subject and object of a sentence. The semantic subject and object are not related to sentential functions. For example, in the sentence "Cats are loved by scholars," the word "cats" is its syntactic subject. Semantically, however, the same word indicates an object, that is, the object of love. Whereas the syntactic subject and object are determined by the syntactic relation of words in a sentence, the semantic subject and object are determined by their semantic relations.

36. A good example of the charge of irrelevance against structural analysis can be found in Michael Riffaterre, "Describing Poetic Structures: Two Approaches to Baudelaire's *Les Chats*."

FIVE: STRUCTURALIST MARXISM

1. Lévi-Strauss, "Le Triangle culinaire," *L'Arc* (1965), 26:19–29.

2. Edmund Leach makes this comparison to demonstrate not the difference but the similarity between the culinary triangle and the traffic-signal triangle; Leach, *Claude Lévi-Strauss* (New York: Viking, 1970), pp. 19–20.

3. Claude Lévi-Strauss, *Structural Anthropology* (New York: Basic Books, 1963), p. 229.

4. K. O. L. Burridge, "Lévi-Strauss and Myth," in Edmund Leach, ed., *The Structural Study of Myth and Totemism* (London: Tavistock, 1967), pp. 91–115, esp. pp. 102–5.

5. Burridge, "Lévi-Strauss and Myth," p. 105.

6. This remark appears in the Afterword to the second German edition of *Das Kapital*. The quoted translation is from Robert Tucker, ed., *The Marx-Engels Reader* (New York: Norton, 1972), p. 198.

7. "Contradiction and Overdetermination," included in Louis Althusser, *For Marx* (New York: Random House, 1970), pp. 87–128. Trans. by Ben Brewster.

8. Louis Althusser and Étienne Balibar, *Reading "Capital"* (London: New Left Books, 1970), p. 186. Trans. by Ben Brewster.

9. Althusser and Balibar, *Reading "Capital,"* p. 187.

10. Althusser, *For Marx*, pp. 94–100.

11. Ibid., pp. 95–96.

12. Ibid., p. 99.

13. Georg Lukács, "What is Orthodox Marxism," in *History and Class Consciousness* (Cambridge, Mass.: MIT Press, 1971), pp. 1–26, trans. by Rodney Livingstone; Karl Korsch, "Marxism and Philosophy," in *Marxism and Philosophy* (New York: Modern Reader, 1970), pp. 29–97. Lukács calls the proponents of economic determinism "the vulgar materialists" and "the vulgar Marxists."

14. Althusser and Balibar, *Reading "Capital,"* p. 97.

15. Ibid., p. 99.

16. Ibid., p. 100.

17. Ibid., pp. 209–308.

18. Ibid., p. 215.

19. Ibid., p. 99.

20. Ibid., pp. 91–92.

21. Ibid., p. 108.

22. Miriam Glucksmann presents a fine comparison of Lévi-Strauss' structuralism and Althusser's Marxism in her *Structuralist Analysis in Contemporary Social Thought: A Comparison of the Theories of Claude Lévi-Strauss and Louis Althusser* (London: Routledge, 1974). However, she does not establish a clear distinction between the two meanings of the word "structure," that is, between that of Lévi-Strauss and that of Althusser. Consequently, the expression "structuralist analysis" in her work has the same meaning as "structural analysis," that is, the analysis of any structured whole.

Althusser employs some empressions which may sound uniquely structuralist, for example, "metonymic causality" (*Reading "Capital,"* p. 188). By this expression he means partial causality or partial determination, which goes together with his notion of relative autonomy of the different social levels. To say that their causality is metonymic means that it is a partial determination rather than a total one. Although the word "metonymy," along with "metaphor," has been extensively used by structuralists, its conceptual content has nothing to do with the unique conceptual mechanism of structuralism. That is, it can be readily replaced by a nonstructuralist term.

SIX: SEMIOLOGY AND GRAMMATOLOGY

1. These structuralist projects and experiments have been presented under the general rubric of structuralist poetics. The nature of this structuralist movement in literary criticism has been the topic of many articles and books, for example, Frederic Jameson, *The Prison-House of Language* (Princeton: Princeton University Press, 1972); Robert Scholes, *Structuralism in Literature* (New Haven: Yale Univeristy Press, 1974); Jonathan Culler, *Structuralist Poetics* (Ithaca: Cornell University Press, 1975); Terence Hawkes, *Structuralism and Semiotics* (Berkeley: University of California Press, 1977). My own account of structuralist poetics will be given in a sequel to this volume.

2. Roland Barthes, *Elements of Semiology* (London: Jonathan Cape, 1967), pp. 26–28. Trans. by Annette Lavers and Colin Smith.

3. F. de Saussure, *Course in General Linguistics* (New York: Philosophical Library, 1959), p. 16. Trans. by Wade Baskin.

4. Ibid., p. 17.

5. Barthes, *Elements of Semiology*, pp. 13–25.

6. Ibid., p. 41.

7. Ibid.

8. Roland Barthes complicates his structural analysis of cultural objects by using another Saussurian distinction, namely, the one between syntagmatic and associative relationships (ibid., pp. 58–63). By using this distinction, he

produces substantially the same result as he has done by using the distinction between *langue* and *parole*. However, he does not tell us how these two Saussurian distinctions are related to each other. Instead, he only observes certain similarity between them: "The associative plane has evidently a very close connection with 'the language [*langue*],' while the syntagm is nearer to speech [*parole*]" (p. 59).

The distinction between syntagmatic and associative relationships is the distinction between syntactic and semantic relationships. Syntagmatic relationships are the rules of combination (combining words) in constructing a sentence; associative relationships are the rules of associating them in terms of their meanings. Both relationships are operative in both *langue* and *parole*. Rules of combination and association can both be applied to objects of nature as well as culture.

9. Jacques Derrida, *Of Grammatology* (Baltimore: Johns Hopkins University Press, 1976). Trans. by Gayatri Spivak. Derrida's theory of written signs also occurs in his other works, notably, *Speech and Phenomena and Other Essays on Husserl's Theory of Signs* (Evanston: Northwestern University Press, 1973), trans. by David Allison; and *Writing and Difference* (Chicago: University of Chicago Press, 1978), trans. by Alan Bass.

10. Jacques Derrida, "Signature Event Context," *Glyph* (1977), 1:181.

11. Ibid., p. 180.

12. Ibid.

13. Ibid., p. 183.

14. Derrida says that the so-called original or natural language "had itself always been a writing" (*Of Grammatology*, p. 56). See also "Signature Event Context," p. 182.

15. Derrida, *Speech and Phenomena*, p. 93.

16. Because of this misunderstanding, Derrida's theory of writing has been said to be "the reversal of everything valorized by McLuhanism." See Jameson, *The Prison-House of Language*, pp. 175–76. About his own project, Derrida says, "It is not a question of rehabilitating writing in the narrow sense, nor of reversing the order of dependence when it is evident." (*Of Grammatology*, p. 56.)

17. Derrida, *Of Grammatology*, p. 9.

18. Derrida's extension of the words "writing" and "text" is continuous with the structuralists' general tendency of overextending linguistic categories to the nonlinguistic domains. Derrida himself recognizes this tendency and calls it the "inflation of the sign 'language'" (*Of Grammatology*, p. 6). It is linguistic or verbal inflation.

19. Derrida, "Signature Event Context," pp. 181–85. Saussure has also recognized the affinity of *langue* to writing: "*Langue* is a system of signs that express ideas, and is therefore comparable to a system of writing, the alphabet of deaf-mutes, symbolic rites, polite formulas, military signals, etc." Saussure, *Course in General Linguistics*, p. 16. In the Saussurian linguistics, a system of writing is not the same as writing or a script; the former is a *langue* and the latter a *parole*.

20. Saussure, *Course in General Linguistics*, p. 14.

21. Ibid., pp. 18–19. Saussure claims not only the necessity of *langue* for *parole*, but the necessity of *parole* for *langue*. He stresses their mutual dependence.

22. Ibid., p. 19.

23. This critique is given in Derrida's *Speech and Phenomena*. Husserl's theory of signs is given in his *Logical Investigations*, 2 vols. (London: Routledge and Kegan Paul, 1970), trans. from the second German edition by J. N. Findlay.

24. "The First Investigation," sec. 1.

25. Ibid., sec. 11.

26. Ibid., sec. 12.

27. Ibid., sec. 2.

28. Ibid.

29. As quoted by Derrida in *Speech and Phenomena*, pp. 37–38.

30. Derrida, *Speech and Phenomena*, pp. 22, 32.

31. Ibid., pp. 35, 81.

32. Ibid., p. 70.

33. Ibid., p. 73.

34. Ibid., p. 43.

35. Ibid., p. 59.

36. Ibid., pp. 79–86.

37. Husserl's theory of internal time-consciousness is given in his *Phenomenology of Internal Time-Consciousness* (Bloomington: Indiana University Press, 1964). Trans. by James Churchill.

38. "Bracketing off" is a technical term in Husserl's phenomenology, and it means suspending judgement. It is also called phenomenological reduction. The consciousness that performs phenomenological reduction and still remains after it is called the transcendental consciousness or ego. That is, the transcendental consciousness brackets off everything uncertain or doubtful; it is the consciousness of only what is absolutely certain.

39. Derrida, *Speech and Phenomena*, pp. 95–96.

40. Ibid., p. 72.

41. Ibid., p. 64.

42. Ibid., p. 88.

43. Derrida, *Of Grammatology*, p. 70.

44. Derrida, *Speech and Phenomena*, p. 156.

45. John Searle, "Reiterating the Differences: A Reply to Derrida," *Glyph* (1977), 1:200. Derrida's complaint about this confusion is expressed in his "Limited Inc," *Glyph* (1977), 2:187–91.

46. Derrida, *Speech and Phenomena*, p. 154.

47. Derrida, "Limited Inc," p. 190.

48. Martin Heidegger, *Being and Time* (New York: Harper and Row, 1962), pp. 172–88. Trans. by John Macquarrie and Edward Robinson.

49. Ibid., pp. 47–48. Heidegger's condemnation of the ontological view that whatever truly exists is located in the present moment is the source for Derrida's derision of the metaphysics of presence. This derision can, however,

be ambiguous, because the word "presence" can have two different meanings. It can denote (1) the relation of an object to time, whatever is located in the present moment, or (2) the relation of an object to a subject, that is, what is present to someone. The former is an ontological notion of presence; the latter is an epistemological one.

Heidegger was aware of these two meanings of "presence" and used two words *Anwesenheit* and *Anwesen*. The former term is used mainly in his *Being and Time* to express his view that all previous ontological attempts have been misdirected by the misconception of being as being in the present (*Anwesenheit*). In his later writings he revises this view and holds that the pre-Socratic thinkers such as Parmenides and Heraclitus did not make this ontological mistake and that the misconception was initiated by Plato and Aristotle and perpetuated thereafter. He also introduces the notion of *Anwesen*, which is quite different from the *Anwesenheit* of Aristotle's *ousia*. *Anwesen* is the presenting or disclosure of *Sein* (Being) to *Dasein*; this relation of *Sein* and *Dasein* is sometimes called *Lichtung* (the clearing). Without this privileged relation with *Sein*, *Dasein* can never know the ontological difference between *Sein* and *Seiende* (the existent).

Since the word "presence" has these two meanings, Derrida's expression "the metaphysics of presence" can mean two things, that is, the metaphysics of *Anwesenheit* and that of *Anwesen*. This difference can be illustrated by the three examples Jonathan Culler gives in his explanation of the metaphysics of presence: (1) the presence of the self to itself (the Cartesian self-presence), (2) the presence of the present instant, and (3) the presence of meaning or intention to the subject. See Culler, "Jacques Derrida," in John Sturrock, ed., *Structuralism and Since: From Lévi-Strauss to Derrida* (Oxford: Oxford University Press, 1979), pp. 161–62. The last is an example of *Anwesen*; the second is an example of *Anwesenheit*; the first is an example of the conflation of the two. Derrida has made no attempt to discriminate *Anwesen* from *Anwesenheit*, probably because he condemns the metaphysics of both *Anwesen* and *Anwesenheit*, whereas Heidegger condemns only one of them and exalts the other.

50. Derrida, *Speech and Phenomena*, p. 139.

51. Ibid., p. 143.

52. Ibid., p. 80; *Of Grammatology*, p. 166.

53. For example, Lionel Abel has pointed out the resemblance of Derrida's theory to Nelson Goodman's nominalism. For Newton Garber's discussion of this point, see Derrida, *Speech and Phenomena*, p. xxviii.

54. Derrida, *Speech and Phenomena*, p. 103.

55. Derrida, "Limited Inc," p. 194.

56. Derrida, *Speech and Phenomena*, p. 13.

57. Ibid., p. 154.

58. Derrida, *Of Grammatology*, p. 61. For the inevitability of endless mediation of a sign by another sign by the third sign and so forth, Derrida cites the authority of Charles Peirce (*Of Grammatology*, p. 50).

59. For the moderate version of Derrida's position, See "Limited Inc," p. 184.

60. Saussure, *Course in General Linguistics*, p. 114.

61. Ibid., p. 66. A sound-image is not the same as a sound. A sound is a particular and a sound-image is a universal. The former is a physical entity; the latter is a psychological entity. The relation of a sound-image and a sound is that of type and token.

62. Ibid., p. 114.

63. Saussure uses a Neoplatonic term "emanation" in describing how linguistic distinctions and values are self-generated. (ibid., p. 117).

64. Ibid., p. 117.

65. Ibid., p. 120.

66. Kant's conceptualism is given in his *Critique of Pure Reason* (London: Macmillan, 1923). Trans. by Norman Kemp Smith.

67. Hegel's conceptual dialectic is given in his *Science of Logic* (London: Allen and Unwin, 1929). Translated by W. H. Johnston and L. G. Struthers.

68. Saussure, *Course in General Linguistics*, pp. 101–90. The relation of synchrony and diachrony in Saussure's linguistics is well explained by Jonathan Culler in his *Ferdinand de Saussure* (Harmondsworth: Penguin Books, 1976), pp. 29–41.

69. This synchronic tendency of Saussure's structural linguistics has eventually influenced the development of French structuralism mainly as a movement of synchronic analysis.

70. This category is the subject of his essay "La Différance," trans. in *Speech and Phenomena*, pp. 129–60. My references are to this translation.

71. "La Différance," p. 140.

72. Ibid., pp. 129–30.

73. Ibid., p. 140.

74. Ibid., p. 145.

75. Ibid., p. 143.

76. Ibid., p. 154.

77. Ibid., p. 141.

78. Ibid., p. 146.

79. Derrida, "'Genesis and Structure' and Phenomenology," in Jacques Derrida, *Writing and Difference* (Chicago: Chicago University Press, 1978), p. 157. Trans. by Alan Bass.

80. Ibid., p. 165.

81. Derrida, *Speech and Phenomena*, pp. 145–47.

SEVEN: CULTURAL DIVERSITY AND HISTORICAL RELATIVITY

1. T. K. Seung, *Cultural Thematics* (New Haven: Yale University Press, 1976), pp. 134–36.

2. Rosalie Colie, *Paradoxia Epidemica: The Renaissance Tradition of Paradox* (Princeton: Princeton University Press, 1966).

3. Quoted in Cleanth Brooks, *The Well-Wrought Urn* (New York: Harcourt, 1947), p. 223.

4. Ibid., p. 224.

5. In his later works, Freud postulates the instinct of aggression and destruction (death instinct) as another primary instinct along with the instinct of love and sex. Freud, *Beyond The Pleasure Principle* (New York: Liveright 1928); *Civilization and its Discontents* (New York: Norton, 1930). Both works trans. by James Strachey. However, this revision does not affect Freud's presumption that his psychological structure is meant to be transcultural and transhistorical.

6. Freud's use of the term "libido" is not always consistent. Although this term in his general usage means sexual instincts, he sometimes uses it to refer to all human instinctual desires. In his 1914 essay "On Narcissism," for example, he distinguishes between the ego-libido or ego-instincts on one hand and the object-libido or sexual instincts on the other. The former is for the preservation of the individual self, while the latter is for the perpetuation of his species. He says that this distinction corresponds to what is generally known as the distinction between hunger and love. Freud, *Collected Papers* (New York: Basic Books, 1959), 4:30–59. The question whether Freud uses the term "libido" in its narrow sense to mean only sexual instincts or in its broad sense to mean all human instincts does not seem to affect the centrality of sexuality he presupposes in his theory of instinctual forces.

7. The instinct of aggression rather than the sexual instinct has been recognized as the primary instinct in the constitution of what has been called the culture of narcissism by Christopher Lasch and others. But this fact alone does not prove the primacy of aggressive instinct in the human psyche; rather it may simply indicate the aggressive character of contemporary American culture. About the social character of psychopathology, Christopher Lasch says: "Every age develops its own peculiar forms of pathology, which express in exaggerated form its underlying character structure. In Freud's time, hysteria and obsessional neurosis carried to extremes the personality traits associated with the capitalist order at an earlier stage in its development—acquisitiveness, fanatical devotion to work, and a fierce repression of sexuality. In our time, the preschizophrenic, borderline, or personality disorders have attracted increasing attention, along with schizophrenia itself"; *The Culture of Narcissism*, (New York: Norton, 1978), p. 41.

8. Freud, *Totem and Taboo* (London: Routledge, 1950). Trans. by James Strachey.

9. Bronislaw Malinowski, *The Sexual Life of Savages* (New York: Liveright, 1929); *Sex and Repression in Savage Society* (New York: Harcourt, 1937). Margaret Mead, *Coming of Age in Samoa* (New York: Blue Ribbon, 1928); *Growing Up in New Guinea* (New York: Blue Ribbon, 1930). Abram Kardiner, *The Individual and His Society* (New York: Columbia University Press, 1939).

10. This attempt is perhaps best represented by Géza Róheim, *Psychoanalysis and Anthropology* (New York: International Universities Press, 1959).

11. Jacques Lacan, "The Insistence of the Letter in the Unconscious," in Jacques Ehrmann, ed., *Structuralism* (New York: Doubleday, 1970), pp. 101–37, reprint of a special issue of *Yale French Studies* 36–37 (1966); *The Language of the Self* (Baltimore: Johns Hopkins University Press, 1968), trans. by Anthony Wilden.

12. Gilles Deleuze and Félix Guattari, *Anti-Oedipus: Capitalism and Schizophrenia* (New York: Viking, 1977), p. 170. Trans. from the French by Robert Hurley et al.

13. Harold Bloom, *The Anxiety of Influence* (Oxford: Oxford University Press, 1973), p. 94.

14. Ibid., p. 122.

15. The Roman tradition of *pietas* and the Chinese custom of ancestor worship embody their sense of communal gratitude. Nietzsche says, "What is astonishing about the religiousity of the ancient Greeks is the lavish abundance of gratitude that radiates from it"; *Beyond Good and Evil* (Chicago: University of Chicago Press, 1953), p. 58, trans. by Marianne Cowan. The sense of gratitude need not be limited to ancient Greek religion; it can be regarded as a universal feature of all religious ethoses especially in contrast to the secular Western ethos of modern individualism. As long as one feels that his being is derived as a gift from God or gods, he is most likely to accept it in gratitude. On the other hand, if he feels that he is the ground and master of his own existence, he has no reason to feel grateful to anyone else.

16. Martin Heidegger, *Being and Time* (New York: Harper, 1962), pp. 172–224. Trans. by John Macquarrie and Edward Robinson.

17. Heidegger, *Being and Time*, p. 233.

18. Concerning the nothingness of contemporary man, Jules Henry makes the following observation: "Ancestor worship puts in every man's mind the certainty that when he is dead people will revere him; and the kinship systems of primitive people, with their compelling social relationships, guarantee that one will never be deserted as long as one lives. Contemporary man suffers from the certainty that when dead *he will mean nothing to everybody*, and from the anxiety that even while alive he may come to *mean nothing to anybody*"; Jules Henry, *Culture Against Man*, (New York: Random House, 1963), p. 350.

19. Heidegger, *Being and Time*, pp. 112–13.

20. Ibid., p. 65.

21. Ibid., p. 38.

22. The culture-boundness of Heidegger's Dasein-analysis has been perhaps most trenchantly pointed out by his Marxist critics. For example, Georg Lukács has branded Heidegger's *Dasein-analysis* as a disclosure of the decadent bourgeois mentality; *Die Zerstörung der Vernunft* (Berlin: Aufbau-Verlag, 1955). Theodor Adorno has made a similar criticism in his *Jargon of Authenticity* (Evanston: Northwestern University Press, 1973), trans. by Kurt Tarnowski and Frederic Will.

23. Personal communication, September 8, 1977.

24. David Hoy, "Hermeneutic Circularity, Indeterminacy, and Incommensurability," *New Literary History* (1978), 10:165.

25. The title essay in Geoffrey Hartman, *Beyond Formalism* (New Haven: Yale University Press, 1970), pp. 42–57.

26. M. H. Abrams, *Natural Supernaturalism* (New York: Norton, 1971).

27. Roland Barthes, *S/Z* (New York: Hill and Wang, 1974), p. 3. Trans. by Richard Miller.

28. See Michel Foucault, *The Order of Things* (New York: Random House, 1970). Trans. from the French.

29. Michel Foucault, *The Archeology of Knowledge* (New York: Harper, 1972), pp. 3–15. Trans. by A. M. Sheridan Smith.

30. Thomas Kuhn, *The Structure of Scientific Revolutions*, 2d ed. (Chicago: University of Chicago Press, 1970).

31. Ibid., pp. 94, 103, 108.

32. Foucault, *Archeology of Knowledge*, p. 203.

EIGHT: RELATIVITY AND SUBJECTIVITY

1. Michel Foucault, *The Archeology of Knowledge* (New York: Harper, 1972), p. 130. Trans. by A. M. Sheridan Smith.

2. Ibid., p. 205.

3. Stanley Fish, "Literature in the Reader: Affective Stylistics," *New Literary History* (1970), 2:123–62.

4. "Literature in the Reader," and also Stanley Fish, "Facts and Fictions: A Reply to Ralph Rader," *Critical Inquiry* (1975), 1:887.

5. The demarcation of semantics from pragmatics and its significance for textual interpretation will be fully discussed in a sequel to this volume.

6. Norman Holland, "Stanley Fish, Stanley Fish," *Genre* (1977), 10:434.

7. Norman Holland, *5 Readers Reading* (New Haven: Yale University Press, 1975), p. 12.

8. Stanley Fish, "Interpreting the *Variorum*," *Critical Inquiry* (1976), 2:478.

9. Ibid., p. 482.

10. Ibid., p. 483.

11. A detailed account of this doctrine is given in my *Cultural Thematics* (New Haven: Yale University Press, 1976), pp. 3–27.

12. The difference between allegory and analogy is explained in my *Cultural Thematics*, pp. 77–89.

13. Fish, "Interpreting the *Variorum*," p. 482.

14. Ibid., p. 483.

15. Ibid., pp. 483–84.

16. David Bleich, "The Subjective Paradigm in Science, Psychology, and Criticism," *New Literary History* (1976), 7:313–34.

17. Thomas Kuhn, "Postscript—1969" to *The Structure of Scientific Revolutions*, 2d ed. (Chicago: University of Chicago Press, 1970), pp. 174–210.

18. Norman Holland, "The New Paradigm: Subjective or Transactive?" *New Literary History* (1976), 7:339.

19. Holland, "The New Paradigm," p. 342.

20. Holland, 5 *Readers Reading*, pp. 113–28.

21. Holland, "The New Paradigm," p. 338; also Norman Holland, "Unity, Identity, Text, Self," *PMLA* (1975), 90:813–22.

22. T. K. Seung, "Semantic Context and Textual Meaning," *Journal of Literary Semantics* (1979), 8:65–83.

23. Friedrich Schleiermacher, *Hermeneutik* (Heidelberg: Carl Winter, 1959), p. 90. Edited with an introduction by Heinz Kimmerle.

24. Wilhelm Dilthey, *Gesammelte Schriften* (Göttingen: Vandenhoeck, 1924), 7:213–16.

25. Martin Heidegger, *Being and Time* (New York: Harper, 1962), p. 194. Trans. by John Macquarrie and Edward Robinson.

26. Hans-Georg Gadamer, *Truth and Method* (New York: Seabury, 1975). Trans. from the 2d German edition, *Wahrheit und Methode* (Tübingen: J. C. B. Mohr, 1965).

27. Ibid., pp. 153–92.

28. Karl Mannheim, *Ideology and Utopia* (New York: Harcourt, 1936), pp. 2–5. Trans. by Louis Wirth and Edward Shils. The word *Seinsverbundenheit* is not easy to translate; it roughly means that our knowledge is always bound by or dependent on the nature of our being. Karl Mannheim sometimes uses an easier word *Situationsverbundenheit* (situation-boundness), which is interchangeable with context-boundness.

29. Gadamer, *Truth and Method*, pp. 235–45.

30. Ibid., pp. 262, 351.

31. Ibid., p. 273.

32. Ibid., p. 261.

33. Ibid., p. 483. Gadamer makes this admission in order to maintain the self-consistency of historicism.

34. Ibid. Gadamer says, "For the thesis (of contextual relativism) is not that this proposition will always be considered true, any more than that it has always been so considered. Rather, historicism that takes itself seriously will allow for the fact that one day its thesis will no longer be considered true, i.e., that people will think 'unhistorically'." Even if they think unhistorically and fail to recognize the historicity of their own thought (hence the truth of Gadamer's thesis), Gadamer's thesis will still be true, that is, true of the historicity of their thought. The truth of his thesis cannot be affected by anyone's recognition or acceptance of it.

35. It is not easy to determine whether Gadamer's historical relativism is meant to be reflexive. Even such a notable Gadamer scholar as David Hoy has pronounced conflicting views on this matter: (1) "Gadamer only hints at a transcendental dimension by claiming universality for his theory of understanding, which is valid for all acts of understanding even though the theory itself emerges at a particular historical time," "Taking History Seriously: Foucault, Gadamer, Habermas," *Union Seminary Quarterly Review* (1979), 34:94,

and (2) "Actually, however, the charge of assuming an unhistorical superiority for hermeneutic philosophy itself cannot be leveled against Gadamer . . . Gadamer explicitly recognizes the inevitability of hermeneutical theory itself being historically superseded"; "Hermeneutic Circularity, Indeterminacy, and Incommensurability," New Literary History (1978), 10:165.

36. R. G. Collingwood, The Idea of History (Oxford: Oxford University Press, 1946); Peter Winch, The Idea of Social Science (London: Routledge, 1958).

37. Benjamin Whorf, Language, Thought, and Reality (Cambridge, Mass.: MIT Press, 1956), pp. 137–47.

38. Martin Hollis, "The Limits of Irrationality," and "Reason and Ritual," both reprinted in Bryan R. Wilson, ed., Rationality (New York: Harper, 1970), pp. 214–20 and 221–39. Donald Davidson, "The Very Idea of a Conceptual Scheme," Proceedings and Addresses of the American Philosophical Association (1974), 47:5–20, and "Radical Interpretation," Dialectica (1973), 27:313–28. The same argument has been restated in terms of the constitution of different worlds or world-views by Richard Rorty in his "The World Well Lost," The Journal of Philosophy (1972), 69:649–65.

39. Fredrick Swoyer ably argues for this version of relativism in his "Conceptual Relativism," (Ph.D. diss., University of Minnesota, 1976), pp. 351–54.

40. Gadamer, Truth and Method, p. 273.

41. Ibid., p. 262.

42. Barry Stroud, "Conventionalism and the Indeterminacy of Translation," in Donald Davidson and Jaakko Hintikka, eds., Words and Objections: Essays on the Work of W. V. Quine (Dordrecht: Reidel, 1969), pp. 82–96.

NINE: OBJECTIVITY AND TRANSCENDENCE

1. William Empson, 7 Types of Ambiguity (New York: Meridian, 1955).

2. Wilhelm Dilthey, Gesammelte Schriften (Göttingen: Vandenhoeck, 1924), 7:151, 208, 251. Dilthey's idea of objective mind has been appropriated by George Herbert Mead in his theory of "the generalized other"; Works of George Herbert Mead, ed. by Charles Morris (Chicago: University of Chicago Press, 1934), 1:154–64.

3. Dilthey, Gesammelte Schriften, 7:151.

4. These two approaches, the evaluative and the nonevaluative, are very much like Bernard Williams' two types of relativism, appraisal and nonappraisal, given in his essay, "The Truth in Relativism," Proceedings of the Aristotelian Society (1974–75), n.s. 75:215–28.

5. Dilthey, Gesammelte Schriften, 5:9. ,

6. Karl Mannheim, Ideology and Utopia (New York: Harcourt, 1936), pp. 105–6. Trans. by Louis Wirth and Edward Shils.

7. Bertrand Russell formulated his theory of types to solve what is known as Russell's paradox. The nature of this logical paradox and its solutions can be found in most textbooks on elementary logic. Russell's own expositions of his theory of types can be found in Appendix B to his *Principles of Mathematics*, 2d rev. ed. (New York: Norton, 1964), pp. 523–28; his *Logic and Knowledge* (London: Allen and Unwin, 1956), pp. 57–102.

8. Israel Scheffler, *Science and Subjectivity* (Indianapolis: Bobbs-Merrill, 1967), pp. 45–66.

9. Jack Meiland, "The Historical Relativism of Charles A. Beard," *History and Theory* (1973), 12:403–13.

10. Ibid., p. 408.

11. Some attempts have been made to employ the idea of agreement and consensus in resolving Kuhn's problem of paradigm choice or theory choice. Notable examples of this trend are John M. Ziman, *Public Knowledge* (Cambridge: Cambridge University Press, 1968) and *Reliable Knowledge* (Cambridge: Cambridge University Press, 1978), and Keith Lehrer, "Social Consensus and Rational Agnoiology," *Syntheses* (1975), 31:141–60.

12. Karl-Otto Apel, "The A Priori of Communication and the Foundation of the Humanities," *Man and the World* (1972): 3–37. An abridged version of this article is reprinted in Fred Dallmayr and Thomas McCarthy, eds., *Understanding and Social Inquiry* (Notre Dame: University of Notre Dame Press, 1977), pp. 292–315. My references are to this abridged version. "Sprechakttheorie und transzendentale Sprachpragmatik—zur Frage ethischer Normen," in Karl-Otto Apel, ed., *Sprachpragmatik und Philosophie* (Frankfurt: Suhrkamp, 1976), pp. 10–173.

13. Apel, "A Priori of Communication," pp. 295–96.

14. Ibid., p. 298.

15. Ibid., p. 299.

16. Jürgen Habermas, "A Postscript to *Knowledge and Human Interests*," *Philosophy of the Social Sciences* (1973), 3:157–89; "Wahrheitstheorien," in *Wirklichkeit und Reflexion: Walter Schulz zum 60. Geburtstag* (Pfullingen: Neske, 1973), pp. 211–65; "What is Universal Pragmatics?" in J. Habermas, *Communication and the Evolution of Society* (Boston: Beacon, 1979), pp. 1–68, trans. by Thomas McCarthy. For a good discussion of Habermas' theory of universal pragmatics, see Thomas McCarthy, *The Critical Theory of Jürgen Habermas* (Cambridge, Mass.: MIT Press, 1978), pp. 272–91.

17. Habermas, "A Postscript to *Knowledge and Human Interests*," pp. 166–72.

18. J. Habermas, "On Systematically Distorted Communication," *Inquiry* (1970), 13:205–18.

19. Habermas, "Wahrheitstheorien," pp. 252–60.

20. John E. Smith, *The Spirit of American Philosophy* (New York: Oxford University Press, 1963), p. 27.

21. Habermas, *Communication and the Evolution of Society*, pp. 2–3. For those interested, it may be worthwhile to compare Habermas' four universal

validity claims with H. P. Grice's fourfold characterization of the Cooperative Principle governing conversational acts; "Logic and Conversation," in Donald Davidson and Gilbert Harman, eds., *The Logic of Grammar* (Encino, Calif.: Dickenson, 1975), pp. 64–75.

22. *Works of George Herbert Mead*, 1:69.

23. Ibid., 1:68.

24. Edmund Husserl, *Ideas* (London: Allen and Unwin, 1931), trans. by Royce Gibson; *Cartesian Meditations* (The Hague; Nijhoff, 1960), trans. by Dorian Cairns.

25. For example, W. V. Quine, *From a Logical Point of View*, 2d rev. ed. (Cambridge, Mass.: Harvard University Press, 1961); *Word and Object* (Cambridge, Mass.: MIT Press, 1960). Keith Lehrer, *Knowledge* (Oxford: Oxford University Press, 1974).

TEN: LANGUAGE AND REFERENCE

1. Roland Barthes, "Science versus Literature," *The Times Literary Supplement* (September 28, 1967), reprinted in Michael Lane, ed., *Introduction to Structuralism* (New York: Basic Books, 1970), pp. 410–16.

2. Roland Barthes, "To Write: An Intransitive Verb?" in Richard Macksey and Eugenio Donato, eds., *The Structuralist Controversy* (Baltimore: Johns Hopkins University Press, 1970), pp. 134–56.

3. Michel Foucault, *Language, Counter-Memory, Practice* (Ithaca: Cornell University Press, 1977), p. 116. Trans. by Donald F. Bouchard.

4. Jacques Derrida, *Glas* (Paris: Édition Galilee, 1974).

5. Paul Bové, "The Image of the Creator in Beckett's Postmodern Writing," *Philosophy and Literature* (1980), 4:50.

6. Jacques Derrida, *Speech and Phenomena* (Evanston: Northwestern University Press, 1973), p. 139, Trans. by David Allison.

7. Benjamin Whorf, *Language, Thought, and Reality* (Cambridge, Mass.: MIT Press, 1956), pp. 137–47.

8. Ferdinand de Saussure, *Course in General Linguistics* (New York: Philosophical Library, 1959), p. 120. Trans. by Wade Baskin.

9. This is a summary of Kant's complex doctrine presented in his *Critique of Pure Reason* (London: Macmillan, 1929). Trans. by Norman Kemp Smith.

10. This is a summary of the first chapter of Hegel, *Science of Logic* (London: Allen and Unwin, 1929). Trans. by W. H. Johnston and L. G. Struthers.

11. Saussure, *Course in General Linguistics*, pp. 117, 120.

12. Derrida, *Speech and Phenomena*, p. 51.

13. Jacques Derrida, *Of Grammatology* (Baltimore: Johns Hopkins University Press, 1976), p. 46. Trans. by Gayatri Spivak.

14. Derrida seldom faces the problem of protention in his account of signs.

I know of only one passage in which he comes close to recognizing the problem of protention in the constitution of traces, and that passage is on p. 66, *Of Grammatology*. Derrida's retentional theory of sign is a causal theory. The relation of an origin and its trace is the relation of cause and effect. Hence the notion of efficient causation is central in his theory of signification, and Derrida uses the word "effect" quite often. On the other hand, the notion of final causation or teleology seems to be alien to his theory of signs, and protention belongs to this alien notion.

15. Derrida's doctrine of semiotic independence may at first appear to be in support of the signs and ideas produced by creative imagination and protention. For instance, let us take those signs which express fictitious ideas such as "a golden mountain" and "a squared circle." The meanings of these signs are said to be independent of any objects which can correspond to their meanings. This notion of semiotic independence may seem to imply that signs can be created without any constraints from what there is in the domain of reality. But the doctrine of semiotic independence concerns the function of signs and not their creation. It asserts only that signs can function in total independence of subjects and objects, and says nothing at all about how they are generated. As far as their generation is concerned, Derrida's theory is emphatically and unequivocally retentional.

16. Derrida, *Of Grammatology*, p. 19; *Speech and Phenomena*, pp. 148–49.

17. Jacques Derrida, *La Dissémination* (Paris: Éditions du Seuil, 1972), p. 290.

18. Derrida, *Speech and Phenomena*, p. 52.

19. Jacques Derrida, "Positions," *Diacritics* (1973), 3:33–34.

20. Jacques Derrida, "Limited Inc," *Glyph* (1977), 2:162–254.

21. Derrida, *Of Grammatology*, p. 46.

22. For his argument of context-independence, see his "Signature Event Context," *Glyph* (1977), 1:172–97, esp. pp. 174, 181–86. This argument is based mainly on the independence of a code from its context. One of Derrida's best examples for his argument of context dependence is his treatment of Nietzsche's statement "I forgot my umbrella," that is, how this statement can have different meanings in different contexts. This example can be found in his "Limited Inc," p. 201.

23. Derrida, *La Dissémination*, p. 241. The logic of neither/nor differentiates the polysemy of *hymen* from that of *pharmakon*, which is governed by the logic of both/and. *Pharmakon* can mean both remedy and poison without contradicting itself, because any medicine can have both beneficial and harmful effects even for the same person at the same time.

24. Jacques Derrida, *Spurs/Éperons* (Chicago: University of Chicago Press, 1979).

25. Ibid., p. 97.

26. Ibid., p. 99.

27. Derrida, *La Dissémination*, p. 249.

28. Ibid.

29. Ibid., p. 250.

30. Paul de Man, *Allegories of Reading* (New Haven: Yale University Press, 1979), pp. 9–10.

31. Ibid., p. 10. This application of Austin's theory of illocution involves some inaccuracy. De Man assumes that every linguistic expression has only one illocutionary mode and that this mode is at once affirmed and denied by its conflicting meanings. In Austin's theory, no linguistic expression, by itself, has any illocutionary mode; it can be given different illocutionary forces through different speech acts. Those illocutionary forces can conflict with one another, but they cannot be in conflict with the constative which has no illocutionary force. The expression "the illocutionary mode" which de Man uses is never used by Austin. For details, see Austin, *How to Do Things with Words* (Oxford: Oxford University Press, 1962).

32. De Man, *Allegories of Reading*, p. 10.

33. Ibid., pp. 131, 290, 298–99.

34. Ibid., p. 10.

35. Ibid., p. 105.

36. Ibid., p. 15.

37. Derrida, *La Dissémination*, p. 249.

38. Jacques Derrida, "Positions," *Diacritics* (1972), 2:36.

39. The same logic of elimination and diffusion may underlie Derrida's rejection of Husserl's "essential distinctions." See *Speech and Phenomena*, p. 101.

40. Rodolphe Gasché, "Deconstruction as Criticism," *Glyph* (1979), 6:177–215.

41. Derrida, *Spurs/Éperons*, p. 51.

42. Ibid., pp. 79–81.

43. Ibid., p. 101.

44. De Man, *Allegories of Reading*, pp. 11–12.

45. Ibid., pp. 111–16.

46. Ibid., p. 16.

47. Ibid., pp. 116, 301.

48. Derrida, *Of Grammatology*, p. 24.

49. Derrida, *Speech and Phenomena*, pp. 101, 133–35.

50. Ibid., pp. 23–24.

51. Edmund Husserl, "First Investigation," sec. 1, in his *Logical Investigations* (London: Routledge, 1970), trans. from the second German edition by J. N. Findlay.

52. Jacques Derrida, "Positions," *Diacritics* (1972), 2:36.

53. Richard Rorty, "Philosophy as a Kind of Writing," *New Literary History* (1978), 10:144.

54. Derrida, *Speech and Phenomena*, pp. xxvi, 101–2.

55. Martin Heidegger, "What Is Metaphysics?" in his *Existence and Being* (Chicago: Henry Regnery, 1949), p. 361.

56. Derrida, *Of Grammatology*, p. 22.

Index